DESIGNING GAMES and SIMULATIONS

To
HARRY C. BREDEMEIER

Mentor,
Colleague,
Dear Friend

DESIGNING GAMES and SIMULATIONS

AN ILLUSTRATED HANDBOOK

Cathy Stein Greenblat

SAGE PUBLICATIONS
The Publishers of Professional Social Science
Newbury Park   Beverly Hills   London   New Delhi

For information address:

SAGE Publications, Inc.
2111 West Hillcrest Drive
Newbury Park, California 91320

SAGE Publications Inc.
275 South Beverly Drive
Beverly Hills
California 90212

SAGE Publications Ltd.
28 Banner Street
London EC1Y 8QE
England

SAGE PUBLICATIONS India Pvt. Ltd.
M-32 Market
Greater Kailash I
New Delhi 110 048 India

Printed in the United States of America

Library of Congress Cataloging-in-Publication Data

Greenblat, Cathy Stein.
    Designing games and simulations.

    Bibliography: p.
    1. Social sciences—Simulation methods.
2. Game theory. I. Title.
H61.G669   1987   300′.724   87-12862
ISBN 0-8029-2956-0

Contents

Figures

Acknowledgments

An undertaking such as this volume always entails a set of intellectual debts far too extensive to acknowledge. My current knowledge about and perspective on game and simulation design is a derivative of considerable reading, listening, participating in demonstration runs, informal conversing, and teaching. Hence I am deeply indebted to those many colleagues and friends around the world who have contributed to my own and others' education about the nature and value of the enterprise in which we are collectively and individually engaged. I also owe a great deal to my students who, through the years, have challenged me to formulate my thoughts more cogently. I am sad that I cannot mention all these people by name, for I am thankful to them all, but I am simultaneously pleased that the field has become so large and vital that the names of the important people in it cannot easily be listed.

I am particularly indebted to several people. Harry Bredemeier, to whom this book is dedicated, spurred my early interest in gaming, and supported and encouraged my enterprises through all the years of my involvement in exploring its many dimensions. My first exposure to game design was as a participant in a workshop run by R. Garry Shirts; those early learnings have remained important ones upon which I have built. I owe a great deal to those people with whom I have worked directly on the design of games and simulations. The intellectual and personal rewards of meeting the challenges of design with Peter Stein, Norman Washburne, Richard D. Duke, John Gagnon, Linda Rosen, Philip Langley, Jacob Ngwa, Ernest Mangesho, Saul Luyumba, and Foday MacBailey, have been enormous. Our working relationships constitute proof that learning and fun can be conjoined. I thank them here for all the instruction and love they have given me.

The original abbreviated draft of this manuscript was written at the invitation of Pier Ayala of UNESCO's Programme on Man and the Biosphere during the fall semester of 1983 while I was on sabbatical leave from Rutgers University. Pier's encouragement was extremely important, and it was sufficiently strong to prevent me from spending the entire semester savoring the London environment in which I was living. An even more abbreviated form of that early draft appears in the *Handbook for the Organization and Design of Courses* (revised version) published by the Man and the Biosphere Programme in 1986. During that year I profited greatly from the contacts I had with several European colleagues who kept me active in gaming enterprises; in particular I thank Ken Jones (who read the entire original manuscript), Don Thatcher, Jan Klabbers, Klaas Bruin, and Eugene Donahue.

During the stages of writing this expanded version, I incurred additional debts. Mary Bredemeier encouraged me to elaborate on many of the ideas in the first draft. Dennis Meadows, who had used the short version in several training courses, not only urged me to expand it, but provided extensive editorial and conceptual assistance on the almost completed manuscript. Diana Shannon opened my eyes to the potentials of the Macintosh graphics programs, and taught me to use them in the preparation of some of the figures. Jeff Negran assisted with the typing, the preparation of figures, the seemingly endless trips to the local photocopy store, and the more amorphous task of keeping me sane and in good spirits through all stages of writing and manuscript completion. My deep thanks to all of them.

As always, I have been sustained in all ways by the intellectual stimulation, professional support, personal nurturing, and love, which I regularly receive from my esteemed colleague, best friend, and life partner, John H. Gagnon. These are beyond a "thank you," but must be acknowledged here.

Cathy Stein Greenblat
Princeton, New Jersey

1

Introduction:
An Approach to Game Design

SOME BACKGROUND

This guide to the design of games and simulations is based upon 16 years of teaching about gaming, of writing and editing in the field, and of designing gaming-simulations.

Through formal university classes and numerous workshop format courses, I have had the chance to teach about the use and the design of gaming-simulations to very diverse groups of students. Within Rutgers University, I offered courses for many years to undergraduate and graduate students in the social sciences, psychiatric nursing, communications, history, and art. Outside my own university I have offered courses of a similar nature, but shorter in duration, more compressed in time, and structured to focus on specific aims or on a particular substantive problem. A major aspect of these workshops often has been the *design* of gaming-simulations. I have offered these workshop courses to teachers, social workers, and health professionals in the United States; to human settlement managers in the Philippines and in Cameroon, West Africa; and to gamers attending meetings of ISAGA (the International Simulation and Gaming Association). Furthermore, I have had the opportunity to watch game design workshops conducted by such capable designers as Richard Duke, Fred Goodman, Garry Shirts, Alan Coote, and Don Thatcher.

Through my own writing interests, in my capacity as Editor of *Simulation and Games,* and through contacts with members of NASAGA, ISAGA, ABSEL, and SAGSET, I have also had a chance to become familiar with much of the written material on gaming published in English and French. My active participation in ISAGA over the past 15 years has permitted me to learn about gaming activities in many other countries, to see gaming-simulations designed outside the United States, and to establish warm friendships. As a result, colleagues around the world regularly keep me apprised of their own work and of new developments in gaming in their countries.

Thus my knowledge of the fullness of the field and of growth in it is tempered by an awareness of the lacunae in the published literature.

Early in my gaming career I found that gaming-simulation *design* was the aspect of the field that I found most interesting and most intellectually challenging. Other obligations and interests have precluded my spending as much time as I would have liked in design enterprises. Nonetheless, I have worked with a number of colleagues on the production of several games of which I am quite proud and that have been used successfully by others. Several of these will be used as case studies in later chapters.

THE MARRIAGE GAME, co-designed with Norman Washburne and Peter Stein, has been used extensively in courses on marriage and the family or home economics, as well as in premarital counseling. Before the second edition went out of print in 1982, Random House (the publisher) had sold more than 30,000 copies.

With Richard D. Duke, I designed three frame games: IMPASSE?, AT ISSUE, and THE CONCEPTUAL MAPPING GAME, all made available in the volume *Game-Generating-Games* (1979). Both of us have received considerable correspondence that suggests that these simple games have been used throughout the world for extremely diverse purposes.

Under a 1974 contract from the National Heart and Lung Institute, John Gagnon and I designed two gaming-simulations: THE HEMOPHILIA CARE PLANNING GAMES and BLOOD MONEY. The former was designed for one-time play by a group of experts, but the written documentation of the experiment illustrates how parallel forms can be developed for other groups. The latter won an award from the National Hemophilia Foundation, and has been used by their regional chapters, by faculty in medical and nursing programs, and by others concerned with the problems of provision of health care to patients suffering from a variety of diseases.

POMP AND CIRCUMSTANCE was designed under

a subcontract from the Ford Foundation by myself, John Gagnon, and Linda Rosen. It deals in an abstract fashion with problems of premarital pregnancy among noncontracepting adolescents. It has been successfully used for research purposes (Philliber, 1982), and testimony from students and teachers involved in the classroom and training sessions in which it has been employed suggests it is extremely successful as a teaching and counseling tool.

Some of my most exciting and rewarding design experiences were in the UNESCO sponsored project that resulted in CAPJEFOS: A SIMULATION OF VILLAGE DEVELOPMENT. I spent a total of 5 weeks in Cameroon, West Africa, working intensely with the wonderful team of Philip Langley, Jacob Ngwa, Saul Luyumba, Ernest Mangesho, and Foday MacBailey. We brought a mix of interdisciplinary training to the task of designing a complex gaming-simulation about village life and problems and processes of development. We began with their content expertise and my design expertise, but we taught each other well. Within a few days, they exhibited considerable sensitivity to and sophistication about gaming options and constraints, while I actively argued about substantive issues.

Through the teaching and workshop enterprises mentioned above, I have worked on numerous other games, some of which have been carried to completion by students, and some of which await the never-appearing additional time to execute the last steps! I have learned a great deal from my students—at least as much as they have learned from me.

Finally, I must indicate how indebted I am to those colleagues with whom I have worked on game design, not only for the products we have jointly produced, but for my own current ideas about the process. My major debt in this regard is to Richard Duke, whose conceptualizations of the design process have had an extraordinary influence on my thinking and work. The general process outlined in the pages that follow is one that leans heavily on Dick's depictions of the design process (1974, 1980). I had designed gaming-simulations before I met and began working with Dick, but his formulations systematized my design work and made it a much more self-conscious and disciplined enterprise. Indeed, it is only after many years of working on modifications of his approach and of developing a more illustrated approach, that I can comfortably set these pages forth.

These diverse experiences—teaching, reading, writing, and designing—have led me to some strong opinions about the limitations of the written materials currently available to guide game designers, and to some firm ideas about how to guide novice and experienced designers through the process more efficiently and effectively.

THE APPROACH OF THIS BOOK

The speed, efficiency, and creative success of game design depends on numerous factors. Of particular importance is the degree of exposure the designers have had to existing materials. Familiarity with a wide range of styles of gaming-simulation, both as a participant and as a game operator, provides invaluable sensitization to the options that can be selected by the designer and to the elements that make up a good gaming-simulation. Hence the best way to learn about gaming-simulation design would be first to participate in and run a great many gaming-simulations, and second to work directly with an experienced designer on a concrete design problem. Many very capable designers have considerable difficulty giving abstract explanations of how they work; many of them can clearly explain what they are doing and why as they go through the process. One would thus learn by doing—a principle endorsed by aficionados of gaming.

Unfortunately, most people cannot easily arrange such a personalized learning program. As a substitute for working with an experienced designer they must use one of the few published articles or books on design. But as noted above, few designers have been able to present a clear systematic guide to the process by which they design gaming-simulations. When I first entered the field, I heard Duane Dillman express concern about the absence of effective guidance to the design process. In so doing, he echoed the statements of other leaders in the field about the lacunae:

> This writer takes the position that much more attention needs to be given the design and development of simulation games and exercises. . . . Yet almost everyone laments the fact that there are no handbooks, few articles or books, and few references which contain any useful technique of game construction (Shubik, 1968: 644-646; Instructional Simulation Newsletter, July 1968; Boocock and Schild, 1968: 266) [Dillman, 1970, p. 3].

Sixteen years later, David Crookall, Danny Saunders, and Allan Coote (1987, p. 2), who are extremely knowledgeable about the current state of the gaming-simulation literature, issued a too-similar lament:

> the newcomer or student has little material, other than the finished game and instructions on running it, to provide guidance on design paradigms in general, or on a particular design procedure followed for a given simulation, or yet on the underlying model. S/he therefore often falls back on intuitive judgment, informal advice from others, theoretical descriptions of the design process, or inspiration.

There are some more materials available now, primarily in the form of articles in *Simulation and Games* and in proceedings of the professional organizations (see, for example, the proceedings of the 1979 ISAGA meeting, which had as its theme, "How to Build a Simulation Game"). Three books devoted to design have also been published since 1970. The first, Michael Inbar and Clarice Stoll's *Simulation and Gaming in Social Science* (1972), consisted of a series of case studies of the design process for games, simulations, and computer simulations. Useful as the individual essays are (and I highly recommend it), the volume does not present a systematic approach to be followed as you undertake your own projects.

In 1983, Ellington, Addinall, and Percival's helpful *Handbook of Game Design* was published. These authors' advice on designing card games, simple board games, simple manual games, and computer games, is very useful; the detailed case study of design of the board game NETWORK is particularly instructive. No attention, however, is given to design of more complex gaming- simulations. Indeed, even in the discussion of simple manual games, the critical stages between the idea for the exercise and the design of a prototype (Stages II, III, and IV in this book) are described as

> a "black box" into which the designer feeds the basic idea for an exercise and out of which eventually emerges a prototype packages suitable for use in field trials (a set of resource materials and an organizer's guide) [Ellington, Addinall, and Percival, 1983, p. 73].

That volume thus helps to fill the need for guidelines for game design, but does not address the need for guidelines to designing more complex gaming-simulations.

The most recent arrival is Ken Jones's *Designing Your Own Simulations* (1986). Those of you who are familiar with Ken's earlier books (1980, 1982) or with his delightful simulations (SHIPWRECKED, RADIO COVINGHAM, and many others), will find the same clear and imaginative writing in this slim volume. Ken and I are close friends, and we greatly admire one another's work. BLOOD MONEY and CAPJEFOS are treated in laudatory fashion in Ken's new book, and a number of Ken's games are cited as exemplars in these pages. Our philosophical and pragmatic approaches to design, however, are quite different, and, as a result, our books do not deal with the topic in the same fashion. *Designing Your Own Simulations* offers both inspiration to the would-be designer, and concrete suggestions for the design of simple simulations, in which scenarios, role cards, and external factors are the primary elements. Ken's own simulations of this sort are quite elegant, and the reader who follows his advice should be able to design interesting, brief (one to two hour), effective simulations of that sort. The volume, however, provides little guidance to the person who wishes to design a more complex gaming-simulation.

While each of the above mentioned volumes are of good quality and are helpful, none offer what I have tried to present in this book: a careful description of the stages of the process, *illustrated with a rich array of concrete examples.* For the reader who has not had much personal experience as a participant or operator, the inclusion of such examples should be particularly important. Even for the person who has had considerable exposure to gaming-simulations, I believe the illustrated approach has much merit. Often we experience the gaming-simulations in which we participate or that we run as *wholes*, not stopping to analyze their component parts nor to think about how they were designed and assembled.

This guide to gaming-simulation design also differs from the others mentioned in that it presents a combination of the "science" and the "art" of gaming-simulation design. I have described the stages of game design in some detail. These descriptions are then illustrated through four case studies of design: THE MARRIAGE GAME, BLOOD MONEY, CAPJEFOS, and POMP AND CIRCUMSTANCE. In addition, I have carefully selected an extensive set of concrete examples of varying form and from a number of subject matter areas to illustrate the wide variety of options open to the designer at all stages in the process.

USING THE BOOK EFFECTIVELY

In his extraordinarily imaginative address to the 1982 NASAGA meetings, philosopher Bernard Suits gave a follow-up set of reflections to his book *The Grasshopper* (1982), in which he reverses the moral of Aesop's fable of the grasshopper and the ant. In the book, the grasshopper argues that the ideal of human existence—that is, Utopia—must consist fundamentally, if not exclusively, in the playing of games. In the NASAGA address, the dialogue between the grasshopper and one of his disciples, Skepticus, concludes with the words of the grasshopper:

> In the vision I see myself and a multitude of other Grasshoppers all engaged in playing the most elaborate, subtle, and challenging games. For a game-playing Utopia need not confine itself to checkers and tiddly-winks, as you suggested earlier. Rather we ought to be devising really magnificent games now, so that when eternal summer finally arrives, we will have all kinds of absorbing things to do.

To this, author Bernard Suits (1982, p. 21) adds:

> And I mean really magnificent games—games so subtle, complex, and challenging that their inventors will be seen as the ludic Einsteins of the future. And the Utopians will look back on names like Queensbury, Naismith, the Parker Brothers, even Rubix, with the same indulgent condescension that today's physicists look back on those ancient investigators who proclaimed air, earth, fire, and water to be basic elements of nature.

The best way to use this book is to read through it in its entirety to familiarize yourself with the materials presented, especially if you have limited experience with gaming-simulations. When you are ready to begin the design process, return to Chapter 5 and work through each chapter, applying the ideas to your own design problem as you go. In this sense, it is like using a cookbook—simply reading about how to cut and chop and stir is insufficient; you must go to the kitchen and *use* the instructions. Remember, the examples are included to spark your imagination, not to cover all the options possible. As you undertake subsequent design projects it will suffice to review the steps and the decisions to be made. Good luck—may you rise successfully to the challenge of the grasshopper!

2

The "What" and the "Why" of Gaming

SIMULATIONS AS MODELS

Have you ever read about or seen a simulation of a large-scale technological system, such as a wind tunnel for testing aircraft and training pilots, or a televised simulation of spacecraft vehicles and maneuvers? These are models of systems—in the former case, showing the wind elements and effects of these on aircraft, and, in the latter case, showing a technological system built to travel and perform operations in space. In neither of these simulations is the entire system represented; that is, they are not simply scaled down versions of the larger referent systems. Rather, some aspects are simplified and others are omitted. Thus the simulated spacecraft was constructed so that the *dimensions* are scaled accurately to the original, but the *weight* of the model is likely to have been a matter of no concern to the modelers.

As changes take place in the referent system, they likewise take place in the model, for a simulation is an *operating* model. Consider, for example, the difference between a diagram of the solar system, and the simulation one finds in a planetarium.

Keeping these examples in mind, consider the following definition of a simulation:

> A simulation is an operating model of central features or elements of a real or proposed system, process, or environment.

This definition stresses the critical dimensions of a simulation, namely, that:

- a simulation is a form of *model*;
- it is a *dynamic*, as opposed to a static, model;
- only *selected elements* of the referent system are included;
- referent systems can be of several *different sorts*.

While simulations of technological systems may be the most familiar to you, there are a great many simulations of social systems. Whether the referent system is a marital couple, a business firm, a neighborhood council, a national government, or an international arms control network, the principle is the same: central features are identified, represented, and constructed into a model that operates in a manner similar to the real-world system.

SIMULATIONS, GAMES, AND GAMING-SIMULATIONS

The term *game* is applied to those simulations that work wholly or partly on the basis of players' decisions. In these gaming simulations, the environment and activities of participants have the characteristics of games: players have *roles* to play, *goals* they seek to achieve, *activities* to perform, *constraints* on what can be done, and *payoffs* (positive and negative) as a result of their actions and the actions of other elements in the system (including chance). In a gaming-simulation, the *game* roles, goals, activities, constraints and consequences, and the linkages between them are patterned from real life, or, in the terms used above, they *simulate* these elements of the real-world systems.

In THE COMMUNITY LAND GAME (CLUG), for example, a few of the more fundamental factors affecting land-use decisions in a community and its environs are abstracted and represented in a gaming-simulation. Players operate within the constraints offered by these factors; they make decisions about how resources are to be employed, and then they build, operate, and maintain their own community. At the beginning of play they are given information about the system of taxation, the range of permissible land use, the payrolls of employers and the incomes of employees, and transportation costs to industry and to workers. Players periodically face reassessment of their properties and must make decisions as to whether or not they will renovate their depreciated buildings. If they do not keep their buildings at moderately high levels of maintenance, they face increased probabilities of loss. CLUG is designed primarily for teaching urban planning courses, and the model does not include many of the social factors and problems that would be of concern to sociologists. It can, however, be fruitfully employed to deal with problems and processes of urban and community development. The act of "constructing their own city" may serve as a catalyst to students' inquiries concerning problems of urban development.

Gaming-simulation, then, is a hybrid form, involving the performance of game activities in simulated contexts.

SOME PROBLEMS OF TERMINOLOGY

The distinction between *simulations* and *games* is often unclear, as the two terms are sometimes used synonymously. In fact, there are many simulations that are not games, such as the wind tunnel and space craft examples above, or simulated disaster situations used to train medical and paramedical personnel. Similarly, some games (particularly many card and board games) are not simulations—that is, their components are not designed to represent a real-world system or process.

My concern in this volume is limited to gaming-simulations—that is, teaching and training materials that contain the central ingredients of both games and simulations. Readers interested in the design of card and board games that are not simulations will find some guidance here, and should refer to the handbook by Ellington, Addinall, and Percival (1983) for further assistance.

The confusion of terms is not simply the result of sloppy usage. It also results from users' concerns that both terms—*simulations* and *games*—have problematic connotations that they dislike. Hence they substitute a less accurate but more "acceptable" name for their enterprises. For some people, *simulations* sounds too complex, too mechanical, too mathematical. Hence they prefer to use the lighter-toned term *games*, which they think will be less frightening to prospective users. Ken Jones (1980) notes that dictionary definitions of simulation stress concepts of unreality and artificiality, offering as synonyms such terms as *feign, mimic, dissemble, invent,* and *pretend.* This, Ken argues, leads many teachers to avoid simulations, and may be another reason some users prefer the term *games.*

This is not necessarily a solution, however, for the term *games,* too, has problematic connotations. To some people, *playing games* may suggest an activity involving too much fun and frivolity for an educational enterprise. To others, *playing games* conjures up the image of people utilizing devious interpersonal strategies to accomplish their aims. In either case, suspicion of and objection to the idea of playing games about serious problems, such as urban administration, or about such emotionally laden topics as racism or poverty, may result.

Ken Jones's (1980, p. 10) solution to the dilemma is to suggest that "instead of thinking of a simulation as being like a game or an informal drama, it is useful to think of it as being like a case study but with the participants on the inside, not on the outside." This may avoid some of the negative connotations, but gaming-simulations are usually more complex than case studies, so this "solution," too, seems unsatisfactory to me.

In this volume, the more cumbersome but more accurate term *gaming-simulation* will be employed most of the time, though I will periodically use the shorter term, *game.*

THE DISTINCTION BETWEEN ROLE PLAYING AND GAMING-SIMULATION

Role playing is an instructional technique that differs from gaming-simulation in several important ways. Role playing is an *element* of gaming-simulations, but the latter also include other components. In most role-playing exercises the participant is assigned a role and given the general outline of a situation; from there the action is freewheeling. In gaming-simulations, on the other hand, roles are defined in *interacting systems.* That is, emphasis is on the role as it interacts with other roles; the model creates the basis for the dynamic interaction, and includes the constraints, rewards, and punishments referred to above.

In addition, in gaming-simulations, there is little "second-guessing" in terms of personalities of particular people or positions. Participants are given not only a scenario and a role profile, but also are given goals to orient their behavior, resources to attempt to meet their goals, rules to govern the actions they may and may not take, and instructions about the order of play. The consequences of their actions and of violations, and the probable responses of other elements of the system that are not incorporated in the roles or actions taken by participants, are also presented. Thus the consequences of actions in terms of goal attainment or failure to achieve desired ends are built into the model.

Gaming-simulations thus differ from role-playing exercises in the degree of structure and formalization they entail and in their emphasis on interaction processes rather than on the playing of individual roles. Furthermore, in many instances of classroom role playing, several students participate while the remainder of the class watches, or the class is broken into small groups that engage in parallel role plays. (These "fish-bowl" and "multiple" formats are most common, but other formats are described by Van Ments, 1983, ch. 7.) When gaming-simulations are used in a class, all students are participants; none are passive observers.

Again, an example may be useful. In GHETTO, the pressures on the urban poor and the choices available to improve their life conditions are simulated. Participants have roles as ghetto residents. Depending upon their family responsibilities, players have different amounts of time to "invest" in education, work, hustling, collecting welfare (if they are eligible), or trying to improve the neighborhood conditions. Any of these or some combination may be selected by players each round in order to maximize their short-term gains and improve their earning power for the future. Success in the enterprises chosen is not guaranteed; one who goes to school may be informed that "you have no place to study at home so you can't do your homework. You failed this year. If you want to continue in school next round, repeat this grade." A worker may be informed, "If you are an unskilled or semiskilled worker, you lose your job due to automation. Toss a die to see if you can get another one. If you throw a 1, 2, or 3 you get the job. If you throw a 4, 5, or 6 you don't. If you lose the job, you also lose the work reward. Reinvest your points elsewhere." Hustlers face the possibility of being caught; if that happens, they go to jail, acquire a "record," and have less chance of getting a job in later rounds. Residents are subject to victimization in proportion to the time invested by hustlers in illegal activities. Women may have additional children during the course of the game, and may thus suffer additional restrictions of their time for "investment."

GAMING-SIMULATIONS AND EDUCATIONAL OBJECTIVES

Gaming-simulations have been successfully designed and utilized to meet a number of teaching and training objectives including the following:

(1) Increasing motivation and interest

— in the subject matter
— in the general field of study
— in doing further research on the topic

(2) Teaching: conveying information or reinforcing information already given in another format

— facts
— *gestalt* or systemic understanding
— the relationship of a specific role to an overall system
— a broadened awareness of options, policies, and issues
— probable consequences of particular policies or events

(3) Skill development

— critical thinking and analysis
— decision making
— interactional skills, such as bargaining and negotiating
— communication skills
— particular skills such as proposal writing, summarizing for radio or newspaper accounts, budget preparation

— preparedness for specific future tasks such as applying for a job, managing workers on a team, or coping with emergencies

(4) Attitude change

— social values, such as competition or cooperation
— empathy for those in other roles

(5) Self-evaluation or evaluation by others

— self-awareness of one's own knowledge, skills, assumptions, attitudes, or leadership abilities
— teacher's (or trainer's or employer's) appraisal of the participant's knowledge, skills, assumptions, attitudes, or leadership abilities.

While the objectives listed above include most of the aims of individual teachers and trainers, surely gaming-simulations are not the only mode of attaining these pedagogical aims. Indeed, through lectures, case studies, role playing, and audiovisual materials, teachers and trainers have sought and often achieved these ends. Gaming-simulations may be a better way to meet some purposes; they will be potent tools to be used in conjunction with these other techniques, replacing them for some purposes, but, in general, supplementing the existing "kit" of techniques of a teacher or trainer.

TEACHING VIA LECTURE AND VIA GAMING

The standard mode of teaching and training has historically been the lecture or the lecture and discussion method. Let me briefly examine some of the limitations of this approach, and see how gaming-simulations may overcome them.

The most critical problem, and hence the first to be mentioned here, is that learners in the conventional classroom are passive recipients of information. They rarely have to put their ideas forward, and their attention frequently wanders to other goals or topics of greater interest. (For a good discussion of this, see Sarason, 1971; for an excellent gaming-simulation dealing with the diverse goals of students in the conventional classroom, see CLASSROOM EXPERIENCING.)

Second, material is presented sequentially by the lecturer, who must select an appropriate place to start in describing a complex topic, and then must try to work his or her way through to the end. With such a linear approach, it is frequently difficult for the learner to grasp the nature of the whole. It is, in the terms of R. H. Rhyne (1975), like an inchworm trying to study the Mona Lisa by crawling over it, viewing one piece of the painting at a time. Linear approaches do not eventually yield a good appreciation of the whole. This is particularly so in instances in which one is trying to teach an appreciation of the *simultaneity* of events and actions.

Likewise, *discussions* in the conventional class usually entail comments, questions, and answers, following the lecture by the teacher. Often such discussions begin with the remarks of the most loquacious person in the group, rather than those of the one with the most important comments. Similarly, the time devoted to consideration of given topics may be more closely tied to the persistence of the speaker (and the hesitation of the instructor to cut him or her off), than to the relative importance of the comment. In addition, discussions rarely begin with the first points made in the presentation and proceed through the points in the order in which they were made; thus in many cases the questions flow in no logical order.

A third, related shortcoming of lecturing or any other use of verbal models is that the form is one in which it is difficult to present *system* characteristics clearly. The multiple connections and consequences of a given element or action are difficult to convey verbally. While it is often impossible to understand a social system by simply immersing oneself in it, because the complexity is too confusing, the verbal description too often suffers from oversimplification. For example, a lecture on national government may include discussion of the functions and operations of the chief executive, the Senate, the assembly, and the judiciary, and the balance of powers among them; then it may turn to processes such as lobbying and bargaining. Each of these can be looked at only one at a time, and the listener may have a difficult time piecing the parts together.

Fourth, without prior experience, words may not call up much imagery, or they may call up different imagery to different members of the class. For example, think of the multiple connotations of the following terms, depending on the national background, social class, and experience of persons who hear them:

- *peasant*
- *conference*
- *environmental damage*
- *politics*
- *urban renewal*

This semiotic confusion (see Barthes, 1964) is particularly likely to arise in cross-cultural education and where teaching/training materials developed in one country are employed in another society.

How is teaching with a gaming-simulation different? There are several answers. First, in a gaming-simulation, in contrast to a lecture situation, the class members are *active learners*. They must make decisions, pay the consequences, articulate positions, and make the system work. After play, postgame analysis focuses on what happened and why, how that relates to the real-world counterpart, and the limitations of the gaming-simulation. Thus the learning experience builds upon the philosophy in the old Chinese proverb:

I hear and I forget
I see and I remember
I do and I understand

A number of learning theorists, such as John Dewey have stressed the importance of the student's active involvement with the material or skill to be learned. Experiential learning permits discovery, experimentation, and reflection. Omar Khayyam Moore and Alan Ross Anderson's (1975) four heuristic principles for the design of learning environments also parallel the arguments for the effectiveness of gaming in teaching. They suggest that, first, the learner should be given the opportunity to operate from various *perspectives*. The learner should not just be a recipient of information, but should at times be an agent, a referee, and a reciprocator. Second, activities should contain their own goals and sources of motivation, not just represent means to some end (such as grades). That is, in an effective learning environment, activities are *autotelic*. Third, learners should be freed from a dependence on authority and allowed to reason for themselves; they are thus made more *productive* in the learning process. And, fourth, the environment should be responsive to the learners' activity. Not only should they be given feedback, but they should be helped to be *reflexive*, evaluating their own progress.

This active involvement aspect of gaming-simulations in the learning process has been well described in the major books in the field (see Abt, 1974; Boocock and Schild, 1968; Duke, 1974; Goodman and Coppard, 1979; Gordon, 1970; Greenblat and Duke, 1975, 1981; Jones, 1980, 1982; Raser, 1969; Sanoff, 1979; Shubik, 1975; Taylor and Walford, 1978).

To say that students are engaged with the material is not to say that the experience is all pleasant or "fun." Linda Lederman and Lea Stewart (introduction to SIM-CORP, p. 6) have described the multiple dimensions and consequences of such engagement as follows:

Finally, years of experience with interactive, instructional simulations have demonstrated that students in simulations have an involvement with learning unmatched in any traditional classroom. Engagement in the activity calls for active learning, and action brings with it involvement. This is not to say, however, that involvement always carries with it a "feeling good" affect. Experiences bring with them challenges, challenges which at times bring with them uncertainty ("how am I supposed to do this?"), ambiguity ("what's the right way?" "why doesn't the professor tell me what to do?"), change ("I have never been in this position before, no one ever told me before that I needed to behave differently"). But, uncertainty, ambiguity, and change, as well as error, diversity, and even at times, confusion are the lifeblood of learning by doing. They provide the raw data out of which participants, through their own methods, in their own ways, and in their own time, construct for themselves patterns, theories, and behaviors that permit them to cope successfully with the simulated environment, and thereby, in the long term, the real-world environment which it models.

Second, rather than being lectured to and then engaging in discussion, students experience the topic as a whole, since many components of the system are presented simultaneously in the gaming-simulation. In addition, discussion and analysis following play is often structured by roles rather than by general outspokenness or assertiveness. Indeed, many teachers have reported that previously silent members of a class sometimes become the most vocal and active participants in a gaming-simulation and in the ensuing discussion.

Third, gaming-simulations are particularly useful for conveying *system* characteristics. It has long been recognized that systems are more clearly described using graphic models, such as diagrams or pictures, or using physical representations, than through using verbal models. Consider, for example, the greater clarity of a diagram as opposed to a verbal description of the human circulatory system. A simulation, or a model of a *system in operation* can be an even more potent teaching tool than a graphic model. Returning to the example of teaching about national government, consider DEMOCRACY, designed by the Academic Games Project of Johns Hopkins University. A legislative setting is used to present the processes of collective action and decision making in a democracy. The game is actually a set of games, each focusing on a different aspect of the democratic process. The games may be played individually or combined into sequences. The three basic games are "Legislative Session," "Citizens Action Meeting," and "Representative Democracy." Advanced versions (all variations of the first game) introduce more complex principles of political decision making; they are "A Legislator's Own Convictions," "The Power of the Floor Leader," and "Passage of a Legislative Program."

Fourth, and finally, as we shall examine in considerable detail in later chapters, gaming-simulations rely considerably on game-specific symbols, not simply on words. Thus students develop orientations to particular concepts ("mayor," "conference," "peasant") within a common context, though there may be different connotations depending upon the role played. These concepts and related principles can then be explored, using an experience shared by all members of the class.

Much research has been undertaken to evaluate the pedagogical results of gaming-simulations (see Greenblat, 1975; Bredemeier and Greenblat, 1981; Wolfe, 1985, for reviews of the evidence and of questions that remain to be answered). While gaming-simulations will not solve all educational problems, it is clear that they offer exciting opportunities for teaching and learning about a great

many social systems and social problems. Such utilizations extend beyond the classroom context, for many public policy considerations require that decision makers obtain the overall perspectives and systemic understandings that emerge so well from gaming-simulation activities (see Becker and Porter, 1986a, 1986b, for some recent interesting applications of gaming-simulations for impact assessment).

GAMING-SIMULATIONS AND COMPUTER SIMULATIONS

On a scale of abstraction, gaming-simulation lies between role playing and computer simulation. Computer simulations employ the capabilities of computers to explore mathematical models of structures and processes. Mathematical symbols or equations are used to represent the relationships in the system, and the calculations indicated by the model equations are repeatedly calculated to investigate changes over time. With the advances in computer technology of the past forty years, computer simulation has become inexpensive and widespread. Roberts et al. (1983) offer an excellent introduction to computer simulation.

Paul Gray and Israel Borovits (1986, p. 238) offer the following summary of the contrasts between computer simulation and gaming, with advice about the conditions under which each should be employed: In making a choice between Monte Carlo simulation and

gaming for a particular application, the strengths and weaknesses of the two methodologies must be considered. Simulation offers the ability to generate random scenarios, extreme case scenarios, and statistical output distributions quickly and easily; whereas, gaming provides only a single or a few replications which are never statistically significant. Simulations provide results that help managers understand the range of issues they must cope with. Gaming, on the other hand, provides a "hands-on" feel and the ability to see how people really respond, not just how the simulationist assumes they will respond. Whereas analytic and simulation tools are preferable for modeling competitive and conflict situations where the dimensionality is small, gaming permits introducing and understanding the multidimensional complexity that is inherent in many real-life situations. Cost is also a consideration. Gaming requires investment in a facility and staff, and can generate the need for a large number of subjects. Simulation can easily generate large computer running costs to obtain statistically meaningful data.

Generally, gaming is to be preferred for exploratory studies in which human responses or interactions are not predictable or in which humans are part of the process being investigated; for eliciting the inputs of experts; and for training people to understand the nature of situations, particularly competitive situations. Simulation is to be preferred for situations in which human decision making input occurs at the beginning or end of the process, and for situations in which the dimensionality of the problem is relatively small.

This book will not deal with computer simulation, but the utility of employing microcomputers in the design process and as an aid to operation of gaming-simulations will be addressed in Chapter 4. Before you begin to read about *how* to design games and simulations, however, you should ask whether there is already one that will meet your needs. That is the topic of the next chapter.

3

Seeking an Appropriate Gaming-Simulation

If the foregoing chapters have kindled or reinforced your interest, you are faced with the problem of finding gaming-simulations suitable for your program of instruction. The emphasis in this book is on *designing* your own gaming-simulations because sometimes it will be necessary or desirable to design them yourself. Such an ambitious and time-consuming enterprise, however, should not be undertaken without first seeking the answers to three questions:

(1) Is there an existing gaming-simulation that you could use?
(2) Is there an existing gaming-simulation that you could modify?
(3) Is there a frame game that you could use?

This chapter addresses these three questions.

IS THERE AN EXISTING GAMING-SIMULATION THAT COULD BE USED?

At the time of this writing it is impossible to estimate the number of existing gaming-simulations that are potentially available to the interested user. The most complete listing of gaming-simulations is the latest edition of *The Guide to Simulations/Games for Education and Training*, edited by Robert Horn and Anne Cleaves (1980). This large volume contains information (e.g., publisher, cost, playing time, equipment, characteristics) about more than 1,000 gaming-simulations for students aged 11 and older. A major criterion for inclusion of an item in the *Guide* was that it be available for sale or distribution. The subject matter headings under which materials are listed include domestic politics, ecology/land use/population, economics, health and health care, communication, and numerous other topics. Many teachers and trainers, with a bit of investigation, will find an existing gaming-simulation appropriate to their purposes described therein.

The items in the Horn and Cleaves *Guide*, however, represent only the tip of the iceberg, since almost all of them are produced in the United States. Numerous additional gaming-simulations written in English have been created in Great Britain, however. While there is no British guide to these materials with the comprehensiveness of the Horn and Cleaves *Guide*, considerable information can be found in the resource lists available from SAGSET (see bibliography for details.)

Again, these sources cover only a portion of gaming-simulations for active professionals who are at work in the Netherlands, Germany, France, most East European countries, and elsewhere (see Stahl, 1983, and issues of *Simulation and Games* for discussion of gaming on an international level). Many of these people have produced materials in their native languages, but sometimes they have published versions in other languages as well. I know of no comprehensive reference guide to these materials, but a search for them might well begin with correspondence with Jan Klabbers, Secretary of the International Simulation and Gaming Association (ISAGA) (see the list of organizations at the end of this volume for the address); issues of *Simulation and Games,* especially the ISAGA News and Notes section; and Stahl (1983). There are also resource lists produced by agencies with specialized foci, such as Amy and Lynn Zelmer's *Simulation/Gaming for Health Teaching*, published by the Canadian Health Education Society (1982).

Finally, there are several sources of information about available business games, including the lengthy section of the Horn and Cleaves volume, the *Handbook of Management Games* by Chris Elgood (1984), and the extensive set of papers delivered at the annual meetings of ABSEL—the Association for Business Simulation and Experiential Learning (see Goosen, 1982, for a listing of papers through 1982; contact ABSEL for information about Proceedings since that time.)

Despite the great number of existing gaming-simulations, you may encounter problems in finding a useful one. The gaming-simulation must not only be in your language and deal with the appropriate subject matter. It must also be suitable for students of the right age, skill level, knowledge, and experience, and it must fit into your training program in terms of the time needed for preparation and play. For example, you may find that there is a game dealing with the substantive problem of interest to you (e.g. the economics of small-scale farming in India) but that it is designed to be played with groups of 25 elementary school students in one or two weeks of class time, while you deal with groups of 6-10 adult professionals who meet for one two-hour block of time. When the producer and the potential user are in different countries, there are also problems of availability, entailing issues of cost, shipping time, and materials needed to run the game (e.g., does it require the user to have access to a computer or to supplies not readily available?).

Even if the description of the parameters and materials and cost of the game suggest it may be appropriate, examination of the materials themselves often reveals it is not so suitable as it initially seemed. Simulations of problems of development, for example, are few in number in the first place. More problematic, however, is the fact that most of them have been designed by white, Western males, often working exclusively from written materials, having no direct personal experience with the problem or geographic area. While this does not guarantee failure to develop an accurate model, unfortunately the models are often weak.

For those gaming-simulations published in the form of participants' manuals and an operator's manual, you can obtain an examination copy of both guides by writing to the publisher on your letterhead. (Review copies of games in kit form are rarely available; check to see if a colleague in your institution or a nearby one has a copy you can examine.) See if the players' instructions are clear and whether they are presented in a manner likely to engage participants' interest. It is probable that you will have to review both manuals to get a feel for the game in operation. Be sure the instructions for the operator are clearly presented. If any technical expertise is required (e.g., computer operation) and you do not possess it, locate a potential assistant and have him or her review that portion of the documentation to make sure it is both sound and specific.

There is probably no substitute for the advice of colleagues who have actually *used* the gaming-simulation. Check regularly with such colleagues at disciplinary professional meetings, or attend the annual meetings of ABSEL (usually in the spring) ISAGA (usually in the summer), NASAGA (usually in the fall), or SAGSET (usually in September). These meetings often feature demonstration sessions, and provide invaluable opportunities for the exchange of ideas and recommendations.

(See the listing for organizations at the end of this book for addresses of the secretariats.)

COULD AN EXISTING GAME BE ADAPTED?

Before starting from scratch on a design enterprise, you should consider whether an existing game might be *modified* to suit your needs. If the basic model is similar to what you need, but a different institutional area or cultural setting makes the gaming-simulation inappropriate, it is possible that a suitable gaming-simulation can be developed by altering the original. THE ACADEMIC GAME, for example, simulates the problems experienced by women faculty in higher education. It can, however, be modified relatively easily to simulate structural impediments to women's mobility in industry (see Bredemeier, Rotter, and Stadsklev, 1981). A gaming-simulation of major elements and relationships in an American college (EDGE CITY COLLEGE) was found to offer a model of the workings of an education institution that could be modified for African trainers concerned with teaching students about bureaucratic form (see Greenblat, 1982).

A careful reading of the rest of this manual will prepare you to modify existing materials. Their component parts can be analyzed using the scheme here, and the relevant portions of the representation and construction stages can be brought to bear on this simpler task of redesign.

CAN A FRAME GAME BE LOADED?

The final possibility to be mentioned here is the use of a special form of gaming-simulation usually referred to as a *frame game*. Richard Duke and I (1979, p. 2) defined frame games in *Game-Generating-Games* as follows:

> Basic mechanisms or frameworks which can be loaded with appropriate subject matter for any occasion. The basic rules, once learned, persist for use after use, even though the subject matter changes. For example, a very simple frame game known to most of you is the crossword puzzle. The format is the same in every day's newspaper, but the content changes from day to day.

That volume presents examples and full instructions for loading three frame games: IMPASSE? AT ISSUE! and THE CONCEPTUAL MAPPING GAME. The first of these is a very simple yet effective tool for generating discussion, and has been utilized in many nations to guide participants to consideration of a vast array of topics. Figure 3.1 presents an example of a fully loaded IMPASSE? game, developed for urban planners in the San Francisco Bay Area (the two pages are in back-to-back format in the actual game materials). Figure 3.2 presents a partial loading of a version for consideration of local

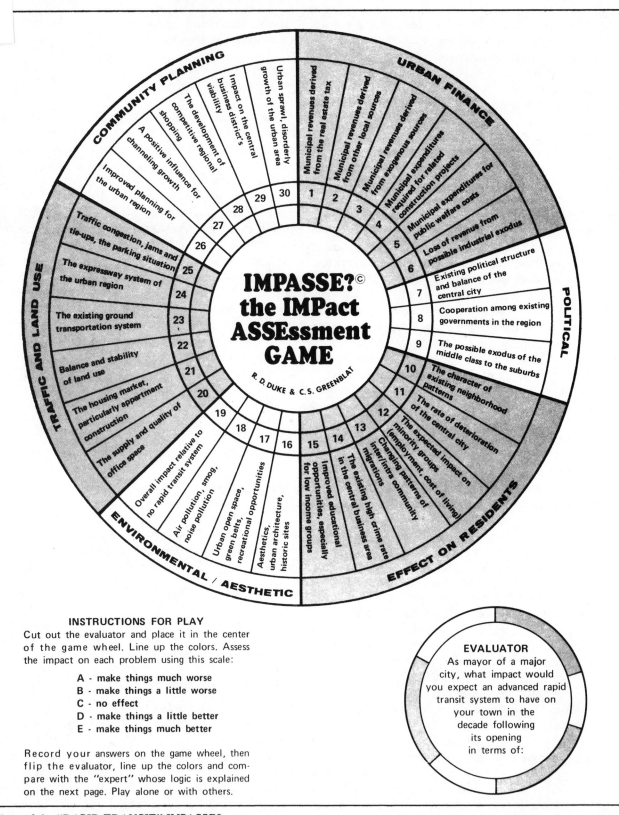

INSTRUCTIONS FOR PLAY

Cut out the evaluator and place it in the center of the game wheel. Line up the colors. Assess the impact on each problem using this scale:

A - make things much worse
B - make things a little worse
C - no effect
D - make things a little better
E - make things much better

Record your answers on the game wheel, then flip the evaluator, line up the colors and compare with the "expert" whose logic is explained on the next page. Play alone or with others.

EVALUATOR
As mayor of a major city, what impact would you expect an advanced rapid transit system to have on your town in the decade following its opening in terms of:

Figure 3.1 "RAPID TRANSIT" IMPASSE?

SOURCE: Duke and Greenblat (1979). Reprinted by permission.

1-(E)   Improved viability of the central business district would result in higher land values.

2-(D)   More active business climate would result in higher tax derived from business.

3-(E)   A successful, advanced rapid transit system will spawn other projects requiring federal aid.

4-(A)   Basic changes in transportation capability will result inevitably in secondary costs for roads, sewers, etc.

5-(C)   Some welfare recipients will be better off, but others will arrive to replace them.

6-(B)   The existing tendancy of industry to decentralize will be encouraged.

7-(B)   Populations will shift as land use patterns adjust to transit capability, affecting wards.

8-(E)   The very magnitude of a rapid transit system requires discussions; perhaps agreement!

9-(B)   The existing tendancy of the middle class to leave the city will be encouraged.

10-(B)   Populations will inevitably shift; construction will intrude on existing neighborhoods.

11-(E)   A viable rapid transit system inevitably makes a city a more viable "central place".

12-(D)   Many actual improvements (low-cost transport, new jobs) will be offset by new indigents.

13-(B)   Construction side effects as well as improved mobility will result in shifting populations.

14-(D)   A more active, viable central area will discourage street crime.

15-(D)   Better transit gives better access, more opportunity to reach a variety of facilities.

16-(B)   Construction of this magnitude inevitably causes damage, some of which is permanent.

17-(E)   Improved mobility brings a greater area of access to residents; more people moved in a given space.

18-(E)   Existing pressures for change will have a better chance for success.

19-(E)   No rapid transit system will inevitably lead to more sprawl and deterioration of the city.

20-(D)   Entrepreneurial response to a new transport system is dramatic; perhaps too dramatic.

21-(E)   The new transport mode will make large areas more accessible to the city.

22-(E)   In the long run, more-dense land uses will locate near the terminals; A more European pattern will result.

23-(E)   Assuming proper integration (!) more people will commit to public transport.

24-(C)   Expressways are here to stay; rapid transport is a complimentary system.

25-(D)   Some improvement is to be expected, however the auto is always with us.

26-(D)   A rapid transport system is a major component in regional growth permitting improved planning.

27-(E)   Growth can be expected to concentrate at the terminals of the rapid transit system.

28-(A)   New shopping centers can be expected at the nodes or transit terminals.

29-(E)   The central business district will be more readily accessible and therefore more viable.

30-(E)   Growth will be channelled by the transit system, planning decisions will be more orderly.

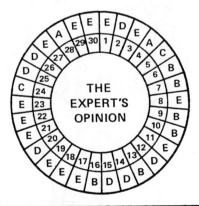

Our "expert" for this game is Dr. William Drake, Assoc. Dean for Research, School of Natural Resources, the University of Michigan. Dr. Drake is director of the Ann Arbor Transportation Authority, which has successfully pioneered in the use of "Dial-a-Ride" mini-buses.

Should your perceptions differ (either with regard to the problems in the impasse wheel, the "expert's" values as assessed, or the brief explanation of his choice) drop a note to the editor marked "Rapid Transit Impasse".

Figure 3.1 Continued

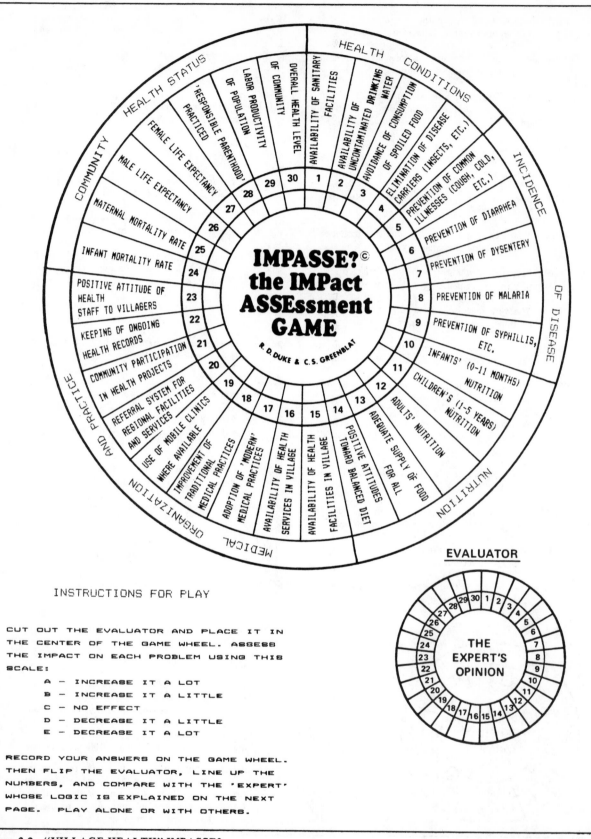

INSTRUCTIONS FOR PLAY

CUT OUT THE EVALUATOR AND PLACE IT IN
THE CENTER OF THE GAME WHEEL. ASSESS
THE IMPACT ON EACH PROBLEM USING THIS
SCALE:

A — INCREASE IT A LOT
B — INCREASE IT A LITTLE
C — NO EFFECT
D — DECREASE IT A LITTLE
E — DECREASE IT A LOT

RECORD YOUR ANSWERS ON THE GAME WHEEL.
THEN FLIP THE EVALUATOR, LINE UP THE
NUMBERS, AND COMPARE WITH THE 'EXPERT'
WHOSE LOGIC IS EXPLAINED ON THE NEXT
PAGE.   PLAY ALONE OR WITH OTHERS.

Figure 3.2   "VILLAGE HEALTH" IMPASSE?
SOURCE: Greenblat. Reprinted by permission.

PREPARATION:

1. Know what your intentions, aims or pedagogical purposes are; review the available games; select the one that seems most appropriate.
2. Integrate the game with other course materials.
3. Become familiar enough with the game to run it well.
4. Be sure you have adequate personnel to run the game; train assistants.
5. Make a time schedule for the game run. Be sure to have adequate time available.
6. Prepare all materials. Careful checking avoids chaos at game time.
7. Decide whether to give out materials in advance.
8. Decide when and how roles will be assigned.
9. Prepare space and furniture arrangement. Check unfamiliar rooms as far in advance as possible.
10. Decide on a policy concerning visitors and/or observers.

INTRODUCTION TO THE GAME:

1. In the introduction to the game, make early reference to:
    a. Gaming-simulation as an instructional medium.
    b. The purpose of the gaming-simulation to be played.
    c. The rules of the game in outline form.
    d. The roles represented by players in the room.
2. Keep the introduction brief.
3. Sound decisive.
4. Explain that initially the participants should expect to be confused.
5. Acknowledge the normality of nervousness and self-conscious-ness in the beginning.
6. Sound enthusiastic.

OPERATION OF THE GAME:

1. Remind players of the rules as situations arise.
2. Give out necessary resources.
3. Collect forms which must be submitted to the game operator.
4. Check forms and other materials that are submitted for accuracy.
5. Perform the necessary calculations.
6. Announce time limits and any time changes.
7. At several intervals announce the time left in the round.
8. Regulate the rhythm of game and non-game enterprises.
9. Deal with unanticipated consequences.
10. The major activity of the operator during this phase is careful observation and assistance to those requiring it.
11. Watch players when they get the results of each cycle.
12. Watch for general lassitude in player behavior.

POST-PLAY DISCUSSION/CRITIQUE:

1. Let players first vent their emotions about the game experience.
2. Then systematically examine the model presented by the game from the perspective of the various roles.
3. Finally, focus on the reality which was represented by the game rather than the game itself.

Figure 3.3 A Guide for Running Gaming-Simulations

SOURCE: Adapted from Greenblat and Duke (1981, pp. 125-136).

health issues in Third World countries. You can consider which issues or policies might be loaded on the reverse side of the "Evaluator" for analysis of their impacts on the 30 variables in the large game wheel, to get an idea of the ease of using a frame game.

One of the most exciting frame games I know of is Fred Goodman's POLICY NEGOTIATIONS. It is described as a "gaming process" consisting of three stages: (1) play of a "priming game," with an emphasis on (2) learning the formal structure of the game, in order to (3) design a new game by modifying the priming game to suit the participants' own situation or interests. POLICY NEGOTIATIONS is a game of the allocation of limited resources type, with the resource being influence. The priming game entails a policy negotiations situation among three school board constituencies and three constituencies of teachers. They negotiate over 24 issues (e.g., increase clerical staff, decrease staff size, replace social studies textbooks). Each constituency can at any point in time be characterized by its influence and its prestige; issues are either internal or external, and the historical propensities of each issue to pass or fail is recorded through play. External social forces that can influence decisions and external events that are "read about in the morning paper" are other structural elements included in the game.

The main goals of play of the priming game are not to have players grapple with the particular substantive issue loaded in the framework (i.e., the school system issues), but rather to have the players learn enough about the structure and process to be able to design a new version, content-specific to their own needs. A vast array of situations lend themselves to this allocation of influence format. While the game design process is immensely easier using the POLICY NEGOTIATIONS frame instead of designing a fully new game, considerable work will need to be done to load the new material. Constituencies must be identified, and their relative influence and prestige assessed. External social forces and external events will also need to be defined. The biggest and most difficult set of tasks have to do with assessment of the impact of passage and failure of each of the issues identified. As the Leader's Notebook indicates, this involves a set of six types of relationships that have to be specified. These are the relationships between:

(1) Each individual issue passage or failure and the historical propensities (including the election probabilities) of all the other issues.
(2) Each individual issue passage or failure and the prestige and influence level of each player.
(3) Each individual issue passage or failure and the influence capacities of each external social force.
(4) Each individual external event and the historical propensities (including the election probabilities) of all the issues.
(5) Each individual external event and the prestige and influence level of each player.
(6) Each individual external event and the influence capacities of each external social force.

These are the kinds of determinations that have to be made in creating the accounting system of a gaming-simulation of this sort. Hence while the task is a highly demanding one, it is one that would have to be done if you were to start from scratch on such a game design project, but you have saved the work of many of the other steps by utilizing this framework.

Other frame games have been described and evaluated by Thiagarajan Sivaisalam in his review article in the Horn and Cleaves *Guide* (1980). Descriptions of the games are also offered in one of the main sections of the volume.

RUNNING THE GAMING-SIMULATION

If you have found a suitable gaming-simulation, you will find there are a number of keys to successful use. A sound educational experience will emerge when the teacher/ trainer pays attention to simple recommendations concerning preparation, operation, and leading the discussion/critique. A short version of such guidelines are provided in Figure 3.3; more elaborate advice can be found in Greenblat and Duke (1975, 1981) and in Jones (1982).

WHEN YOU WANT TO DESIGN YOUR OWN MATERIALS

If the above three questions do not yield usable materials, you may find it necessary to design your own gaming-simulation. Even if you *do* find and use existing materials, the temptation to design your own is likely to arise eventually. The rest of this manual is devoted to that enterprise.

4

An Overview of
the Design Process

The process of design can be thought of as consisting of five stages.

Stage I: setting objectives and parameters
Stage II: model development
Stage III: decisions about representation
Stage IV: construction and modification of the gaming-simulation
Stage V: preparation for use by others

Each of these stages entails a number of steps that will be described in detail in the following chapters. Since decisions in the early stages profoundly affect options available later, it is helpful to begin with an overview of the entire enterprise in this chapter.

STAGE I: SETTING
OBJECTIVES AND PARAMETERS

At the outset it is crucial that the gaming-simulation designer consider carefully what he or she is trying to do and to what ends. This means first delimiting as clearly as possible the subject matter, purpose, intended operators and participants, and the context of use for the proposed gaming-simulation. This stage is too often skipped or undertaken casually, and the would-be designer's initial enthusiasm is translated into only a vague formulation such as "I want to design a game about local politics," with no thought given to what the gaming-simulation is supposed to convey, to whom, and under what conditions of play. The result is often total failure or a product that is totally inappropriate for the intended audience. It is critical to make these decisions *before* anything further is done, and the good designer will spend considerable time formulating such a statement, for it offers much needed guidance later in the process. Wise choices among alternatives in Stage III can be made only by reference to criteria that are explicit or implicit in Stage I specifications.

In Stage II, the designer must also assess the constraints of time, money, and other resources for development and utilization. If you have about 10 hours and

$50 to spend on design, you will make different decisions than if you have 3 months to work under a $15,000 grant! This may seem too obvious to warrant stating, but novices are likely to find they have tremendously underestimated the time and resources needed for effective completion of the project. The resources of potential *users* must also be assessed. Later decisions about the levels of abstraction, time reduction, specificity, complexity, paraphernalia, and computing methods, and so on cannot be made soundly without estimations of the knowledge, time, and monetary resources of the purchasers and operators. A gaming-simulation to be used by experienced trainers with small budgets and one-day sessions should be designed differently than one on the same topic for a large company prepared to invest sizable amounts of time and money in using the product, but having operators with little background in group work or gaming.

In working with student designers I have found it helpful to insist that they develop a brief but cogent set of responses to these questions before proceeding to model development. The same demands made upon myself have likewise forced me to develop greater clarity about what I was proposing to undertake.

It must also be stressed that the answers to these questions may lead to a decision to abandon the project. Gaming-simulation may prove an inappropriate medium for your message, or the resources may be deemed insufficient for the task. In some instances modification of the intent or inflation of the resources may be possible, but often this will not be feasible or desirable. Then the project should be scrapped or shelved for some future time.

STAGE II:
DEVELOPING THE MODEL

The second stage entails developing a conceptual model of the system to be simulated and deciding which elements are to be included in the gaming-simulation. To me, this is the most critical phase, and the point at which many potentially good games fail to achieve their effectiveness. During this stage, the designer must first spell out verbally (and graphically where possible) the system as he or she understands it from the literature and other sources—that is, indicate the *substantive content* of the real-world system. Here roles, goals, activities, constraints, consequences, and external factors must be identified.

Although psychological factors can be brought in by players who are stressed in the same way their real-world counterparts are stressed, this necessitates that the most critical of these psychological factors be identified, and that the roles, goals, resources, constraints, and contingencies that create them be identified as well, so that the sources of the stresses can be simulated.

All too often this stage is undertaken carelessly, and the result is a model that bears little relation to the referent system and is unlikely to operate as it does. *Unless you take the time required to understand the system, you cannot simulate it, even in highly abstract form.*

The model should be written out and shown schematically where possible. With students, I require that 3-10 pages of prose accompanied by diagrams be approved by me before they proceed. Consultation with others at this point may help you to unearth omissions or inaccuracies in your conceptualization and may lead to promising hints or clues about how to proceed with the other task of Stage II: selecting which elements should be included in the gaming-simulation. Guidance in this process of assigning priorities to elements will come from a serious review of your *aims and audiences* as specified in Stage I.

STAGE III: DECISIONS
ABOUT REPRESENTATION

When the basic model has been developed and decisions about elements to be included have been made, you are ready to proceed with translating it into an *operating* model. Here you must make a set of decisions that relate to both style and form.

First, you must decide about the *style* of gaming-simulation, considering four important questions:

(1) What is the appropriate level of abstraction?
(2) What time frame should be employed?
(3) Should there be a linear, radial, or interactive structure to the flow of activities?
(4) How much and what type of interaction should take place between participants?

At this point, review of a number of existing games will give you a sense of basic styles of games.

Second, the *form* of the gaming components must be determined. Here decisions must be made about *how*

each model element that has been selected for inclusion in the gaming-simulation is to be represented. Each element can appear in one of several ways: in the *scenario*, in the *roles*, in the *procedures and rules*, in the *visual imagery and symbols* (e.g., in maps, a game board, blocks, or beans), in the *external factors* (e.g., as chance cards or radio broadcasts or letters received by a player or players, or as an announcement by the operator), or as part of the *accounting system* (e.g., the statements or submodels governing the initial distribution and subsequent redistribution of resources). The creative designer will often find elements in others' games that can be modified and incorporated in the new one. This is not plagiarism; it reflects the wisdom that avoids reinventing the wheel. If the borrowing is extensive, of course, there is an obligation to cite the source.

STAGE IV: CONSTRUCTION
AND MODIFICATION

Now the actual game must be put together and appropriate data must be loaded into it. In Stage III you decided which pieces of the model would be included in the scenario and which in roles; now scenarios and role descriptions must be *written*. Other game elements must likewise be constructed and materials must be acquired. When all parts are assembled into a prototype, the gaming-simulation must be field tested, debugged, retested, and so on until it operates successfully. Considerable trial and retrial is usually necessary before the game generates the behaviors and outcomes characteristic of the referent system. Each "bug" leads the designer back to a reexamination of the conceptual model and the design decisions as well to possible failures in the construction process, in search of a missing element or one inaccurately linked to others. Here considerable creativity and fortitude are required, for the point at which you are "almost there" may be more frustrating than the initial stages when you knew a final product was far distant. When the game has run smoothly 10 times, you are ready to proceed.

STAGE V: PREPARATION
FOR USE BY OTHERS

When you are satisfied that the gaming-simulation works well, it must be prepared for use by others. This means an operator's guide must be prepared and tested, for *you* must not be one of the "necessary materials" for a successful run! Arranging for reproduction and dissemination of a kit or of materials or of instructions for users on how to assemble their own kits involves such considerations as copyright, publication, packaging, and distribution. These are often complicated problems.

Consequently, many fine gaming-simulations have never been made available beyond a limited circle of colleagues.

THE STAGES RECONSIDERED

There are two additional points that must be made here. First, the sketch presents the process as unidirectional: The designer moves from Stage I to Stage II, then to Stages II and IV, and finally to Stage V. In fact there is much moving back and forth among these stages. This was suggested in noting that problems in the test-retest procedure lead the designer back to the conceptual model for modification. Likewise, insights developed in the design and construction phases about the complexity of the system or the costs of high realism may lead to a redefinition of the objectives or parameters (Stage I), as decisions made earlier prove impractical. The decision to publish (Stage V) may lead to revision of some of the construction decisions (Stage IV), as the cost estimates of mass production of some elements indicate they are prohibitively high. In general, however, the "push" is in the forward direction—that is, the process is basically sequential, though there is considerable iteration.

The second caveat is that this is an outline of how games *should* be created rather than a description of how they usually *are* created. As described, the process entails a high degree of discipline that is often not present. Having taken both routes, however—stumbling along doing things in varying sequence, and following these guidelines—I must stress vigorously that the second approach is much more efficient and effective.

GAME DESIGN AND THE MICROCOMPUTER REVOLUTION

In the past decade there has been an enormous growth in computer utilization by game designers for two main purposes: as an aid in the design process, and as a tool for game operation. In the mid-1970s a few quite elaborate and sophisticated gaming-simulations employed computers, including METRO-APEX, CITY 1, INS, and a number of business simulations. On the whole, there was a sharp separation between this handful of computerized gaming-simulations and the rest of the materials in the field.

There were two major impediments to the greater adoption of computer use in design and operation. First, in general, game designers did not have the necessary expertise to design computer models for their games. Second, both the computer hardware and software were expensive and cumbersome. If the game operation was to entail a computer as an element of the paraphernalia, the operator was dependent upon personnel at various locations, and needed to have a compatible system and language at each of the sites at which the game was run.

Neither of these conditions could be comfortably anticipated. Hence some of us recall long nights of trying to make the advance preparations for a complex game run at a host institution, seemingly endless hours of hand-computing results when the computer went "down" in the midst of a run, and considerable frustration as we found ourselves unable to run some games in locations that did not have the hardware, the personnel, or the regular electric current needed for continuous computer operation.

The first signs I saw of the effect of the microcomputer revolution on the game-design enterprise followed fast on the arrival on the market of the Hewlett-Packard programmable calculator. Richard Duke, designing the SNUS game, was concerned with making a portable game "kit" that could be used by ministers in Third World countries that had the above-mentioned limitations of hardware, trained personnel, and regular electric current. He programmed all the model relationships into the HP, and included this $300 item as one of the game materials.

It was not long after this that the first microcomputers were developed for public consumption. The arrival of Apples, IBM-PC's, BBC-Acorns, and the many other brands of microcomputers that were soon available was followed by quantum leaps in memory size, the development of a wide range of software, and improvements in user friendliness. The microcomputer was ideal for game designers, who found they could convert mainframe programs or could directly program their games for these smaller, more readily available machines, which did not require the same level of computer expertise to employ them. Furthermore, the regularly dropping prices of such small machines as the NEC PC-8201A, the Tandy 100, the Sinclair ZX81, and the Commodore 64, meant that even where operator resources were low, computers that offered both low price and high portability could be used. As a result, as this section is being written, computers are increasingly employed in our field. Indeed, David Crookall and Rebecca Oxford (1987), in an introductory essay to a section of a volume on the state of the art in the 1980s, pointed out that,

> although Section Two contains a high proportion of papers dealing with computers, this was not by design, their inclusion here having been determined by substance. Moreover, computers, being essentially content-free, are treated in all sections. This is indicative of the growing use of computers in simulation, and it is becoming increasingly difficult to publish a substantively organized collection, such as this one, which contains a section exclusively devoted to computerized simulation. Indeed, it can easily be argued that computers constitute just one in a whole array of simulation support paraphernalia, along with such items as boards, dice, and forms.

A number of gaming-simulations that formerly ran only on mainframes have now been rewritten for micros (e.g., THE EXECUTIVE SIMULATION, METRO-APEX). New games are more frequently written directly for micros. (There are several papers on this issue in the volumes of proceedings from recent ABSEL meetings; a special issue of *Simulation and Games* was devoted to microcomputers in gaming, and the *Simulation and Games* special issue of June 1987, dealing with the state of the art of business gaming, makes frequent reference to microcomputers.)

The discussion here will necessarily be a limited one, given the restricted scope and scale of this volume, and the limited expertise of the author! For fuller guidance, consult one of the references mentioned herein or a colleague/friend with computer expertise. While mainframe games are surely still in use for some gaming enterprises, I am assuming that most readers will have easier access and greater facility with microcomputers, and hence I will limit my discussion to them.

MICROCOMPUTERS AS
AIDS IN DESIGN

There are four main ways in which computers (microcomputers in particular) can be used as wonderful adjuncts to the design tasks sketched in this chapter and elaborated upon in the ones to come: word processing, graphics, thought organizers, and computer modeling. Readers, I assume, are most likely to be familiar with word processing.

From the first stage of design to the last, your job will be eased considerably if you use a word processor. Many of the materials you draft in Stages I and II will be employed, with minor modifications, in the operator's manual you write when you arrive at Stage V. Hence having these materials on disk means that you can make the needed revisions and be well underway with the preparations for use of the game by others.

When you actually begin construction of the prototype (Stage IV) and then revise it (endlessly, it sometimes seems), the word processor is again a blessing. A change in any part of the gaming-simulation will often necessitate minor or major changes in many other components. With the word processor, clean versions of the revised materials can be produced with little trouble.

The first materials for CAPJEFOS (one of the case studies to be introduced in the next chapter) were prepared by hand and on old typewriters in Cameroon. When I returned home, I typed them all onto disks on the Apple II+ that I used at that time. The bulk of the construction and modification work was undertaken in Cameroon in January 1985. I brought my Apple and my data disks, and we were freed from dependence upon the limited secretarial staff, the ancient typewriters, and the nonexistent photocopying facilities. Every page of materials underwent at least 5 revisions, and all were produced rapidly in the "Greenblat Computer Room" by members

of the team, who were taught to use the program the first day. Had this rapid turnaround not been possible, the time for field testing and modification would have been at least 10 times as long—an impossibility, given the short-term UNESCO contract under which we were working. Pierre Corbeil has made the French translation of these materials by using an IBM compatible microcomputer and we have been able to coordinate tasks on preparation of this new set of materials through my use of a laptop IBM compatible machine.

At the stage of preparation for use by others (Stage V), the word processor again will give you great flexibility. Desktop publishing programs, coupled with laser printers, make it feasible for you to produce operator's and players' materials of high quality, and hence to "publish" attractive game kits without typesetting. Those who do go the route of professional publishers may find that typesetting can be done from the computer disks you provide, eliminating many errors.

The use of graphics programs for the creation of forms and diagrams is a second arena in which the microcomputer may be an invaluable aid to the gaming-simulation designer. At present, the best materials I have seen are made for the Macintosh, but each day brings news of improved graphics programs for other machines (e.g., PC-Paint for the IBM family). These programs permit inclusion of graphs, pies, diagrams, and basic graphic designs that may enhance both the presentation and the clarity of the materials. As an example, consider Figure 4.1, which shows the form to be completed by the player in charge of the Population and Household Consumption sector in the first published version of STRATEGEM-1. Figure 4.2 shows the next version of this form as Diana Shannon created it on the Macintosh. The information given the player and the entries required of him or her are identical, but I would argue that the psychological impact of the newer form is far more positive, and it should elicit considerably more enthusiasm and general interest in the game.

As I began to write this section, I decided to take advantage of an offer by Dennis Meadows and Diana Shannon to come to Dartmouth and have them show me the ease with which such graphics could be done on the Macintosh. Within three hours of the beginning of my instruction, I was saying "I *have to* have a Mac...," and I anticipate acquiring one in the near future. I know of no other way, shy of professional publication (with typesetting at high costs), to obtain the extraordinary quality of graphics for cards, boards, forms, and so on that are possible with relative ease through the use of such programs such as MacDraw; Illustrator; Ready, Set, Go!; and PageMaker. They are a game designer's delight.

The third use to be mentioned here is that of "thought organizers," such as MaxThink, ThinkTank, THOR, and the Idea Processor, and the fourth is the utilization of

Figure 4.1   Form from the First Published Version of STRATEGEM-1

SOURCE: Meadows (1985). Reprinted by permission.

Country # _____, Name _____

Population Minister Decision Sheet

Your Sector's Stocks

	years 0-4	years 5-9	years 10-14	years 15-19	years 20-24	years 25-29	years 30-34	years 35-39	years 40-44	years 45-49	High Equilibrium
PO:1 Population	200										500
PO:2 Total Food Available (last cycle's imports and production)	3300										12500
PO:3 Total Goods Available (last cycle's imports and production)	3500										68600

Useful Information

	years 0-4										High Equilibrium
PO:4 Food Per Capita (per year, last cycle)	2										5
PO:5 Annual Deaths Per 1000 (per year, last cycle)	18										10
PO:6 Goods Per Capita (per year, last cycle)	2										15
PO:7 Human Services Capital Per Capita (last cycle)	2.25										18
PO:8 Annual Births Per 1000 (per year, last cycle)	41										10

DECISION #1 Allocate Total Food Available

	years 0-4	years 5-9	years 10-14	years 15-19	years 20-24	years 25-29	years 30-34	years 35-39	years 40-44	years 45-49
PI:1 Food for Population (total for this cycle)										
PI:2 Food for Export										
TOTAL (must equal PO:2)										

DECISION #2 Allocate Total Goods Available

	years 0-4	years 5-9	years 10-14	years 15-19	years 20-24	years 25-29	years 30-34	years 35-39	years 40-44	years 45-49
PI:3 Goods for Population (total for this cycle)										
PI:4 Goods Available for Investment										
PI:5 Goods for Export										
TOTAL (must equal PO:3)										

Figure 4.2 Form from the Second Published Version of STRATEGEM-1

SOURCE: Meadows (1985). Reprinted by permission.

modeling programs (such as DYNAMO). Both of these are too technical to discuss in these pages, but some preliminary information is available from sources in the References section (see Fuhs, 1986; Richardson and Pugh, 1981; Roberts et al., 1983).

MICROCOMPUTERS IN GAME OPERATION

The second domain to be addressed is the utilization of computers in the *operation* of the game. There are several reasons the designer may wish to include a computer in the materials to be employed by either the operator or the players or both. (See Crookall et al., 1986, for a lengthier discussion.)

First, one objective of the gaming-simulation may be to make players more familiar with and/or comfortable with microcomputers or particular software applications. For example, Daniel Sherrell, Kenneth Russ, and Alvin Burns (1986) wanted to have business students learn to use Lotus 1-2-3 in a simulated management environment; they employed a microcomputer decision support system (DDS) using this software in conjunction with play of COMPETE, a mainframe game.

Second, the microcomputer may be employed for calculations of outcomes of players' decisions as either an optional or a mandatory element. For example, operators of CLUG can hand calculate between rounds of play or can enter players' decisions into a short program to save time and reduce errors. Likewise, THE GREEN REVOLUTION GAME manager's handbook contains a small program for the Sinclair ZX81, which, if used, provides similar assistance to the operator. And several business games such as COLLECTIVE BARGAINING SIMULATED include optional computer disks to be employed by the game operator. (See Biggs, 1986, for an introduction to and overview of computerized business games.)

Third, in some cases, the computer is not simply an optional aid to the operator, but a mandatory element, for the gaming-simulation includes a simple or complex model that involves calculations beyond those that might be done by the operator between rounds of play (e.g., FISH BANKS, LTD., MANSYM, STRATEGEM-1, STRATEGEM-2). Players may turn forms in to the operator, who enters the figures into the computer, or players may themselves have disks and do their own data entry, giving these to the operator for the additive operations. In addition to the option of having the microcomputer do calculations in COLLECTIVE BARGAINING SIMULATED, the game can also be run with individuals or groups representing management negotiating with the computer, which "plays" labor; the time frame is reduced from 1-4 weeks of play to 2-4 hours.

Fourth, the microcomputer may be used for communication between teams. In ICONS, the necessary communications between player teams in different countries are handled through local computer terminals, network user identifiers on the various national telecommunication packets, and a central mainframe at the University of Maryland (see Crookall and Wilkenfeld, 1985, for more details).

Fifth and finally, microcomputers can be productively employed to give players access to a data base. In THE MARBLE COMPANY, an (optional) computerized data base is available to players and the operator through the REFLEX program on the IBM-PC. Jan Klabbers's PERFORM simulates a university with two faculties, a governing board and a planning staff. These players are concerned with policymaking processes related to manpower planning. Each faculty has its own computerized planning system, FORMASY, and they communicate through computer terminals (Klabbers, 1984, 1985). Sherrell, Russ, and Burns (1986) use microcomputer software to give players access to a historical data base of past teams' strategies and successes.

THE COSTS AND REWARDS OF DESIGN

The design enterprise is one that should not be undertaken casually. First of all, it is time consuming. Occasionally, designers, when asked how long it took to complete work on their latest product, can offer a clear answer. More often, however, they give an answer such as the following hypothetical one (which resembles the answer we would have given concerning design of THE MARRIAGE GAME):

> Well, we started in January, working "officially" one day a week on the project while all of us were also teaching and writing. Then at Easter time we spent an intensive 5 days on design. In the next few weeks an assistant reproduced materials, typed forms and gathered paraphernalia, and the next time we met we put a set together. Early in June we ran the game for the first time. It worked quite well, but there were several problems which we worked out in the next several months through meetings, more trials, more meetings, and more trials! We thought we were finished in early November, but we hadn't yet written the operator's manual, and had done nothing about arranging for publication. I don't then really know how long it took us, because we've been working over a 10-month period, but it has been only one of several things we've done in that time. On the other hand it would be unfair to count only the days we "officially" worked on the gaming-simulation, as there were many times I thought about it while riding the bus, washing my hair, and trying to fall asleep—and some of those moments yielded the best solutions!

A very small percentage of designers work on their projects under contract from clients who demand that a time schedule be met but who also provide funds to free the designer from many other obligations. (Richard Duke is one of the exceptions, and his extensive output is partly a result of his success in securing external support.) Even fewer persons are full-time designers (again noteworthy exceptions are Chris Brand and Terry Walker of Maxim Consultants in Brighton, England). The rest of us (and, I assume, most readers) must engage in gaming-simulation design during scant "free time" or at least in conjunction with numerous other obligations. In such cases, the process is likely to stretch over a long period.

Persons who have never been involved in gaming-simulation design tend to underestimate this time investment. I periodically receive calls from people who want to hire me to design a product that can be employed in an event scheduled for 3 weeks from the time of the inquiry! However tempting the idea (or the fee!), I must turn them down, explaining the impossibility of fulfilling such a commitment.

Second, it must be noted that designing a gaming-simulation demands hard work as well as imagination. The time problem outlined above is compounded by the fact that, as with any creative enterprise, it is impossible to make plans with knowledge of when inspiration will strike! I have had game design projects in which I felt "stuck" on a problem for 2-3 weeks, and then suddenly "knew" what to do and proceeded with great speed for a time afterwards. As suggested in the introduction, prior familiarity with a range of existing gaming-simulations can make the job much easier, as can taking a systematic approach. Thus undertaking design with the aid of this manual should help you to be successful, but you must bring your own talents, discipline, and perseverance to the task.

Third, I do not believe that game design should be undertaken as a single-person effort; rather, a *team* of at least two people (and preferably three) should be assembled. Most good ideas in gaming-simulation design result from considerable interaction with others: brainstorming, dividing up jobs, trying out various alternatives, and "playing out" some of the ideas. If others are not on your design team, you will either lack this essential interaction, or you will find yourself dragging your spouse, children, parents, roommates, students, or colleagues into the venture!

There is, however, a bright side to the bleaker picture painted above. It is true that your enthusiasm for undertaking a gaming-simulation design project should be tempered by a realistic assessment of the time needed, the work and imagination you are willing to put forth, and the difficulties of working alone. If, on the other hand, you are not working under heavy time pressure, if you are willing to continue the work over more than just a few days, and if you can find others to work with you, you are likely to find design an extremely rewarding process— one that is enormously instructive even to the designer who already knows a great deal about the referent system. This derives from the demands of design: the need for clarity in thinking about what the critical elements are; the need to think at various levels of abstraction; the push for concreteness to specify the conditions under which posited relationships hold; and, primarily, the need for *systemic* understanding—seeing the connections among roles, goals, resources, constraints, and contingencies. Thus you may design your gaming-simulation to instruct others, but you will learn a great deal yourself! Dennis Meadows has told me that after 20 years of teaching students to build computer-simulation models, he now requires them to take a course in game design, because it imposes a very strict and rigorous discipline on the effort to model a system.

William Gamson (1975, pp. 306-307) has described the excitement of designing SIMSOC as follows:

> I have found the process of continual modification of SIMSOC a peculiarly absorbing and rewarding intellectual experience. It has a concreteness and immediacy which is lacking in much of the intellectual work I do. . . . With the development of a simulation . . . it is as if I have a complicated Rube Goldberg device in front of me that will produce certain processes and outcomes. I want it to operate differently in one way or another but it is difficult to know where and how to intervene to achieve this purpose because the apparatus is delicate and highly interconnected. So I walk around it eyeing it from different angles, and imagine adding a nut here or a bolt there or shutting it off and replacing some more complicated parts.
>
> Each of these interventions must take the extremely specific form of a rule. To intervene, one must play a mental game in which the introduction of *every* specific change must be weighed in terms of how the whole contraption will operate. Such mental games force one to develop a clear picture of what the apparatus looks like and why it operates as it does. Each hypothetical alternative must be put in place and imagined in operation. Finally, an explicit choice has to be made and the game actually run under the altered rules, and one has a chance to discover whether he really understands the contraption or not. When a rule-change has the effect it is supposed to have, the experience can be very exciting— as exciting as predicting a non-obvious outcome in any social situation and having it turn out correctly.

This personal report emphasizes the final point to be made here about the rewards of design: it is an involving, exciting, and intellectually challenging enterprise. If the project is undertaken well and carried to completion, it is likely to leave you "hooked" on the process as a fine way to refine your thinking about a great many topics.

5

Setting Objectives and Parameters

Let me begin with a summary of the questions to be answered in Stage I—setting objectives and parameters. When you set to work, write the underlined words on separate sheets of paper or index cards and write the answers as you develop them for the proposed gaming-simulation:

What is the *subject matter*?
What *purpose* is to be served?
Who are the likely *players*?
Who are the likely *operators*?
What is the probable *context of use*?
What *resources* (time, money, other) are likely to be available to the users?
What *resources* (time, money, other) are available for development?

THE SUBJECT MATTER

The first and most obvious consideration is that of the *subject matter*. In many instances you will have decided to design your gaming-simulation because you know about a topic and wish to find a better way to teach about it or communicate about it to others. (If you are a novice designer, it is unlikely that you have been approached by someone else and asked to design a gaming-simulation about a topic with which you are not familiar. This will happen when you have designed several successful products. In that case, you must work with the client for careful specification of the subject matter and parameters.)

At this early point you need not be concerned with a detailed statement, but you must narrow the topic somewhat. For example, it is insufficient to say that the subject matter is "marriage," or "sexism," or "village life." Rather you need to translate these general formulations into more limited statements such as the following:

"The major decisions that must be made by couples in the early years of marriage, and the cumulative consequences of these decisions . . . " (from THE MARRIAGE GAME);

"The factors that impede female academics from advancing up the promotion ladder in institutions of higher education as readily as their male counterparts do . . . " (from THE ACADEMIC GAME);

"The character of traditional village life in Africa, and the factors that facilitate and factors that hinder development in these villages . . ." (from CAPJEFOS: A SIMULATION OF VILLAGE DEVELOPMENT).

Simple as it sounds to write such statements of the subject matter, you will often find that design-team members will have different ideas about *which* facet of the topic should serve as the basis for the gaming-simulation. One person may wish to emphasize the role of elders in structuring village life; another may want to focus on the role of development agents in bringing about change; and a third may be concerned with patterns of communication among village residents and between them and the outside world.

It is often helpful to begin by "brainstorming" for suggestions about specific subject matter—that is, make a list of those foci that *might* be emphasized. Generate a long list at first, withholding judgment about the suitability or interest any suggested topic has to you. Then consider each possibility independently. Finally, narrow the list down to those two or three statements that look most promising. If you cannot reach agreement on the one to be adopted as your subject matter statement, you may wish to leave several options for the moment, and move to other questions, later returning to make the final choice. (Of course, if you are doing work for a client, many of these statements will be given to you.)

PURPOSE

The question of purpose is closely connected with that of subject matter. Indeed, in some cases, particularly where *skill development* is of special concern, the question of purpose may be more important than that of subject matter. For example, if your main purpose for the gaming-simulation is to develop players' communication skills, it may not matter to you very much whether the subject matter is in the domain of local politics or hospital administration. Rather, you will select a subject matter area that you know something about and that is likely to interest the players and stimulate them to engage in verbal interaction.

In many cases there will be more than one purpose. If this is so, you should list several aims, but you must put them in some order of priority, because there are always trade-offs to be made during the overall process.

If you do not already have a set of purposes in mind, review the list of objectives in Chapter 2 and select the one(s) of most concern to you, add others if you choose, and phrase the statements with as much specificity as you can. For example, instead of "communication skills," you might list "developing and presenting an argument, negotiating and bargaining, preparing written reports, public speaking, chairing a meeting." Instead of "business skills," you might list "learn how to read and use financial statements, how to relate decisions and transactions to their financial statements, how to plan and control their businesses" (as in THE CONDENSED BUSINESS EXPERIENCE PROGRAM).

PLAYERS' CHARACTERISTICS

Who will the likely players be? You must answer this by listing as many of their characteristics as possible, but particular attention must be given to their age, knowledge of the subject matter, level of relevant skills prior to play, social and/or occupational positions, and to the degree of *homogeneity* of typical groups of players. A gaming-simulation about health care for terminally ill patients, designed to create empathy for both medical personnel and patients, for example, will be differently designed depending upon whether it is to be played by high school students, or nursing students, or the elderly. Similarly, the characteristics of a game about some aspect of business management should be different if it is to be played by audiences of community members to show them the pressures on business leaders than it would be if it is to be played by corporate executives to sensitize them to the problems of coordination of departments in the firm. It is important, then, that you state your target group of players and think carefully about their characteristics. These have implications for the degree of complexity you can present, the degree of formality that must be included, and the need for background information.

OPERATOR CHARACTERISTICS

A question directly related to the characteristics of the players is that of the characteristics of the likely oper-

ators. In the case of commercially produced entertainment games, players themselves are likely to choose a game and organize themselves to play it. In the case of gaming-simulations, however, the players are likely to be invited or "forced" to play a game selected by a teacher, group leader, or conference organizer. You must thus think about who *these* people are and what aims, interests, and abilities they have. A gaming-simulation that would have enormous appeal to secondary school social studies students will not be adopted for their use if it does not appeal to secondary school social studies *teachers*; a gaming-simulation designed to strengthen players' communications skills by focusing on complexities in irrigation project management is unlikely to be selected by a trainer with a limited economics background.

CONTEXT OF USE

How do you envision the gaming-simulation will generally be used? Will it be incorporated in courses on the topic offered in schools? Is it to be used at professional meetings or conferences by player groups created for the occasion but with no continuing contact? Will it be used as the "opener" in a 2-3 day workshop or course, or, alternatively, as a finale to a short course, giving participants a way to try out what they have learned? Will preparatory or follow-up sessions be possible? Will the topic also be dealt with through lectures, films, and reading assignments, or is the gaming-simulation the main vehicle to be employed?

Specification of the context of use will give you the ability to determine how many players must be accommodated in play sessions. If the gaming-simulation is directed at classes that are typically composed of 20-25 students, you must design a gaming-simulation with that number of roles, or one in which the class can be divided into smaller groups for simultaneous play (recall that teachers may not be able to find assistants, so one operator will have to be able to run the game with these parallel groups . . .). If the training sessions in which you want the gaming-simulation used are typically composed of 5-10 participants, you will have different constraints in design.

The answer to the question of context of use will tell you something about how *long* the gaming-simulation can last, and also about how much follow-up can be expected. It is also directly keyed to the question of resources of the users, as discussed below.

RESOURCES FOR PLAY

You must decide approximately how long play is to last. This answer is likely to flow directly from the above considerations, but there may be some latitude. Thus if training sessions typically last for 3 days, you could design a one-hour, a half-day, or a three-day exercise. Again, advance specification of the approximate time that you think operators will be willing to devote to the enterprise will affect later decisions about what to simulate and how to incorporate it in the gaming elements. On the other hand, the complexity of what you want to teach will effect how long the exercise should last, as indicated by Duane Dillman (1970, p. 7):

> The length of a simulation exercise should probably be governed by the amount of time necessary for the participants to uncover the governing relationships of the exercise and then develop the appropriate strategies and ideas and observe the results of their actions. . . . Decision periods would vary from twenty minutes or so to several hours depending upon the activity being undertaken.

If you know something about the monetary resources that will be available to potential users you will also be guided in design decisions. Expensive paraphernalia should not be included if users have limited financial resources to buy such a kit; rather you should use very inexpensive materials or instructions for self-made kits. On the other hand, if the gaming-simulation is to be used by a corporate training program, you may need to use printed forms rather than mimeographed ones, and other materials will have to look "professional" to these people, or they may not take the gaming-simulation seriously.

Some users (such as those in training-program offices, secondary schools, and corporations) must usually purchase the gaming-simulation from their budgets, but in other cases a portion of the costs can be passed on to players (e.g., university students can each be asked to purchase a manual as part of their course material). Information about this may affect the form in which you put the final product.

Finally, what do you know about the other resources available to potential users? What kind of *space* do they have to work in, for example? Are the rooms they have access to large or small? Do they have desks or tables in them or can such desks or tables be obtained easily? If not, are the players likely to be willing to sit on the floor (secondary school students will usually be happy to do so; physicians and business executives will not)? Is the furniture movable or fixed in place? How far will they have to move the game materials when it is run?

What about facilities for photocopying? Computing (via hand calculators or computers)? What kind of materials can readily be purchased in stores in the locales of users? Again, this will affect your decisions about what to include as symbols, and about whether to provide complete kits or instructions for assembling kits.

RESOURCES FOR DEVELOPMENT

The questions concerning time, money, and other resources must also be asked about the design team. How much time do you have to meet and work on the gaming-simulation? Are there deadlines for completion? Will you be able to work together or must much be done separately? Do you have funds available from your employer or an outside source, or must you personally pay for all materials used? Are some resources, such as photocopying and typing, available to you free of charge? These answers should be seriously considered before you start.

WRITING OUT THE ANSWERS

When you have developed the answers to the questions discussed above, you should have information on your index cards or sheets that will permit you to prepare a 1-3 page statement of objectives and parameters. Do not trust to memory about your answers, but write them out and keep the statement in front of you to serve as a reminder and to help narrow the options at each later step. Furthermore, it will be helpful to have such a statement prepared if your boss or others ask what you are doing! Finally, as we shall see in Chapter 11, this statement can be used with only minor editing, as the beginning of the operator's manual and as an essential summary about the product. Thus writing it out now will save you work later.

SOME SAMPLES

The following are examples of statements of objectives and parameters written early in the design process for BLOOD MONEY and CAPJEFOS, two of the case studies that will be presented in later chapters.

INITIAL STATEMENT OF OBJECTIVES AND PARAMETERS: BLOOD MONEY

(1) *Subject Matter*

The game is to simulate on an abstract level the general character of the experience of the hemophiliac and of those concerned with providing him with care. The basic game should be alterable to simulate the situation of another patient group with similar basic characteristics: i.e., disease is chronic, attacks are unpredictable, costs of care are financially catastrophic to the patients.

(2) *Purpose*

The game is designed to serve as a "motivator" to present issues and problems, "priming" the player for more information to be presented in a more traditional manner (e.g., reading material in pamphlet form). The creation of empathy is a major purpose.

(3) *Intended Players*

There are three major potential groups of players:

(a) Medical and medical school personnel desiring further understanding of the problems of hemophilia, particularly from the perspective of the patient;

(b) students of medicine, nursing, and health care; and

(c) lay people involved personally with hemophiliacs (parents, blood bank staff, employers) or interested in learning about the disease and its consequences (e.g., students). The game should be the same for all groups, but post-game discussion and follow-up material provided should be different. The game should be playable by groups of approximately 25-35 participants.

(4) *Intended Operators*

This game is being developed under contracts from the National Heart and Lung Institute, in cooperation with the National Hemophilia Foundation. The Foundation might be the ultimate disseminator of game instructions and/or materials to member chapters and others interested. Operators will be teachers or members of NHF chapters.

(5) *Context of Use*

This would depend upon the player-group. For students, the game would be used as part of an educational program. For others, it would most often be used as part of a brief program: e.g., Introduction—15 minutes; play 1 hour 15 minutes; discussion 1 hour or discussion 1/2 hour and lecture 1/2 hour. Hence the game could be utilized as the basis of a meeting sponsored by NHF or at a conference. Follow-up would consist of players' receiving a "data book" which would amplify their experiences. Three "levels" of data book might be prepared, directed at three audiences.

(6) *Resources*

(a) Financial, for design, construction and testing: Enough days remain on these contracts to develop a preliminary version for trial at the April 24-25 session in New York City. Further work, if warranted by that run, would require additional time for working out bugs, trials, and write-up of the instructions in final form for use by others. It is difficult to estimate that time now—I would guess 10 days each, but would be able to make a more educated estimate after seeing the shape the game is in on April 24th.

(b) Materials: These costs are being kept relatively low. Our vision of the game at this moment is that it should consist of materials that could be readily assembled and disseminated at low cost. A "kit" should be constituted of re-usable materials, so that once purchased it could be readily re-used with a number of player groups. It should be possible for the interested person to construct a kit himself, so standard, readily available materials will be used wherever possible. I would, however, hope we could

find a way to disseminate pre-packaged "kits." The total kit should be portable and easily put together into use [Greenblat and Gagnon, 1976].

The next statement was developed by a team of 23 Africans and myself, working in the context of a game-design workshop sponsored by UNESCO and the Pan African Institute for Development (PAID) in Buea, Cameroon in November 1983. This game was later developed into CAPJEFOS by a smaller subgroup. The specifications remained the same.

INITIAL STATEMENT OF OBJECTIVES AND PARAMETERS: AFRICAN VILLAGE DEVELOPMENT GAME

(1) *Subject Matter*

Factors which hinder and/or promote rural development at the scale of the village. Particular attention will be paid to self-help programmes for health and agriculture systems and the manner in which village actions are influenced by regional/national planning objectives and policies.

(2) *Purpose*

(a) Understanding factors of development and their interaction;

(b) more empathy for villagers and knowledge of their rationale;

(c) exploration of what development agent's role could/should be.

(3) *Intended Players*

Development agents in service or training:

(a) first priority for village level workers;

(b) second priority for division/sub-division/micro-region workers;

(c) third priority for provincial and national level agents.

Size of group: 20-25 would be a suitable group, given the number of roles. It also corresponds to a batch or 1/2 batch in a training institute and represents a reasonable number of people to be assembled for a short in-service training session.

(4) *Intended Operators*

Training Institute staff with regular students, or for refresher courses for graduates and in-service training sessions organized on request from grass-roots development agents.

(5) *Context of Use*

See #4 above.
Time frame for play including breaks and discussion: Minimum: 5 hours; Maximum: 1 day (about 8 hours).

(6) *Resources (for design)*

• 23 highly qualified participants with active development and/or training experience, in different African countries

- Student case studies of 2 villages
- Case studies of effects of migration
- PAID facilities (blackboard, classroom(s), typing, running off mimeographed materials)
- Limited monetary resources (necessarily limits costs of reproducing copies of the game)

USING THE STATEMENT OF OBJECTIVES AND PARAMETERS

As you progress through the next stages of the process, you will make regular references back to this statement. Many of the decisions about representation and about construction entail making trade-offs between options, and there will be no right and wrong answers. The useful advice of Duane Dillman (1970, p. 6) is consistent with this thesis:

> Although it may sound trite, a guideline regarding simplicity is that in designing a simulation exercise one should make it simple enough to be understood and played without hours of advanced study of the rules and scenario and yet complex enough to be interesting and challenging to an experienced participant. Simplicity applies to at least four areas in simulation: participation, computation, administration and construction. Trade-offs will probably be necessary to get an optimum balance between these four items. Another balance between the realism discussed earlier and the simplicity must be made by considering the degree of each desired as contrasted with the degree of each attainable with available resources.

You will have to make judgments, then, about what to do *given your objectives, the anticipated players, operators, and context of use, and the resources available to you and the users.* These decisions will often be difficult, but they will be easier to the extent that you have thought about those elements in advance. When you have completed this statement of objectives and parameters, you are ready to move to Stage II: developing the conceptual model.

6

Model Development

GETTING STARTED

Stage II, developing the conceptual model for your gaming-simulation, is extremely important, for as Chapter 4 indicated, you cannot simulate a system if you do not understand it. However, you will find that this stage of the overall process entails many relatively familiar activities. Your task at this point is to describe in writing, and when possible also in diagrammatic form, the most salient aspects of the system you wish to simulate. In that sense, developing the conceptual model is somewhat similar to writing a report or short "term paper." This report will present a simplification of the real system (as does *any* model, whether it be verbal, graphic, physical, mathematical, or a simulation); it is likely, however, to be far too complex to translate it fully into a gaming-simulation, particularly if play is to be relatively short (i.e., 1-2 hours). You will then have to review your model, identifying those elements and relationships you believe to be of greatest importance for inclusion.

This stage of gaming-simulation design, then, will take you to the library, to your own prior work, to case studies, and perhaps to some direct fieldwork. How much effort is involved depends upon your existing knowledge of the system. In some cases, designers work on topics on which they have previously done considerable research. Then they are likely to have already identified the salient elements, and they can start at the point of identifying the most critical ones to be included. The model development stage of POMP AND CIRCUMSTANCE, to be discussed later, was very short, as all three designers (myself, John Gagnon, and Linda Rosen) had read and written extensively on the topic: premarital pregnancy. Thus we were able to work from our own prior conceptualizations. While decisions had to be made about the elements to be included in the gaming-simulation, extensive research on the topic was not necessary as design began.

Even if the designers are already familiar with the topic, they typically will want to conceptualize it in a form close to the gaming format (see case studies 2 and 3

below). Gaming-simulation design demands that one think quite *concretely* and that one develop an overall or *systemic* understanding. You have to ask not only about definitions and specific linkages, but also about interconnections among roles, goals, resources, and rules.

When a gaming-simulation designer is hired by a client to design a teaching/training tool about a subject relatively unfamiliar to the designer, much preliminary investigation must take place before design decisions can be approached (see case study 1 below and Duke, 1980). Direct experience by the designer may supplement written sources, if the coverage is incomplete. In designing THE CONFERENCE GAME, a tool for training participants in planning a large conference, Chris Brand and Terry Walker supplemented information gleaned from the literature by making inquiries of hotels, speakers' bureaus, printers, and others. Through direct experience with difficulties and "dead-ends," they were able to identify many of the problems typically encountered by the conference planner. Later they were able to build these into the gaming-simulation.

THREE CASE STUDIES

Three case studies of model development will be described here to illustrate some of the ways the work of developing the conceptual model might proceed.

BLOOD MONEY
(Cathy Stein Greenblat and John H. Gagnon)

As Chapter 5 indicated, the purpose of BLOOD MONEY was to simulate on an abstract level the general character of the experience of the hemophiliac and of those who provide him with care and blood. Our model development began with reading documents about the disease, including some biographical studies. We focused our attention on the social and psychological conditions, paying limited attention to the more technical medical characteristics (we were not physicians, nor were we interested in teaching detailed medical facts).

This search of the literature and a number of meetings with experts on hemophilia care led to the development of a conceptual model consisting of two basic interacting role sets: the sick and those desiring to aid them. The first set consisted of patients whose goals are to engage as fully as possible in the ongoing "normal world" composed of school/job/family/friendship networks with their rewards of money, prestige, and social interaction. Patients are hindered in this by the periodic but unpredictable advent of attacks of bleeding, which require expensive and sometimes not readily available medical care and infusions of blood. The second role set is made up of those in one way or another concerned with the goals of providing medical treatment. Some of these people gather and disseminate blood; others provide care and perform special treatments (operations); others are charged with helping pay for the services and product. The easy accomplishment of these tasks is hindered by the unpredictable timing of demand, the limits of supply of blood and care relative to the demand, organizational problems that limit efficient delivery, and the absence of adequate information about patients.

The character of the patient world was diagrammed in the form of Figure 6.1 (which does not elaborate upon the problems relating to interface with the medical care system. These problems will be described later). The main actors and interdependencies in the health care system are shown in Figure 6.2. This latter is a simplified diagram that omits a number of other actors, such as those engaged in research and education and funders of these programs.

The quality of care the patient receives was seen to depend upon at least the following factors: (a) ratio of patients to doctors with knowledge and ability to treat; (b) availability of care facilities (hospitals, surgery, materials, and so on); (c) availability of blood; (d) cost of care; (e) cost of blood; (f) financial resources of patients (personal funds or insurance or access to public payment); (g) organization of M.D.'s, clinics, and blood banks; (h) linkage of patients to networks.

This material was followed by one- to two-paragraph discussions of some of the details of relevant subtopics in the figures, including medical problems (sources, symptoms); medical treatment and costs; psychological problems; absences; school and job problems and failures; public ignorance, stigmatization, and discrimination; and insurance limitations. The entire document was about 8 pages long.

After carefully reviewing this document, we made a list of the most important factors to be simulated:

(1) Ongoing, unpredictable medical problems that are cumulative in their impacts and that require treatment;
(2) need for medical treatment and blood, and scarcity of both;

(3) need for money for medical treatment;
(4) a rigid school/job world;
(5) public ignorance of medical problems; and
(6) insurance limitations.

A second list was made of factors that we wanted to be *emergent* in most runs of the game—that is, factors that should *develop* through play:

(1) absenteeism;
(2) school/job/family/friendship problems and failures;
(3) job discrimination against the more severely handicapped;
(4) psychological problems: anxiety, tension, fear, negative self-image;
(5) bureaucracy and red tape in the medical arena;
(6) frustration experienced by those trying to deliver care; and
(7) varying degrees of distrust between the two sectors.

Finally we made a diagram of the *linkages* between these elements, viewing the problem as one of a continuing downward spiral, as shown in Figure 6.3. At that point, we were ready to proceed to Stages III and IV: turning the model into a gaming-simulation (this will be described in Chapter 9).

CAPJEFOS: A SIMULATION OF VILLAGE DEVELOPMENT
(Cathy Stein Greenblat, with Philip Langley, Jacob Ngwa, Saul Luyumba, Ernest Mangesho, and Foday MacBailey)

Design of this gaming-simulation began in the context of a training workshop on gaming-simulation design sponsored by UNESCO and the Pan African Institute for Development in Buea, Cameroon. The objectives and parameters of the game have been described in Chapter 5. Workshop participants were highly knowledgeable about dimensions of life in African villages and about the problems of introducing change in such contexts. In addition, PAID provided four recent case studies of villages to all participants at the start of the workshop. Model development was possible using only limited additional documents.

Participants developed a conceptual model by working in subgroups, each devoted to identification of one of the three major sets of information needed for subsequent easy translation to the gaming format. One group worked on the identification of major actors in the real-world system, with the task being to define the main *roles*, and for each role, the goals, activities, and resources. A second group worked on listing factors that hinder development in villages and identifying the linkages between them. Finally, a third group worked on identification of the natural and social characteristics (other than roles and development factors) in a typical village

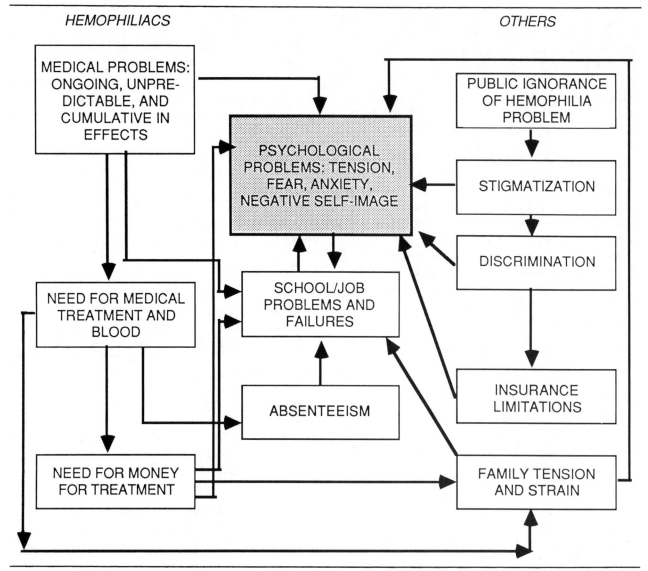

HEMOPHILIACS   OTHERS

Figure 6.1 BLOOD MONEY—The Social Psychological World of the Hemophiliac

SOURCE: Greenblat and Gagnon (1976). Reprinted by permission.

and the kinds of external events that might affect these. They were also asked to produce a map of a "typical" village. Figure 6.4 represents a portion of the piece of the model developed by the group concerned with roles; Figure 6.5 presents a portion of the list of factors identified by the second group. Later discussion by the whole design team was directed at narrowing down these lists by identifying the factors that were most important to the team for inclusion in the final product.

In January 1985, following much interim correspondence, a second workshop was held under UNESCO sponsorship in Cameroon. This time the express purpose was to have a smaller team complete design of the game and test it with development staff trainees and trainers. The current version of CAPJEFOS is the result of work of this second, smaller, but still international group:

Cathy Stein Greenblat (USA), Philip Langley (Great Britain—resident of Africa for 20+ years), Jacob Ngwa (Cameroon), Saul Luyumba (Uganda), Ernest Mangesho (Tanzania), and Foday MacBailey (Sierra Leone).

The six designers included five experts on development issues and one expert on gaming-simulation design. The conceptual model was further elaborated using general texts, field-study reports and visits, interviews in several villages (with the chief, town crier, palm wine tapper, several farmers and traders, a teacher), and interviews with development staff.

The full model contains numerous component parts, a few of which can be illustrated here. Figure 6.6 shows the time and capital allocations in a village, and Figure 6.7 shows the factors related to sickness and loss of productive time due to sickness. Further discussion of the

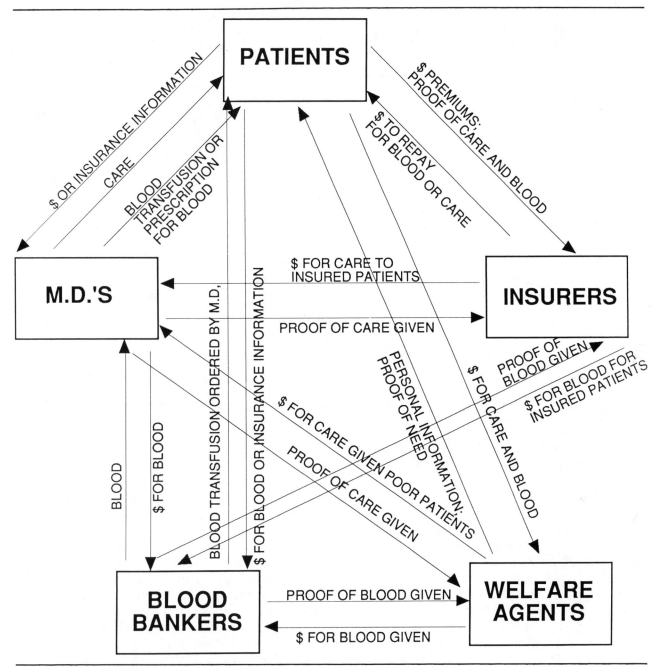

Figure 6.2 BLOOD MONEY—Hemophilia Care System: Major Actors and Functional Relationships
SOURCE: Greenblat and Gagnon (1976). Reprinted by permission.

design of CAPJEFOS will be given in subsequent chapters.

THE MARRIAGE GAME
**(Cathy Stein Greenblat, Peter Stein,
and Norman Washburne)**

THE MARRIAGE GAME began with a pedagogic concern of the authors, all three of whom are sociologists. We had found that students entered courses on Marriage

and the Family with mixed motives and emerged with mixed reactions. Sometimes a Marriage and Family course was simply one of many courses making up a "major" in sociology, home economics, or social work, and it was approached by students in much the same way they approached other courses. Often, however, the course attracted students because it promised them— explicitly or implicitly—insight into states most hoped eventually to enter: marriage and parenthood. Sur-

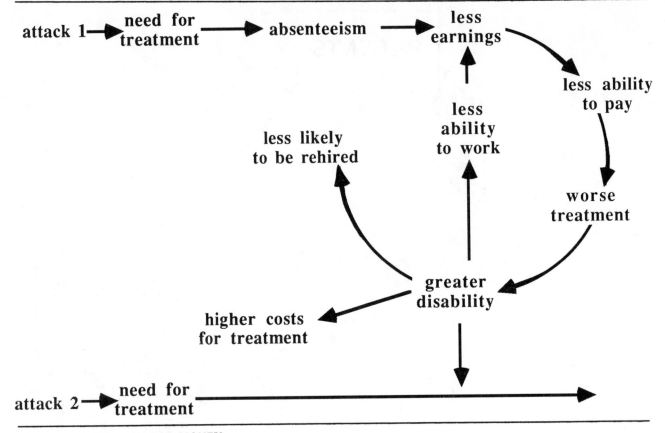

Figure 6.3 Linkages: BLOOD MONEY
SOURCE: Greenblat and Gagnon (1976). Reprinted by permission.

rounded by mystique and highly idealized, yet simultaneously shrouded in prophecies of doom based on rising divorce rates and laments about the "death of the nuclear family," marriage seemed to many undergraduates both promising and perilous. They looked to Marriage and the Family courses for personal guidance in addition to (or in lieu of) scholarly documentation and analysis of a major social institution.

Given these dual motives—academic and personal—it was of little surprise that many courses were defined as failures. Few modes of teaching could convey both the descriptive and quantitative material needed for objective analysis *and* the elusive, subtle sense required to think about one's future. Much of the scholarly material made little sense to those devoid of personal experience beyond that acquired vicariously from limited views of the marriages of parents, relatives, or friends. However much the student read about family budget-making, for example, he or she was likely to be unable to appreciate the pressures on a marriage that accompany economic decision making until he or she struggled to make ends meet in a family that includes young dependent children and a spouse whose desires conflict, in part, with his or her own. Hence students lamented that assignments of

readings that attempted to systematize existing theory and data about marriage were dry and meaningless to them.

When the opposite approach was taken, however, and the course was structured to offer more "personal" advice, accolades were also lacking. The "how-to-do-it" approach promising clues to marital success was attacked as nonacademic and fraught with folklore and homey advice. The lack of intellectual credibility of such a course often spread to the entire discipline, for exposure rates to the course were higher than to almost any other course in sociology.

Gaming-simulation seemed to us to be a promising medium for meeting these diverse aims, for transmitting some of the wisdom of the field to students in a way that had personal meaning to them. It appeared to us that through a gaming-simulation students might both gain a better understanding of marriage in *system* terms and might simultaneously engage in self-testing and future testing.

A number of characteristics of the conceptual model employed in design of THE MARRIAGE GAME must be understood in terms of our decisions concerning the purposes of the game, the intended context of use, and

Actors	Goals	Activities	Resources
1. Village male farmers	-increase cash crop production -feed himself and family -educate children -increase family size -enhance prestige -participate as a community member -increase personal and family health	-farming -hunting -fishing -house construction -attending meetings -trading -participating in traditional activities -pursuit of pleasure -contributing efforts to voluntary enterprises (e.g. road construction)	-land -farming implements -farming animals -time -fishing equipment -hunting equipment -friendship -children
....			
7. Chief	-progress of the village -enhance his prestige -effective leadership -maintenance of law and order -maintenance of traditional customs	-presiding over traditional meetings -settling disputes -representing the village -collecting taxes -presiding over ceremonies	-land -wives -children -animals -farming implements -time -wages given -friendship -authority

Figure 6.4 Portion of CAPJEFOS Model: Actors
SOURCE: Greenblat et al. (1987). Reprinted by permission.

the anticipated age, experience, and sophistication of prospective participants. We had several communication or learning purposes as we began the design process:

(1) to project or teach principles about marriage and family systems;
(2) to provide a concrete, experiential base for reading and lecture materials;

NATURAL/DEMOGRAPHIC:
Balance of immigration with emigration
Existence of fertile soil
Good housing and resettlement
Clean streams with fish and sand
Adequate game/gaming
Use of minerals
Reasonable size of population
Low mortality rate
Birth control and family planning
Existence of forests for lumbering
SOCIAL, CULTURAL, AND HEALTH:
Cultural
  Acceptance of changes in food habits
Social:
  A good organisation of the population
  A good integration of ethnic groups
Health:
  Nutritional education including use of local products
  Sanitary education
POLITICAL AND ADMINISTRATIVE:
Solidarity and cohesion between different groups
Village Council is well run and represents all groups within the village
Dynamic leadership of village institutions
Awareness of the political aspects of under-development (How inequitable N-S
   relations are worked out on a village level)
ECONOMIC:
Use of appropriate technology
Use of natural resources
Adequate food production for domestic consumption
Maintain fertility of the soil
Accumulation of capital in the village
Invest surplus income in the village
Land tenure system, with land for all
Acceptance of recommended/improved production techniques
Local efficient marketing services
Suitable agricultural education of the people
Efficient transportation system

Figure 6.5 Portion of List of Factors Fostering Village Development: CAPJEFOS
SOURCE: Greenblat et al. (1987). Reprinted by permission.

(3) to allow the testing of alternative strategies in a relatively consequence-free environment;
(4) to provide anticipatory socialization for players, giving them greater insight into their own ideas, values, skills, and fears; and
(5) to promote dialogue between players concerning alternative values and decisions and their interrelations.

The game was designed as an instrument for the teaching of Marriage and the Family at the college level. We wanted a vehicle that would project more than the gestalt of marriage, such as might have been conveyed through a simple group-dynamics game or a role-playing exercise. The game would have to transmit crucial ideas about the types of decisions marital partners have to make, the contingencies from outside the system that affect these decisions, the costs and rewards attached to the decisions, and the ways in which decisions in one area affect options in other areas.

These considerations concerning purposes, context of use, and participants necessitated construction of a conceptual model of a more complex sort than might have been developed for other purposes. They also had

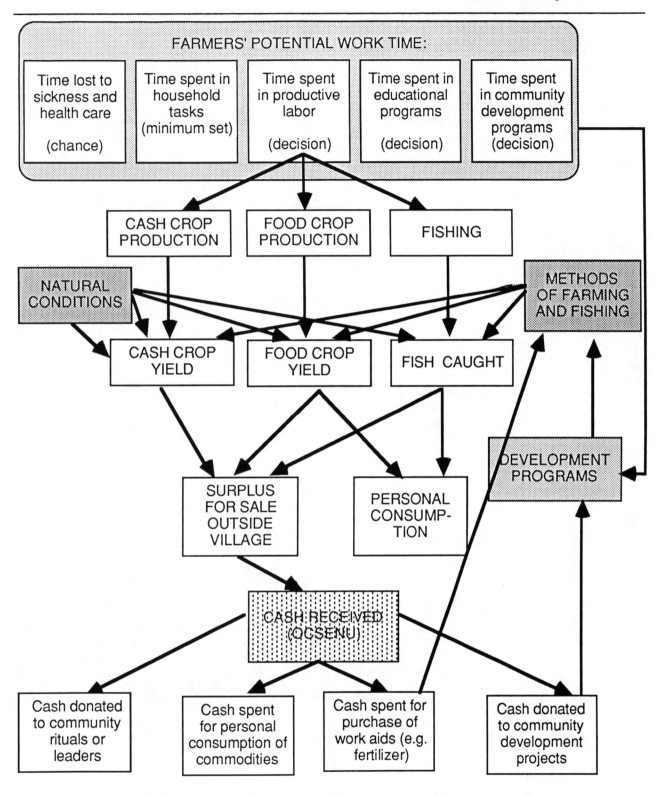

Social time, group meeting time, and community meeting time are dealt with in real time. Small supplements to farmers' productive work time are given if they do not enroll older children in school.

Figure 6.6 CAPJEFOS: Farmers' Time and Capital Allocations

SOURCE: Greenblat et al. (1987). Reprinted by permission.

NATIONAL AND REGIONAL
FACTORS AND RESOURCES

COMMUNITY FACTORS, CULTURAL
PRACTICES, & COMMUNITY AND PERSONAL
RESOURCES

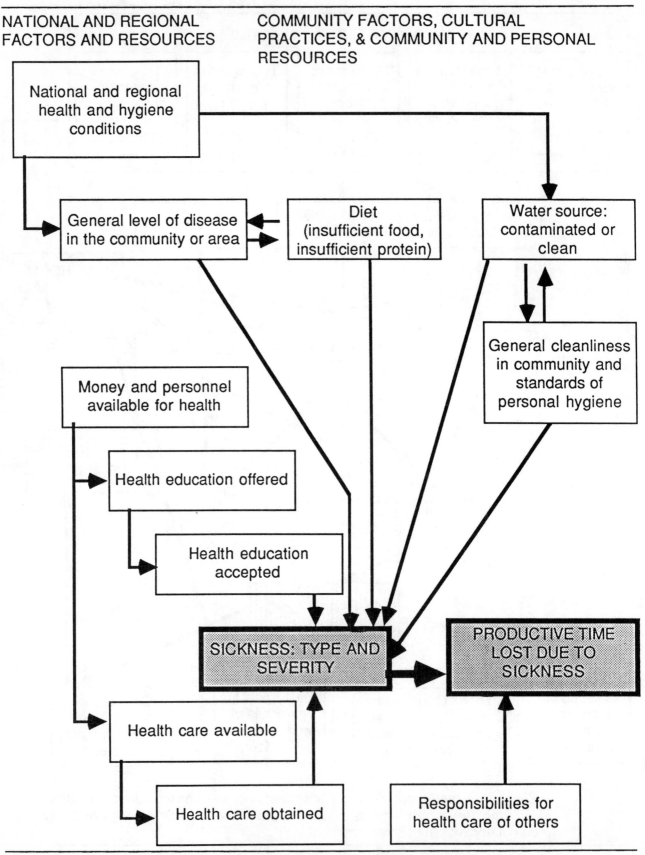

Figure 6.7   Sickness and Loss of Productive Time Due to Sickness in Villages: CAPJEFOS
SOURCE: Greenblat et al. (1987). Reprinted by permission.

consequences in terms of the pragmatics of use. The complexity of the purposes and of the model meant we would have to allot considerable time for play (several class periods at a minimum) and that more paraphernalia would be required.

The conceptual model is nested in a theoretical tradition that holds that marital decision making has to be understood in terms of two sets of elements: those in the society at large, and those in the individuals making the decision. It posits that marital interactions take place between individuals who live in a world of external social facts, many of which have been internalized, affecting conceptions and values.

The elements and relationships of the underlying theory are summarized in Figure 6.8. The left side indicates that the opportunities available to system members derive from two elements: (1) general system states (reflected in unemployment rates, health conditions, levels of technological achievements) and (2) generally accepted definitions of categorical identities of individuals (such as age, sex, marital status). Thus the job opportunities vary with the overall state of the economy, and the opportunities for males and females, young and old, black and white, often differ. These opportunities carry with them objective costs and rewards. Occupational status roles, for example, bring resources of property, power, and prestige to all who occupy them.

The right side of the diagram indicates that individuals living within the society possess (1) categorical identities (such as age, sex, and race) defined by the society as good and bad, better and worse; and (2) sets of values resulting from prior experiences or "biographies." The individual's choices from the opportunities provided by the society reflect both the identities and the personal value-frame. A woman choosing a job chooses from a limited set of options available to her *because* she is a woman and chooses in terms of values she has developed through her life's experiences. The subjective costs and rewards experienced from this choice result from both the objective costs and rewards attached to the opportunity and the extent to which these types of costs and rewards are valued by the individual. Thus the occupational prestige received by two people objectively may be the same, but it will be experienced by one as much less because of the lower value he or she attaches to prestige. The subjective costs and rewards received from new experience may also modify the value-frame used to make future decisions.

The overall marital/family system model was reduced by our concern to focus upon the decision-making elements of marriage, their consequences and interconnections. The model we developed was an exchange theory model that, roughly stated, holds that each decision made by an individual will accord him or her

certain costs and certain rewards. Three basic elements of the model therefore had to be defined and the linkages specified: (1) major decision points, (2) the units of cost and reward involved in each, and (3) the factors accounting for similarities and differences in the amount of cost or reward experienced.

The third decision was critical and was decided first. The relevant categorical identities we enumerated included age, sex, marital status, parental status, social class, race, subculture, and region. It was clear at an early stage that considerable limitation of these sources of diversity would be required if the game were to be playable. We decided that the basic game would be constructed to represent the situation that we believed pertains for middle-class college graduates in the metropolitan areas of the United States. Variations by class would be put into substitute materials. Variations by race, subculture, and region were eliminated.

Decision points and units of cost and reward were also reduced from the real-world range to those we considered most salient. The decision points represent those we considered most critical over the course of a year of marital interaction, including decisions concerning jobs, basic budget expenditures (housing, maintenance, transportation), allocation of free time, sexual relations, use of contraception, luxury purchases, interaction with others, giving of ego support, and deciding upon marital status for the next year. The units of cost and reward were narrowed to security, respect and esteem, freedom, enjoyment, sex gratification, marital and parental status rewards, and ego support—all units that could be roughly quantified.

A graphic model was then made to represent the linkages among these three elements, as shown in Figure 6.9. Factors leading to variation in opportunities and/or in costs and rewards are indicated on the left. In the center are the decision areas, presented in the order they must be dealt with in the game. On the right, the nature of the cost and reward consequences of such decisions are indicated. In Chapter 9, you will see how this conceptual model was represented in the gaming-simulation.

SUGGESTIONS FOR PROCEEDING

There are several different forms the conceptual model can take. The strategy recommended to you is the one I have found most amenable to easy transition to Stage III: that is, research the referent system and

(1) identify the major *actors*, including their goals, activities, and resources, and the interactions between them (remember resources are not only monetary, but include such things as power, and access to information);
(2) identify and, if possible, schematically describe the major *system characteristics and linkages* (for example,

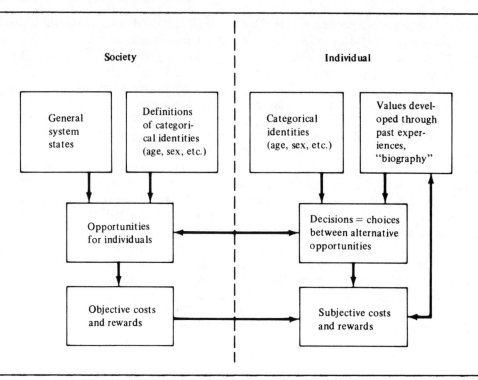

Figure 6.8   Theory Underlying THE MARRIAGE GAME
SOURCE: Greenblat, Stein, and Washburne (1977). Reprinted by permission.

in designing THE MARBLE COMPANY, a game dealing with organizational communication and information management, the designers had to specify the rules for interaction in an organizational structure: who reports to whom about what, what tasks are to be accomplished, what rewards and punishments are there for task accomplishment);

(3) indicate the types of *external factors* that may effect the system.

If the design team is small (i.e., 2-5 persons), you should work together on each of these; if the design team is larger, it may be more efficient to subdivide into groups of at least three persons and initially divide the tasks, later coming together for refinement of the conceptualizations.

You may find it extremely useful to study or review a basic system dynamics text that explains the creation of causal loop diagrams, plots of variables against time, and computer flow diagrams. Two particularly useful texts are *Introduction to Computer Simulation: A System Dynamics Modeling Approach* by Roberts et al. (1983) and *Introduction to System Dynamics Modeling with DYNAMO* by Richardson and Pugh (1981). The most deliberate effort to show stages of model conceptualization in system dynamics is to be found in *Dynamics of Growth in a Finite World* (Meadows et al., 1974), which is highly recommended for gamers intent on clear model development.

Next, review the materials you have developed and decide which components you consider most important for inclusion. These decisions should depend partly on your judgment of which factors are primary and which ones are secondary in the real world. They should also depend on your design objectives: That is, how much simplification is essential given the decisions you made in Stage I? Take out your statement of objectives and parameters and *use* it to generate a list of the major elements of the model you want to be sure to include in the gaming-simulation. Allan Feldt and Fred Goodman (1975, p. 4) urge in this regard that:

The important principle in good design is how to keep things out of games, not how to put them in. It seems possible that many games fall into one of three classes of design and use, reflecting their level of complexity and the number of "variables" represented within them. Games containing less than ten variables seem amenable to play in periods of one to two hours although more extended use can be made of them. . . . Other games which deal with 25-50 variables seem to require four or five hours at a minimum for adequate representation and play. They are less conveniently used in a simple classroom setting and often require more elaborate preparation and assistance in their conduct. . . . Substantially more elaborate games generally require computerized assistance or very large staffs to assist in their management and frequently require several days or weeks to play. . . . Within the constraints of the purpose and necessary levels of detail

Sex	Marital status	Parental status	Other	Decision areas	Other possible consequences	Security	Esteem	Freedom	Sex gratification	Enjoyment	Marital-parental status	Ego-support
			Factors affecting opportunities and/or costs and rewards						Cost-Reward consequences:			
X	X	X	Savings	1. JOB CHOICE		X	X	X	X			X
X	X	X		2. GENERAL EXTERNAL EVENTS (e.g. sickness)		X	X	X	X	X		X
X	X			3. FIXED COSTS PAYMENT (e.g. repayment of debt, taxes, alimony)		X						X
				4. BASIC BUDGET DECISIONS								
X	X	X		A. Housing		X	X		X			X
	X	X		B. Maintenance		X	X					X
			Occupational status	C. Transportation		X	X	X		X		X
X	X	X		D. Household help		X	X	X				X
				5. INTERACTING WITH OTHERS								
				A. Allocating free time		X	X			X	X	X
				B. Sexual relations								
				1. Partner:								
				a. spouse						X		X
				b. non-spouse ——→ chance of VD			X			X		X
				2. Amount						X		X
				3. Contraception								
				a. Yes		X						X
				b. No ——→ chance of conception:								
				birth		X	X	X			X	X
				abortion		X						X
				C. Luxury purchases		X	X			X		X
				D. Choosing primary partner								X
				E. Comparing with others								X
			Overall quality of relationship	6. ASCERTAINING QUALITY OF SEX RELATIONS						X		X
				7. RATING PRIMARY PARTNER AND RELATIONSHIP								X
				8. CALCULATION OF SCORES: OBJECTIVE AND SUBJECTIVE								
				9. DECISION: MARITAL STATUS FOR NEXT ROUND								

Figure 6.9 THE MARRIAGE GAME: Model Elements

SOURCE: Greenblat, Stein, and Washburne (1977). Reprinted by permission.

which a particular purpose may require, the game designer is urged to follow Thoreau's advice and "simplify, simplify."

In making decisions about the reduction of elements, you must keep in mind that the gaming-simulation must not have so much detail and complexity that it is either unplayable or that the lessons you wish to teach through it are lost in a forest of ideas. When you have identified the salient elements in your model, you are ready to proceed to Stage IV: making decisions about representation.

7

Decisions About Representation
Questions of Style

The decision to divide the discussion of Stage III into two separate chapters is somewhat arbitrary. I have found it useful to think of the decisions involved in moving from the conceptual model to a gaming-simulation—that is, the decisions about representation—as questions of the *style* of the gaming-simulation you wish to create, and questions of the *form* to be taken by each element. The first of these sets of decisions is dealt with here, and the second, in the next chapter. There is, by necessity, considerable overlap.

THE STYLE OF A GAMING-SIMULATION

The dimension of style can be divided into the following four questions:

(1) What is the appropriate *level of abstraction*?
(2) What *time frame* should be employed?
(3) Should there be a linear, radial, or interactive *structure*?
(4) How much and what type of *interaction* should take place among players?

At this point, a familiarity with the wide range of existing gaming-simulations will prove invaluable. If you have seen many gaming-simulations you will be able to supplement the examples given here; if not, the ones offered should give you a basis for making choices.

LEVEL OF ABSTRACTION

Like a book, a simulation is an explicit statement of what the designer believes about some aspect of reality. As we noted earlier, however, the model does not have to *look like* the referent system, but should *behave* like it. The decision to simulate thus forces the designer to decide what the essential features of the referent system are, and which ones shall be included (Stage II), and then to decide upon the appropriate level of abstraction for his or her purposes. The job is to transform and substitute—to find dynamically analogous mechanisms and surrogate functions. The solutions generally can take a variety of quite different forms. Some substitutions represent reductions in scale (iconic representations), while others entail the introduction of properties that are different in form, but that produce the same consequences (analogue or homologue representations).

The process of thinking about what it is that is really important and how to represent it so the system will "work" may foster new insights, for one must think at different levels of abstraction. Furthermore, as R. Garry Shirts (1975, p. 4) notes, "The designer might want to exaggerate, simplify, limit, distort, and redefine it [reality] in order to create an experience that teaches what he or she wants to teach." (Of course it is essential that such simplifications and distortions be pointed out in the operator's manual, so the user can bring them up in postgame discussion.) Several concrete examples should make this more clear. I will begin with iconic representations, which involve the least abstraction.

Players in CLUG (the COMMUNITY LAND USE GAME) are asked to bid for land, decide upon the location and extent of public utilities, set tax rates, construct buildings, decide upon renovation of deteriorated buildings. Of course, they are only "playing" at these things; they don't bring in bulldozers or moving men to displace tenants in urban renewal areas, but the gaming-simulation demands that they make the same decisions and go through the same steps the real-life developer or planner goes through. It is a *reduction in scale*.

Likewise, in some international relations games, such as INS, DANGEROUS PARALLEL, or CRISIS, "diplomats" confer with their ministers, examine indicators of social, political, and economic states of their countries, meet formally and informally with delegates of other "countries," and engage in related activities. Again the parallels between the real world and the simulation behaviors are quite close; the latter are abstracted from the larger number of things done by politicians, and then they are reduced in scale.

A final example of this sort of iconic representation is

RADIO COVINGHAM. Players are told they are journalists on the local radio station. They have to use handouts, letters from listeners, and items of news to create a ten-minute radio broadcast. The amount of material they have to work with is considerably less than what confronts "real" program producers, but the process is very realistic, and players are confronted with similar problems of choice of material, integration of themes, and order of presentation.

In some other games it is the *function* rather than the *structure* that is considered important. It may be the feelings or attitudes experienced by real-world role players that one wants to simulate, rather than the specific mechanisms that create them. In this case, abstraction may lead you to use *analogue* or *homologue representations*.

Allan Feldt and Fred Goodman (1975, p. 175) are advocates and practitioners of the idea of using analogues and homologues in games. They offer several examples:

> In designing games, processes and components are often selected because they provide clear and workable *analogs* to some more complicated aspect of the real world. Such components or processes behave in substantially the same way as their real world counterpart for substantially the same reasons, although in a more simple or more obvious way. Occasionally, however, the game designer will stumble across a homolog which may be equally useful, although initially confusing. A *homolog* is like an analog except that the reasons it behaves the same as its real world counterpart are absolutely irrelevant or even wrong. Good usable homologs are rare and must be examined carefully before being put into use. Well chosen ones are useful, however, and they may be legitimately employed in game design in the same manner as analogs. A simple example is . . . where the shape of certain blocks makes it impossible for them to be piled upon each other, thereby making certain combinations of land uses physically impossible in the game when in fact those same combinations should be prevented from occurring for some entirely different reason. Similarly, players seated in the back of the room may have problems seeing or hearing all that is occurring in the front of the room. Instead of writing larger or speaking more loudly to correct the problem, it might be desirable to use their disadvantage as a surrogate for cultural or geographic isolation in the game for some particular set of players . . .

Some of the most creative analogues and homologues I have seen appear in Fred Goodman's END OF THE LINE. In order to simulate the decreasing physical-geographic mobility that comes with increasing age, Goodman rejected mobility "points" to be forfeited and decided to use ropes. Players are tied to their chair legs, with different lengths of rope representing the amount of mobility they have. Some people can get around more than others, and as the players "age," their ropes are shortened. Similarly, players' loss of their memories is simulated through their progressive loss of pieces of the paper on which they can record the state of the system, and eventually in loss of their pencils.

Another example of the extremely creative use of analogues and homologues is ME, THE SLOW LEARNER. Designers Don Thatcher and June Robinson designed the game to promote empathy with learning problems. The game focuses on difficulties in tasks requiring reading skills, comprehension skills, mathematical skills, motor skills, and motor control. Participants are all physically handicapped in some way as play begins, and hence are, in varying degrees, inhibited in the performance of what would appear to be six relatively simple tasks. The "classroom" is meant to be silent, with strong discipline, and there are severe time limits for accomplishment of the tasks. Controllers and assistants ensure that participants do not talk and are under continuous pressure, sometimes including denigration and ridicule. Scores (usually very low ones) are received by each player for each task, and are posted on the board, making the failure public information. Following completion of the 45-minute to one-hour period of play, an intense discussion generally emerges about the strong feelings generated by the experience. (For an example of the handicaps used, see Figure 10.41.)

Other examples also show the role of thinking at various levels of abstraction about what should be represented.

Several years ago I consulted with two graduate students trying to design a gaming-simulation for sensitizing expectant parents to the demands of infants, and to the factors that lead to mothers taking major responsibilities for infant care, even when fathers are home from work. They had worked diligently but fruitlessly on designing a very realistic gaming-simulation in which players were mothers and fathers who had to perform tasks very close to reality with doll-infants. After a few minutes' discussion of their problem, I said, "Tell me in more abstract terms what you want the players to experience about new parenthood." When their answer emphasized "the feelings of unfamiliarity with the character of demands of an infant and the appropriate ways of satisfying them," I proposed that they consider *that* as what had to modeled. Following this advice, they created a more abstract model of three roles, in which members of a dyad have to respond to unclear demands from a third party to whom they are linked. One dyad member also has responsibilities away from the unit, while the other must spend full time trying to figure out the cues and appropriate responses from the "boss." From this more abstract conceptualization, a gaming-simulation was successfully designed.

Particular aspects of the model may be construed abstractly. A frequent example is "work." You must ask again, "What is it about this that I want to reflect?" It may not be that "workers" have to do the same tasks their real-life counterparts engage in, but that the character of the enterprise or the consequences of it are what are important.

In STARPOWER, for example, players accumulate points through trading and bargaining with little colored chips. Surely this is not a familiar or regular activity for most players, yet the mechanism of trading chips generates the desired outcome variable: differential success in the "marketplace."

In BLOOD MONEY, it was determined that the important elements of work were that (1) one had to be present at the times set by the employer, not when it was convenient to the employees, and that (2) those present gained rewards that helped purchase needed medical care and supplies. For the purposes of the gaming-simulation we felt it did not matter much what *type* of work was done. What was crucial was that hemophiliacs have problems of absenteeism due to the need for immediate care when they have attacks, and that (2) the more disabled are less skilled at tasks requiring manual coordination. Work was simulated by players being hired by an employer for a turn or turns at throwing darts. The player earned a set salary from the employer, whose income was, however, dependent upon the score earned by the dart thrower. Players who were not present when their turn was called (because they were sick and receiving medical attention) missed their turn and were not paid; likewise the employer missed out on production from this employee. Players with greater disabilities had to "work" with handicaps that reduced their likely productivity—sitting down to throw or throwing with their nondominant hand—earning full salary, but generating less income for the employer. In play of the game, employers soon learn which players have high rates of absenteeism and which have greater disability. By the second and third rounds, employers do not hire these persons, who, as a result, have even fewer financial resources to pay for their subsequent medical needs.

In other gaming-simulations, work has been simulated by having players make things from tinker toys (HORATIO ALGER) or solve word problems (THE ACADEMIC GAME; the third edition of SIMSOC; ADVANTIG). In BALDICER, a simulation concerned with the population explosion and limited capacities to deal with it, an important variable is differential ability to generate enough produce to feed the nation's people. Each player has responsibility for feeding the people of a country of a specified population. At one point in the round, he or she is given a sheet on which to write "Push, Pull, Dig, Sweat" as many times as he or she can in thirty seconds. The number of completed phrases equals the number of thousands of persons that can be fed that year

without obtaining outside assistance. Obviously, this is a far cry from planting, fertilizing, and harvesting, but it symbolically represents differential capabilities, generates scarcity for some, and propels players to examine interdependency.

In CAPJEFOS, we wanted to show the sacrifices that had to be made by persons who elected to work on difficult, time-consuming community projects with little equipment and supplies, and the reasons such enterprises may be abandoned. The *particular* project was not as important as the general principle. As designed, villagers can choose to try to build a new road that gives them easier access to the main road to the market. To do so, however, they must give up their social time (drinking palm wine and singing and dancing with friends) and instead must work on stringing together small safety pins. If (and when) the string is 12 feet long, the road project has been completed. Players soon find it is very difficult to obtain that degree of investment in the enterprise, and roads are often abandoned after a short stretch has been completed.

In THE MARRIAGE GAME, different neighborhoods are represented by different physical conditions. Those who elect expensive housing are seated in a comfortable area of the room where there is much space to write and shuffle papers, easy access to "shopping," and ease of reaching the coffee pot. Those who economize by electing to live in poor neighborhoods are crowded in a small area of the room without chairs, with little space in which to work, and with restricted access to the coffee and "shopping."

The point, then, is that you must decide *what aspect* of the system is important and whether you wish to deal with it in a fairly realistic fashion through reduction in scale, or to simulate in a more abstract fashion the processes or outcomes or feelings it generates. At this stage, you need decide only upon the level of abstraction that is appropriate, not on *how to create* the element in the gaming-simulation.

TIME FRAME

Another aspect you must consider is *time*. You need not specify the time represented when the game is quite abstract (e.g., BAFA-BAFA, ACCESS, THE COMMONS GAME, THE HEX GAME, and POMP AND CIRCUMSTANCE make no mention of the time represented by a round or step of play). The more "realistic" the gaming-simulation is, however, the more likely it is you must say something about the relationship between play time and real time, such as:

—"each round represents one year" (GHETTO, THE MARRIAGE GAME);

— "each round represents one season" (GREEN REVOLU-
TION GAME);

— "each round represents one day" (CARIBBEAN FISH-
ERMAN; RED DESERT);

— "play represents one two-hour segment in the lives of the
radio program producers" (RADIO COVINGHAM).

You must decide upon the period to be represented. This should be tied to the subject matter and purpose you specified in Stage I. For example, if you want to deal with decisions in the early years of marriage, you will probably want to make each round represent a year so that several years' decisions can be simulated. If you want to show the cumulative problems of debilitating attacks of a disease (as in BLOOD MONEY), you must represent enough time (at least implicitly) for each person to experience several attacks. A simulation of school board negotiations (POLICY NEGOTIATIONS) or politics (ST. PHILIP) might well focus on much shorter times and a few issues. This point is urged by Dillman (1970, pp. 7-8) when he states:

> Time compression or expansion (the relationship of the amount of real world time to its simulation in the exercise) depends upon the objectives and problem type. If a person in a top management position in education (dean, college president, or state superintendent) is being trained to look for certain concerns, he might best look at conditions over a long period of time (five years or so). On the other hand, if a teacher is being trained in classroom behavioral analysis he might more profitably look at a five minute segment or a single class period.

There are actually two aspects of time you must consider: the length of total time to be represented by a game session, and the length of time to be represented by a cycle. The former must be long enough to encompass the full expression of the behavior and to show the response of the system to the players' principal decision options. The latter must be fine enough to show the true shape of the dominant dynamics. Thus you might decide to have a cycle represent 5 years and to have a typical run last for 10 cycles of play if changes are slow or consequences are not felt for a long time.

Once again, Feldt and Goodman (1975, p. 176) offer useful advice:

> In designing and seeking to control the length of time a game requires, the designer should bear in mind that it may be perfectly legitimate and even desirable for the game to distort certain time frames from reality. Thus, it may be very useful for the purpose of the game to get players to spend an hour or more on one aspect which in the real world might only take a few hours while on some other aspect or decision players might spend five minutes when in the real world the analogous situation would have consumed months of effort and time. The distortion of time to help emphasize and control the attention and focus of the players is a useful and

highly productive way in which the nature of the learning and communication process may be enhanced.

Just as the level of abstraction has implications for the time frame to be represented, the decision concerning time frame has implications for the level of detail that must be presented. The shorter the time represented, the more detailed the activities must be, but the more the long-term influences must be ignored or represented as exogenous inputs.

STRUCTURE

Ellington, Addinall, and Percival (1983) suggest that gaming-simulations have one of three basic structures—linear, radial, interactive—or a composite of these. Their conceptualization is both clear and valuable, and will be used here in abbreviated form to explain this dimension of style. According to these authors:

> A linear structure is one in which the participants all work systematically through the same essentially linear programme of activities—usually using the same resource materials. This structure is an extremely versatile one, and can be used to achieve a wide range of educational and training objectives. In addition, it has the following specific characteristics.
>
> — the progressive nature of the linear structure enables a complicated case study or procedure to be broken down into easily-manageable stages, and clearly illustrates the relationship of each part to the whole;
> — the structure is particularly suitable for developing high-level skills.
>
> In a typical linear exercise . . . the participants are led systematically through a programme of activities that become progressively more complicated, more sophisticated and more demanding as each stage builds upon the work of its predecessor [Ellington, Addinall, and Percival, 1983, p. 66].

Figure 7.1 is taken from their discussion; it shows the structure of their collaboratively designed game, WHAT HAPPENS WHEN THE GAS RUNS OUT?

The second basic structure, the radial structure, is described by Ellington, Addinall, and Percival (1983, pp. 67-68) as follows:

> Here, each participant (or group of participants) first carries out a set of preparatory activities specific to a given role in a scenario or particular point of view in a problem situation, and then presents information or argues a case at a plenary session or simulated meeting of some sort. In this case, the participants usually have different resource materials. Like the linear exercises discussed above, radial exercises can be used to achieve a wide range of educational or training objectives related to their particular subject content, and also have a number of characteristics that are specifically related to their structure:

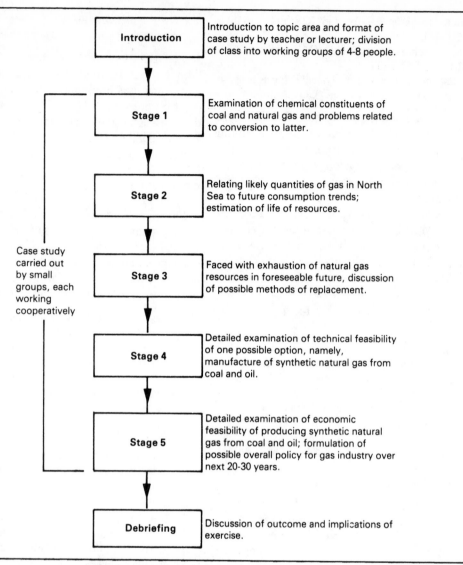

Figure 7.1   Linear Structure: **WHEN THE GAS RUNS OUT**

SOURCE: Ellington, Addinall, and Percival (1982). Reprinted by permission.

— they enable the different arguments or points of view in a complicated problem situation to be identified, examined in detail, and subjected to informed criticism and discussion;

— they can be used to foster a wide range of useful skills (particularly those related to the preparation, presentation and defense of arguments) and desirable attitudinal traits (such as a willingness to listen to the points of view of other people or an appreciation that problems can generally be viewed in a number of different ways.

The radial structure can be illustrated by a game already mentioned: ST. PHILIP. In this short, but very useful exercise, students deal with arguments for and against the development of large-scale tourism in Third World countries. The simulation is based on a real-life event but it is set in the mythical Caribbean island of St. Philip. Twelve participants take the roles of Members of Parliament, and another 2-6 serve as directors of Holiday, Inc. The activity proceeds through 8 steps:

(1) explaining the activity
(2) introduction of general theme
(3) organizing roles
(4) distribution of papers
(5) study of papers
(6) informal meetings of groups
(7) the meeting of Parliament
(8) debriefing

Figure 7.2 illustrates the structure of the game.

Linear and radial structures are most commonly employed in short (less than two hours), simple gaming-

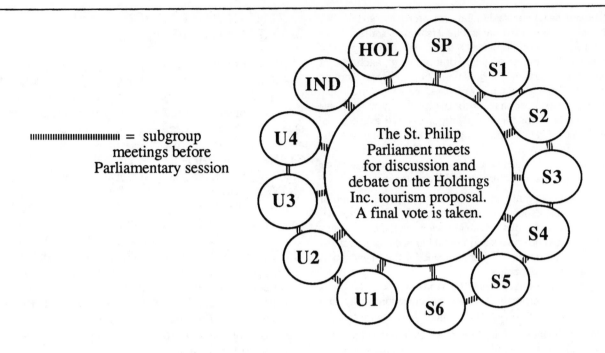

|||||||||||||||||||||||||| = subgroup meetings before Parliamentary session

SP: Thomas Crowe: M.P. for Queenstown - Speaker of the House

S 1-6:   Members of S.P.N.I.P. - the Government Party

                  S-1 Sam Wells - M.P. for N. Queenstown & Prime Minister
                  S-2 Jessie Wells - M.P. for Queenstown Harbour
                  S-3 Evelyn Talbot - M.P. for Queenstown Royal
                  S-4 Fred Southcott - M.P. for South Queenstown
                  S-5 James Ramirez - M.P. for Purple River
                  S-6 Brian Samuel - M.P. for Mid-Island

U 1-4:   Members of United Party - the opposition's party

                  U-1 Ernest Tyreman - M.P. for Queenstown East
                  U-2 Bob Ballinger - M.P for Mountain
                  U-3 Francis Smythe - M.P. for Western Margins
                  U-4 John Holder - M.P. for Warner

IND: Independent M.P.:
                  IND Robert Willett - M.P. for North Bay

HOL: Director of Holidays Inc.

Figure 7.2 Radial Structure: ST. PHILIP

SOURCE: Reprinted by permission of the Cambridge Publishing Services, Oatlands, High St., Conington, Cambridge, CB3 8LT, England.

simulations (many of which are quite elegant in meeting their purposes). Most of the gaming-simulations used as examples in this book are larger and they have what

Ellington, Addinal, and Percival (1983, pp. 69-70) refer to as an interactive structure, which they describe as follows:

An exercise can be said to have an *interactive structure* if the most important organizational feature is some form of multi-way interaction between individuals or groups. The interaction can take a variety of forms (e.g., exchange of information, trading, negotiation, lobbying) and can be organized in a large number of ways, but almost invariably gives such exercises a much looser, more informal and less predictable character than tightly-structured exercises of the linear or radial types. Like linear and radial exercises, interactive exercises can be used to achieve a wide range of educational and training objectives, but also share a number of more general structure-related characteristics:

— they constitute an ideal vehicle for the simulation of complex social, organizational, political and international situations (which involve several individuals or bodies and can evolve in a number of different ways—ie are basically open-ended), and for the investigation of group dynamics;
— they can be used to develop a wide range of useful skills (e.g., interpersonal and communication skills) and desirable attitudinal traits (e.g.,social awareness).

A further feature of many interactive exercises is that play takes place in a series of cycles, a series that may either be closed (with the game coming to an end after a predetermined number of cycles) or open (with play continuing until the participants or game controller decides to call a halt).

As was indicated above, most of the examples used in this volume are of this third sort, and numerous examples could be employed (indeed all four case studies are of games with an interactive structure). Because these examples are extensive in the volume, only diagrams of an interactive structure game will be given here. The example in Figures 8.3 and 8.4 is THE MANAGEMENT GAME as employed at New York University Graduate School of Business' Management Decision Laboratory (MDL). This is an elaborate, semester-long gaming-simulation that incorporates a unique combination of organization processes, business community relationships, and a sophisticated computer program. Bank officers, insurance company long-term lenders or underwriters, business consultants, attorneys, labor union negotiators and labor management consultants, external auditors, and high-level executives, many of whom are on the boards of publicly held companies, meet on an occasional basis with students to represent interpersonal business relationships in a realistic and meaningful manner. Students meet in teams of 8 for long periods during the semester in which the MDL is their major activity.

Figure 7.3 gives an overview of the full operation of the gaming-simulation; Figure 7.4 elaborates on the activities of the students (the company management) and their interactions with the external consultants named above during the operating phase. (For more details on the MDL, see Kenner and Uretsky, 1986.)

EXTENT OF INTERACTION BETWEEN PLAYERS

Whatever the structure, there will be some degree of interaction between players, but gaming-simulations differ considerably in the degree of interaction they demand. Some are highly interactive. They usually require more space, generate more noise in the room, and seem to elicit more emotional involvement from players (e.g., STARPOWER, BAFA-BAFA, THE HEX GAME, THEY SHOOT MARBLES . . . , END OF THE LINE, BLOOD MONEY). Others are more "intellectual," pitting players against a model or putting them into interaction with a smaller group of other players (e.g., CARIBBEAN FISHERMAN, THE GREEN REVOLUTION GAME, GENERATION GAP). They generally require less space and are quieter to run, and the emotional involvement is sometimes lower. In general, if you are trying to generate *empathy*, you should probably work toward a more interactive game; if you are trying to teach facts and principles you may wish to reduce the players' interaction with one another, and involve them in more individual and dyadic tasks.

A FOURTH CASE STUDY INTRODUCED

POMP AND CIRCUMSTANCE
(Cathy Stein Greenblat, Linda Reich Rosen, and John H. Gagnon)

As an illustration of the representation decision making discussed in this chapter, a fourth case study will be introduced. This is POMP AND CIRCUMSTANCE, which deals with adolescent contraceptive decision making. The nature of the problem led us to design this gaming-simulation at a high level of abstraction, with no specified time frame, with a cyclic structure, and with a low degree of interaction between the full set of players, but a high degree of dyadic interaction. Much of this discussion (and the continuation in the next chapter) is taken from a report by the three designers (Greenblat, Rosen, and Gagnon, 1978).

The design problem had several dimensions. First was the clear need for a new pedagogical tool for sex-education courses for adolescents 13-18 years old. Many factors in American society promote the use of effective birth control techniques: contraceptives and contraceptive information are legally available, relatively inexpensive, and socially approved. American culture generally supports the notion of limiting family size and spacing childbearing over time, while strongly disapproving of births that take place out of wedlock. Nevertheless, the illegitimacy rate—that is, the number of children born to unmarried females—has increased dramatically in the

```
┌─────────────────────────────────────┐
│           PRE-ENTRY PROGRAM          │
│                                      │
│  Student managers and  business      │
│  community participants receive      │
│  manuals, other documents,  and      │
│  orientation regarding the  MDL      │
│  simulation.  Assignment  of         │
│  individuals   to   simulation       │
│  companies is distributed.           │
│  Actual Time: approx. 1 week         │
└─────────────────────────────────────┘
                   │
                   ▼
┌─────────────────────────────────────┐
│          ORGANIZATIONAL PHASE        │
│                                      │
│  Student company managers  and       │
│  boards of directors  organize:      │
│  familiarize themselves  with        │
│  the operating history of their      │
│  fictional companies; and  make      │
│  a dry run of operations.            │
│  Actual Time: approx. 2 weeks        │
└─────────────────────────────────────┘
                   │
                   ▼
┌─────────────────────────────────────┐
│            OPERATING PHASE           │
│                                      │
│  Competing "company" teams make      │
│  management decisions for  each      │
│  16 simulated    months  while       │
│  operating  in  a  simulated         │
│  business environment.               │
│  Actual Time: approx. 11 weeks       │
└─────────────────────────────────────┘
                   │
                   ▼
┌─────────────────────────────────────┐
│           OPERATIONS ANALYSIS        │
│                                      │
│  Company teams  explain  the         │
│  results of their  operations        │
│  and make recommendations to         │
│  future management.                  │
│  Actual Time: 1 week                 │
└─────────────────────────────────────┘
```

Figure 7.3 Interactive Structure: The Simulated World of MDL
SOURCE: Kenner and Uretsky (1986). Reprinted by permission.

past few decades. For instance, among a random sample of women aged 15 to 19, there were about three times as many illegitimate births in 1970 as there were in 1940. About 400,000 births were recorded in the entire United States in 1973, with half coming from teenaged mothers. Since a large number of out-of-wedlock pregnancies end in marriage or abortion, it is possible that as many as a half million teenage pregnancies per year occur in the United States.

Some of the efforts to reverse this trend have focused on making contraceptives more accessible to the adolescent and on educating the potential contraceptive user. Some form of sex education is available in many secondary school systems. At present, however, these programs generally teach the adolescent about the biological facts of reproduction and the hazards of premarital pregnancy, but they neglect the student's personal concerns about sexual activity.

Often both the students and the teacher are made equally uncomfortable by the discussion of sexuality within the traditional classroom format (assuming such discussion is even permitted by local authorities). Both student and teacher are understandably hesitant to reveal personal information, and so discussions of a deeply personal topic may become impersonal and detached from real-life problems. It is generally agreed that conventional forms of classroom sex education have made little impact on adolescent sexual or contraceptive

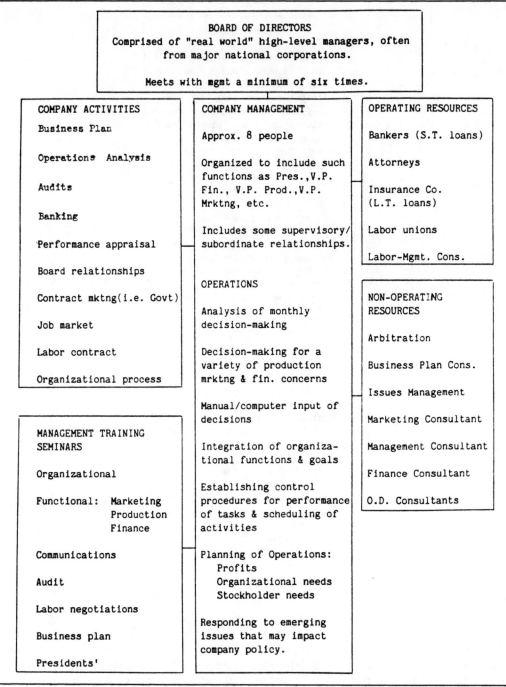

Figure 7.4   Interactive Structure: MDL Company Activities Overview
SOURCE: Kenner and Uretsky (1986). Reprinted by permission.

behavior, and teenage pregnancy remains a serious social problem in the United States.

Our second problem was how to design a game that would permit attention to personal and social factors involved in adolescent sexual and contraceptive decision making. We were not concerned with describing the female anatomy or the reproductive process—topics covered moderately well in other materials.

Third, we believed that the most important value of a game on this topic would be its potential for creating an environment for more relaxed discussion between students and teacher and among students. Thus we were not concerned with teaching many facts, but rather with presenting a set of general principles that would serve as the basis for discussion of personal values and dilemmas and possible modes of dealing with these.

The fourth concern is partly the obverse of the third. We wanted to provide a vehicle for thinking about personal values and actions, but wanted to make sure that players were protected from revealing these if they did not wish to do so. Particular concern was with the possibility of female players in the game revealing sexual codes that would then lead to postgame negative consequences from male players. It appeared to us that we had a moral obligation to offer our players "privacy," considering the possible serious postgame consequences of our not offering such protection.

Of course, this presented us with a dilemma. How could we have players participate in a simulation in which (1) they would have to take actions and make decisions; (2) they would learn about the social and personal factors that affect adolescent decision making about sexual behavior and contraceptive use; (3) they would gain better understandings of the costs and rewards of decisions made; (4) the risks of noncontracepted intercourse would be highlighted; while, at the same time, (5) they would be protected from during-play discussions in which they might feel uncomfortable; and (6) they would be protected from postplay interactions in which their game revelations became a new variable?

I believe our solutions have been extremely successful. The main element introduced to deal with the problem of need to reveal one's values is that we have set the players into fairly stereotypical roles, giving them values that have been found through research to be typical of their gender and age. Of course many of the players diverge from these values in their own thinking. But decisions that are most "rational" in the game are so in terms of the assigned values. Thus at the end of play a student can use as "protection" the explanation that "I did that because it was consistent with what I was told to maximize." While an individual's decisions might not be consistent with what he or she would do "in real life," play by a group of 10-30 persons generates behavior and outcomes very similar to those of a group of adolescents engaged in real-life decision making about sex and contraception.

The second element of "solution" is even more important: We have designed the game on a very high level of abstraction. Although it is possible to run it otherwise, in the typical form of play, players are not told in advance what the topic is or what the gaming symbols represent. The POMP in the title stands for premarital pregnancy, and the title, too, is deliberately kept ambiguous. Instead, participants play with a set of abstractions, choosing partners, negotiating the balance of costs and rewards in partnerships, and making decisions about whether to engage in activities that offer high returns but contain risks of substantial loss. These risks can be avoided altogether or reduced by the expenditure of points and the willingness to interrupt play to perform a repetitive task. Dyads must also decide who will pay the costs and perform the task, if risks are to be reduced.

Following play of the game, there is a discussion of how it was played and why. For instance, players are asked "Why did you choose A instead of B? How did you and your partner reach that decision?" Then players are told what the real-life parallels to the game elements are (see Chapter 9 for this information). They engage in further discussion of the extent to which their decision making and its consequences in the game simulate what we know about teenage sexual and contraceptive decision making in the real world. Finally, discussion centers on these real-world issues, as players and the operator elaborate upon the model represented in POMP AND CIRCUMSTANCE.

FINAL THOUGHTS

Decisions about style are the most difficult to describe and verbal descriptions may not suffice to give you the "flavor" of the style of a game. The best way to get a feel for the alternative styles you can adopt is to examine a wide variety of games, many of which may not deal with subject matter of concern to you. Following a discussion in Chapter 8 of the nature of the representation decisions concerning the form of gaming elements, all four case studies will be expanded with descriptions of their style and form and what they look like in operation (Chapter 9). Then an array of game elements will be used as illustrations in Chapter 10, which deals with construction and modification of a prototype.

8

Decisions About Representation
Questions of Form

When it comes to explaining *how* to incorporate each element of the conceptual model into the gaming-simulation, most manuals fail. Some simply say "that's what you have to do," and leave the rest to your imagination. Ellington, Addinall, and Percival (1983, p. 73) describe the development process as involving two components: "detailed structure" and "resource materials"; these stages of design are then "explained" in one paragraph stating that this "is a 'black box' into which the designer feeds the basic idea for an exercise (the proposed content and basic structure) and out of which eventually emerges a prototype package suitable for use in field trials (a set of resources and an organizer's guide)." Duke (1980), on the other hand, instructs designers to decide in which of the twelve "systems component/game element matrix cells" each part of the model will be represented (scenario, pulse/event, roles, decision sequence, cycle sequence, steps of play, accounting system, model, indicators, symbology, paraphernalia), offering complex *definitions* of each of the forms, but no *examples* of what these might look like nor criteria for making the choices.

My approach is to "open the black box," taking a midpoint position between Duke's extensive formulation and Armstrong and Hobson's (1969) discussion of gaming-simulations being reducible to three components: scenario, roles, and accounting system. Six elements of form—scenario, roles, procedures and rules, external factors, visual imagery and symbols, and an accounting system—will be discussed here. These will be illustrated in Chapter 9 through descriptions of the four gaming-simulations introduced earlier in the case studies: BLOOD MONEY, CAPJEFOS, THE MARRIAGE GAME, and POMP AND CIRCUMSTANCE. Then, in Chapter 10, further discussion and description will be given of each element, and an extensive set of examples of each from an array of gaming-simulations will be offered.

Your eventual job for this second part of the representation decisions of Stage III will involve two tasks:

(1) Decide in which form each model element will be included (e.g., will it be introduced in the scenario, or in the external events?).
(2) Decide on the precise character of each of the 6 elements to be constructed for your gaming-simulation.

If you are working through a design process while reading this book for the first time, it is recommended that you read this chapter and the next two before proceeding.

SCENARIO

Players must be introduced to the game through a short description of where they are and what the problem that they will be coping with is. This can be announced by the game operator, played on a cassette, illustrated through a slide show, or handed out to players to read. Generally, all players should collectively be given some "stage setting," and then introduced to their particular roles. Sometimes this presentation of a common scenario is followed by subdivision into groups, each of which receives a second scenario (e.g., BAFA-BAFA, CAPJEFOS). The scenario should also make reference to what they will be doing in the course of play of the game (see procedures and rules below), to the objectives, and to the main roles represented. When they are to be in a hypothetical country or town, it is often helpful to include visual material, such as a map (see visual imagery below) included in the scenario (as in ST. PHILIP). In addition, some designers have found it helpful to include slides of similar places. As the examples in Chapters 9 and 10 will illustrate, scenarios can be very simple or quite complex.

ROLES

Players must be given roles to play, including goals to strive for, resources available for them to control or allocate (e.g., time, influence, votes, land, money), and an overview of the activities in which they will engage during play.

Not all roles you identified in the conceptual model need to be represented by *players*. Indeed, only those persons who make decisions that affect the outcome should generally be included in the role set. Players in different roles will have different learning experiences (see Greenblat, 1980, and Lederman, 1983, for elaboration) and players who have little or nothing to do for much of the game are not likely to learn much. The decisions of actors whose roles are not played can be incorporated into the operator's role, into external events, or into the accounting system.

As Chapter 10's discussion and illustrations will demonstrate, an examination of a variety of gaming-simulations reveals considerable variation in role specificity, the number and type of roles, and the resultant form of player organization. As a result, role descriptions can be very simple or quite complex.

PROCEDURES AND RULES

We will consider procedures and rules in terms of three levels of design: *overall* play (i.e., the macro level), play of a *round* or *cycle* (i.e., the micro level), and within-cycle activities (e.g., applying for a job, allocating boats to different fishing areas, paying taxes). The cycle steps of play are likely to entail different activities for those in different roles or role sets.

The macro-level steps of play have already been illustrated in Chapter 7 (Figures 7.1, 7.2, and 7.3) in the discussion of structure. Having decided on the overall structure of the gaming-simulation, you must now determine what is to happen in the full time from the briefing to the debriefing. Where the structure is interactive and play takes place in cycles, the steps each player engages in may be the same from one round to another, but it should be pointed out that the cumulative effects of earlier decisions and events will affect what he or she can do.

It is sometimes possible (and often desirable) to begin with a simple first round and then add new elements (as in THE COMMONS GAME). If you do this, however, it is usually necessary to inform players that there will be additional rules or options introduced later. Otherwise they are likely to turn to the operator with complaints that it was not fair, because they did not know what would come next when they planned their strategy. (In a few instances, such warnings are deliberately not given, as emphasis in the gaming-simulation is on some "unfairness" of rule changes. The best example of this is Garry Shirts's enormously popular STARPOWER.)

On the micro level, you must then determine what actions are to be taken, and in what order, by all players and the operator, at each stage of play. Each player (or role) need not know the micro-level steps for *all* players, but must receive instructions on his or her own activities. Those steps of play must specify things that *must* be done, things that *can* be done (but are optional), and things that *cannot* be done by players. The latter category should usually be subdivided into natural laws that cannot be violated (e.g., players cannot decide that they do not need to eat in order to survive) and man-made laws (e.g., you cannot steal from others) that they may choose to violate, though such violations are likely to be sanctioned by others.

An extremely important dimension of procedures and rules involves *communications* between players. Communication may be open, restricted to written messages, or nonexistent, depending on the system you are modeling. For example, if players represent diplomats from different nations they should be free to communicate only with members of other nations at particular points of play. In THE CONFERENCE GAME, conference planner players communicate with hotel personnel and speakers bureau staff (played by the operators) only by letter or telephone (in this case, via walkie-talkies in different rooms), to simulate the character of restricted communications in the real world. To make such communication realistic, game letters sometimes go astray or are not answered for long periods of time; the parties are often not available when called; telephone messages are sometimes not delivered or are ignored; and "wrong numbers" are often reached!

Two other critical points in planning the procedures and rules concern *the timing of breaks* and *the rules for ending the game*. If the period of play is to be a long one, players must be permitted coffee/tea breaks and meal breaks. If play is to be spread over several days' time, even longer breaks will occur. Thus the designer must pay careful attention to structuring play so that breaks do not occur at inopportune moments. Careful attention to the parameters set out in Stage I will alert you to the need to take these into account.

Similarly, it is important to guard against artificial ends of play. Sometimes the end is obvious and reasonable: a period of time is given to the culminating parliamentary session, and play ends when the decision is reached; a vote is taken to see who has won the election toward which play has been directed; the radio program is produced and disseminated. In other instances, especially where there is an interactive structure, the "end" may not be so obvious.

It is also important to avoid players' engaging in "end-of-the-world" strategy. That is, they are told there will be five cycles or rounds, and in the fifth one they invest all their funds in a "win or lose" action, hoping to come out the winners, while their prior play was much more cautious. One way to avoid this is to have the operator announce that there will be six rounds and then end the game at the end of the fifth one. Another option is to have an indeterminate number of rounds, for example, by throwing a die at the end of each round after the minimum number have been played and announcing that if a 6 turns up the game is over. The former strategy may create annoyance to the operator, though it is usually easily deflected by an explanation of why play was terminated prematurely; the latter strategy makes it difficult for the operator to know how long a period is needed for play.

As with the other elements described, procedures and rules may be simple or complex.

EXTERNAL FACTORS

As indicated earlier, not all roles have to be *played* and not all external events have to be introduced in the scenario. As play progresses, other actors, natural events, or social changes may affect the options available to players or affect the consequences of their actions. These may be introduced according to a predetermined sequence; they may be dependent upon players' actions; they can be introduced by decision of the operator; or they can appear by chance. Too often only the last option is used, to the detriment of the realism and impact of the gaming-simulation. Pointing to the problems of an over-reliance on chance, Samuel Livingston (1973, p. 15) offers advice on how to design a *bad* simulation game:

> Have the players' success or failure in the game determined almost entirely by chance. There are at least two ways to make your simulation a game of chance. One way is to have a roll of the dice or a spin of a spinner determine the actions that a player is permitted to take. The other way is to include a step in which the players draw a chance card with results that will overwhelm the results of their plans and strategy. Often just adding a deck of chance cards can turn a good simulation game into a bad one. For example, if the object of the game is to make money, and if by skillful play, clever strategy, and careful planning a good player can earn two or three hundred dollars more than a poor player, the chance cards can provide random bonuses or penalties of four or five hundred dollars.

VISUAL IMAGERY AND SYMBOLS

Visual imagery and physical symbols can add much to a gaming-simulation. Here I have reference to markers, badges, blocks, chips, "money," and other physical representations. Carefully selected, these can lead to greater engagement of players in the action, and can also provide much easier means of identifying who is who and what score one has. Some examples have already been provided in the discussion of levels of abstraction, and further examples will be provided in Chapter 10.

Large charts are another form of imagery that are often helpful to players to remind them of rules, steps, pay-offs, or to show them their relative standing. Sometimes they take the form of a map to remind players of the geographic characteristics of the area.

A major form of visual imagery found in a number of games is a *playing board.* Many designers (including me) began with initial opposition to boards, assuming that they forced one into a circuit form (such as MONOP-OLY) or a race track form, in which players moved markers according to a dice throw to see who would reach the end first. More careful examination of the options, however, reveals that in addition to these forms (which I still don't like), very creative and fruitful use can be made of a board, as the examples in Chapter 10 will demonstrate.

ACCOUNTING SYSTEM

The accounting system refers to all quantifiable elements and their linkages. For example, in gaming-simulations with a simple accounting system, each player may have one vote to cast at the end of play, and the only calculation is the addition of votes. On the other hand, a complex accounting system with many submodels is involved in gaming-simulations in which players have several resources (e.g., money, influence, land) that can be exchanged, and in which consequences result from a combination of players' actions and outside factors, such as the stock market, bank interest rates, and the total amount of product developed by production "teams." Gaming-simulations with this level of complexity of the accounting system (e.g., METRO-APEX, THE MAN-AGEMENT GAME, STRATEGEM-1) almost invariably employ a computer. (The use of computers in the design process has been addressed in Chapter 4.)

In designing the accounting system you must determine all the places at which there will be quantifications. That is, you must go through all the other items: scenario, roles, procedures and rules, external factors, visual imagery and symbols, and see where quantifications are needed. You may have referred to such factors as size of population, salaries earned by various players, amount produced by a factory with full staff, degree of loss from drought or flood, mortgage rates, costs of importing items, cost per military unit sent for defense, price of parcels of land or of various building projects. In this representation decision stage, you must list each of these quantifiable elements and indicate how they are linked to one another; in the construction stage, actual numbers must be put into charts and graphs and calibrations must be worked out and refined. Then charts for conveying this information to players and/or operators must be made, and forms for recording units gained, spent, and transferred must be generated.

FORM

MODEL ELEMENT	Scenario	Roles	Procedures and rules	External factors	Visual imagery & symbols	Accounting system
Changing population						
Uncertain weather						
Transport						
Group conflict						
Deference to authority						
Gender inequality						
Etc.						

Figure 8.1 Decisions about Form Matrix

MAKING REPRESENTATION DECISIONS

Having read the options here and the case studies, you must begin narrowing the choices and making design decisions for your gaming-simulation. You are urged to read Chapters 9 and 10 first to gain a fuller understanding of the range of possibilities. Then do the following:

(1) Decide what form each of the elements of your model will take. You will have to make choices yourself, as each problem has a number of different possible solutions. Take a page of paper, and make seven columns, headed "Model Element," "Scenario," "Roles," "Procedures and Rules," "External Factors," "Visual Imagery and Symbols," and "Accounting System." Then list in the first column the major model elements you selected in Stage II for inclusion in the gaming-simulation. As you decide which *form* each element should take, make a check in the appropriate box as in Figure 8.1.

(2) Next, by reading down each column, make detailed lists of what must be constructed for each form: for example, what must be mentioned in the scenario?; what *roles* should be designed?; what elements are to be represented symbolically or visually? Be as specific as you can in these. It will be helpful to do this by heading one *page* (instead of one column, as above) with each of the six forms, and then detailing your plan. You are likely to encounter the greatest difficulties in describing the accounting system; although all decisions are inter-

dependent, this set depends most fully on the others. Indicate at least *what* linkages must be determined.

Remember—you are not actually writing the scenario, the role cards, and so on, until the next stage: construction. Here you need to detail what is to be done—that is, your representation decisions. If you know any game designers it will be helpful to review the document with them.

LAST THOUGHTS: ON DIGGING HOLES AND CHIPPING AWAY

As you proceed through this step, consider and try to follow the sound advice of two experienced game-designers, R. Garry Shirts and Ken Jones:

"Let's get going. There's a job to do, let's do it. Work, work, work, that's the only way to get anything done in this world." When I start on a project, I have to restrain those driving forces for a while to say to myself "Wait, there's probably a hundred ways of approaching this problem and you've only discovered ten. Give yourself some overnight think time. Ask yourself some more dumb questions. How would a child look at the problem? A person from another planet or culture? If this situation were boiled for an hour and a half what would be left after draining off the juices?" What if you had to design the game with colored buttons and drawing pins? DeBono, in his book *New Think* points out that once a person starts digging a mental hole, there is a tendency to persevere, to keep digging, to take satisfaction in perfecting the shape and size of the hole without considering whether it is in the right place. To increase the probability of digging the hole in the right place, one should dig many shallow holes all over the area before selecting one to develop. In the beginning stages of game design, one must resist the temptation to accept the first idea with merit as the final idea. Dig more holes [Shirts, 1975, p. 2].

There is a story about a sculptor who had just finished making a stone elephant. He was asked, "How did you do it?" He replied "I chipped away those bits that did not look like an elephant."

Simulation design can be rather like this. Most people think of creative work as building, but it might be just as useful to think of it as chipping away. The simulation designer starts with a thousand potential simulations and ends up with one.

Creation involves closing options. Should the simulation be closed or open-ended? Should it be on a national or a local level? Should there be group roles or individual profiles? As each of these questions is decided, a great many possible simulations have been chipped away.

When a teacher inspects a package of simulation material, he or she may think that the author started off with a nice clear objective and the simulation was arrived at by some sort of logical deduction. What the teacher does not see is the author's wastepaper basket [Jones, 1982, p. 31].

Finally, I urge you to try to keep in mind that *this is not an easy task!!! Do not rush and do not become frustrated when you can't figure out how to include something right away.*

9

From Representation to Construction
The Four Case Studies Continued

Before proceeding to the guidelines for constructing and modifying the gaming-simulation, let us return to the four case studies begun in earlier chapters to see how the conceptual models were converted to operating ones. Each of these final products, of course, represents only one set of solutions to the problems of representation, construction, and preparation for use by others. You may find it interesting to think about how *you* would have created the games, based on the descriptions of objectives and parameters, and the short versions of the conceptual models offered in prior chapters.

BLOOD MONEY
(Cathy Stein Greenblat and John H. Gagnon)

The conceptual model for this game was described in Chapter 6; deciding how to represent the model elements in the gaming-simulation was the next step. The "game within a game" model developed by Fred Goodman in THE HELPING HAND STRIKES AGAIN (which deals with general problems in the helping relationship) and subsequently refined by him in later games, was adopted. BLOOD MONEY differs from these Goodman games in its higher level of specificity and concreteness, and in the degree to which assumptions about the operation of the system are simulated rather than left to emerge from player predilections.

To simulate the relationships between actors (see Figure 6.2), two sectors of players were created. In the first sector are the citizens who are victims of hemophilia. Their goal is to achieve success by gaining white chips representing money, prestige in the community, and positive relationships with others. The citizens are periodically limited in their ability to attain these goals by the advent of an attack (described as moderate, severe, or catastrophic) that necessitates that they go to the

medical sector for care (blue chips) and blood (red chips). They are under rigid time constraints to obtain these necessities rapidly enough to avoid further disability (which restricts their abilities at work) and to avoid missing their turn (hence failing to earn the white chips that must be paid to obtain care and blood).

If you were watching the game in operation, you would see that there are two dart games (with velcro darts) "owned" by two players called "employers." These games represent not only jobs in the occupational sense, but the school/work/social worlds in which people earn money and gain other satisfactions. In the first 5 minutes of each round, employers have an opportunity to hire citizens for 25 turns at throwing darts. No citizen can be hired for more than 6 turns per round. The employees are hired at a fixed salary of white chips (payable at the time of performance), but the employers are paid white chips (at the end of the round) based on the scores that their employees make. Employer B pays less but has a higher tolerance for absenteeism.

In a typical run of the game, there are two 45-minute rounds with 5-minute hiring periods preceding each. (Players are generally told that there will be three such rounds, to prevent their engaging in an end-of-the-world strategy in Round 2.) Citizens seek employment in order to earn white chips, which are goals in themselves and also may be exchanged for medical care and blood products. Since the goal of the employers is to make white chips, it is rational for them to (a) disperse employees over the twenty-five trials, rather than giving them sequential turns, in case they become ill during a part of the round; (b) to hire the least disabled citizens; and (c) to hire the best dart throwers. The employers are not given these suggestions, but they usually develop such strategies over the course of play.

When citizens are hired they are given numbered stickers indicating their turn numbers. Employees' names and turn numbers are also listed on an Employment Roster, which is given to Operator 1. When the major part of the round starts, Operator 1 calls out the numbers in sequence. He or she checks the medical status of all citizens who are present when their turns are called, and reminds those with more serious disabilities of the constraints on the manner of their throwing. Those absent (i.e., elsewhere getting medical treatment or financial aid) miss their turns. Those absent from Employer B's roster are recalled when everyone has been called once).

Citizens enter the game having either moderate or severe hemophilia, which affects the frequency of attacks to which they are subject. They also differ in the impairment they already suffer as a result of their prior health history and of the quality of prior care they have received. The degree of disability is indicated by small red dots on their name tags. As play progresses, citizens are likely to become further disabled unless they avoid severe and catastrophic attacks (by luck), and either obtain high-quality care for attacks in a short period of time, or spend resources on rehabilitative care.

The degree of *severity* affects work performance indirectly through absenteeism at times of attacks; the degree of *disability* affects job performance directly, since those with greater disability are constrained in the manner in which they can throw darts. With 0-2 dots there are no constraints; with 3-4 dots the player must be seated to throw; with 5-6 dots they must throw (standing) with their weaker hand; with 7 dots they cannot be employed, but are confined to "bed" unless they are in the medical sector obtaining treatment; and with 8 dots they die and go to the "cemetery."

During the course of play, citizens are subject to new attacks of bleeding. These attacks require the citizen to obtain medical care and transfusions of blood. The citizens are approached during the round by one of the operators, who has a standard deck of playing cards. The citizen is told to cut the shuffled deck and show the operator the bottom card. This card will be translated into an "attack level" as follows:

- Heart—no attack
- Diamond or Club—moderate attack
- 2-10 of Spades—severe attack
- Jack, Queen, King, or Ace of Spades—catastrophic attack

The attack can be ignored, though this has serious consequences in terms of further disability. Medical care and blood can be sought to alleviate the attack and to reduce the disability caused by it. In either case, the citizen must report to the operator who gave the attack within 5 minutes for "on time" care, in 5-8 minutes for "overtime" care, or immediately thereafter if no care was

received. Additional dots are then allocated to indicate further disability.

Medical care and information is available from the two M.D.s and blood is available from the Blood Bank with a prescription from an M.D. The M.D.s and Blood Bank operators are given information about alternative treatment modes to offer, depending upon severity and prior disability, and about costs (in white chips) of each of the levels of care. The M.D. will recommend specific treatment or offer the options; the citizen can then purchase an agreed-upon number of units of medical care (blue chips), and can obtain a prescription for blood (red chips). Citizens may also purchase rehabilitative care from M.D.s, which will reduce the degree of disability (by eliminating red dots), thus making them more effective participants in the world of work. Such care is expensive in both economic and resource terms (it requires a lot of the M.D.'s services and the Blood Bank's blood).

There are limited amounts of blood and care to be dispensed, and the players in the care sector face a considerable record-keeping task in the face of high patient demand. In addition, the welfare agents, who have limited funds and must develop effective and efficient modes of allocation, demand proof of receipt of care and blood.

Briefly stated, then, we elected to simulate some elements of the system, and left others to emerge over the course of a typical run of the game, as shown in Figure 9.1. Following an initial play of the game, those so inclined can use it to examine ways of making the health sector work better by replaying with alterations of record-keeping procedures, ratio of patients to doctors, organization of medical care and blood banking services, flexibility in employment, and so on. This may lead to hypotheses about ways to make the real-world system operate more effectively.

There was little problem with the preparation of the game for use by others. The specifications of the objectives and parameters had been written out, and a clear document about the model had been drawn up; these then made up important sections of the operator's model. We tape-recorded our instructions to several groups of players, and from the transcripts we were able to produce clear "scripts" for the operator. Similarly, through observing one another running the game, we were able to clarify what had to be included in the operator's instructions for other people to run BLOOD MONEY. The client—the National Heart and Lung Institute—was enthusiastic about the game, and arranged for manuals to be produced and distributed by the U.S. Government Printing Office. We had intended from the start to produce a manual that would enable potential users to produce their own kits easily and inexpensively, and this manual contained the needed guidelines. The

MODEL ELEMENT	SIMULATED OR EMERGENT	HOW/WHERE MANIFESTED
A. Medical problems: -ongoing and unpredictable -cumulative in effects	Simulated Simulated	Attacks given by Operator 2 Disability dots with work impairment and other consequences
B. Need for medical care	Simulated	Additional disability dots and possible death for no care, too little care, or late care; limits on care and blood available
C. Need for $ for treatment	Simulated	Minimum costs given for care and blood; M.D.'s and Blood Bank officials may raise costs above minimum
D. Psychological problems: fear, tension, anxiety, negative self-image	Emergent	Citizens are upset by limitations in work participation, interruption in work, difficulty in getting care, time pressure on getting care and increasing disability. Others: M.D.s do not understand system, have limited time; Employers have limited income set by disabilities of Citizens and absentees; Blood Bankers have limited resources; Welfare Agents have limited funds and often have no contact with M.D.'s or with Blood Bank.
E. Absenteeism	Simulated & emergent	Order of turns is set so that most who choose to get care (in an inefficient system) will miss at least one turn at the dart game (and the resulting income)
F. School/job failures & problems	Simulated & emergent	Dart games structured to be inflexible and intolerant of absenteeism (invariant order of turns), limited in total amount of rewards available (25 turns/round limit) andto favor employers who discriminate by skill and lack of disability (employers are paid a percent of total scores. Problems and failures then are likely to be experienced by increasingly harassed and disabled players dealing within such a system.
G. Public ignorance H. Stigmatization I. Discrimination	Simulated & emergent	Most other players are not told much about the Citizens' role, and (see F) there are more rewards for dealing with the less handicapped. These elements, however, are weakly introduced because of the absence of non-hemophiliacs in the Citizens' role.
J. Insurance limitations	Simulated	These limitations are total in the game (something of an exaggeration) since there is NO insurance available.
K. Family tension and strain	Omitted	The decision to eliminate all other players led to elimination of the role of family members. This element should be dealt with at length in post-game discussion.

Figure 9.1   Simulated and Emergent Elements in BLOOD MONEY

SOURCE: Greenblat and Gagnon (1976). Reprinted by permission.

National Hemophilia Foundation awarded the designers a Special Achievement Award at its 1977 annual meeting, and numerous regional and local chapters assembled kits. These chapters employed the game extensively with diverse groups of players, and fostered adoption of BLOOD MONEY in other local training and education programs.

Shortly thereafter there was an abortive attempt to

arrange for production of kits through a game publisher. This company obtained price quotes for materials and began preparation of kits. Unfortunately, other problems within the company forced it into bankruptcy and it went out of business before the contract work had been completed. The kits were never produced.

CAPJEFOS: A SIMULATION OF VILLAGE DEVELOPMENT
(Cathy Stein Greenblat, Philip Langley, Jacob Ngwa, Ernest Mangesho, Saul Luyumba, and Foday MacBailey)

CAPJEFOS simulates on an abstract level the factors that hinder and/or promote rural development at the scale of a village. Particular attention is paid to self-help programs for health and agriculture, and the manner in which village actions are influenced by regional/national planning objectives and policies. Through their experience with CAPJEFOS, players should:

(1) develop a better understanding of factors in development and their interaction;
(2) develop greater empathy for villagers and better knowledge of their rationales;
(3) find a "safe" means for exploration of what the development agent's role could or should be.

While CAPJEFOS is modeled after problems typical of African villages, the designers believe that the development problems simulated are similar in many other areas of the world. CAPJEFOS can be played by a number of different types of players. It was initially designed as a training tool for development agents in in-training or in-service programs. The game is also useful as an educational tool for students of development, African studies, rural agriculture, rural economics, and so on at the university level. Bright secondary school students could also play CAPJEFOS in the context of courses dealing with development issues.

Two operators are required to run the game. Both should be familiar with it from a thorough reading of the manual. If possible, a third person should be recruited to serve as an assistant to Operator 1.

There are several ways to run CAPJEFOS, depending upon the time available, the teaching/training objectives, and the experience of the operators. A minimum of 5 hours is required for the simple version (village only—no development agents); a full day is required for the basic version; and a day and a half is needed for the full version.

Two rooms—one large and one small—are required for play. The first is set up as the village of Capjefos, and the second, as the regional market town and headquarters of the Development Agency. It is helpful to have a third room for the introduction.

When players arrive, they are greeted and introduced to the general character of the exercise by one of the two operators. Within a few minutes, they are divided into two groups: villagers (20-25) and development agents (3-5). The latter are taken by Operator 2 to another room that is thereafter known as "Somnas," the regional center of the Pawafra Division. There they are informed that they are the recently hired staff of the newly formed Rural Development and Industrial Agency of Pawafra. They are given role cards and instructions about the activities they are to perform each round. A document about the region and the general characteristics of the rural villages within it is given to them to read, and specific role assignments are made (1 Divisional Officer, 1 or 2 Health Field Officers, 1 or 2 Agricultural Field Officers).

At the same time, villagers are given their briefing by Operator 1. All are residents of the village of Capjefos, named for its founding ancestors:

—**CA**thy, **P**hilip, **J**acob, **E**rnest, **FO**day, and **S**aul

They are told of the demographic, economic, social, and cultural characteristics of the village, and are informed that the development agents will soon be coming to visit and work there. As the development agents are not informed of the specific cultural traditions and needs of the villagers, so too, the villagers are not told the specifics of the development agents' aims. Villagers are informed that the agents intend to introduce some projects, but they must, through interaction with them, learn about the nature, costs, and rewards of these projects.

Specific role assignments (chief, traditional doctor, religious leader, teacher, town crier, 10 men and 10 women farmers) are made. (See Figures 10.4 and 10.5 for an example.) Four of the farmers are told that they have found it more profitable to engage in trading than in farming, and are given special instructions about buying food and cash crops in Capjefos and selling them in Somnas, or about buying commodities in Somnas and selling them to the villagers. All these players then move to a large room set up as "Capjefos" and play begins.

Play takes place in 2-5 rounds that last approximately 1 hour, each representing one year. The game begins part way through 1980 (Round 0); the first part of this preliminary year has been "played" by the designers, so participants are given record sheets indicating what they have done so far. These records can then serve as guidelines for the next year's decisions and for completion of the next year's forms, though players may make quite different decisions.

The rhythm of life in the two locations differs. In Capjefos, a round is divided into 5 steps: Work Time, Market/Time, Group Meetings, Community Meeting, and Social Life. In Somnas, there are three major periods: Divisional Development Committee Meeting, Office and

RELIGIOUS LEADER
RECORD SHEET: 198*0*

CONVERTS:

Man farmer 5 _____

Woman Farmer 6 _____

Man Farmer 8 _____

Woman Farmer 7 _____

_____   _____

_____   _____

_____   _____

Number of persons you consider serious converts: *0* (Put an asterisk next to their names)

OCSENU:

INCOME:

Received from Regional Church	*150*
From villagers' donations	*100*
TOTAL INCOME	*250*

EXPENDITURES:

1. *new pews*	*250*
2. _____	____
3. _____	____
4. _____	
TOTAL EXPENDITURES	*250*

YOUR ESTIMATION OF THE QUALITY OF VILLAGE LIFE THIS YEAR:
circle one: A   B   C   (D)   F

Figure 9.2   Sample 1980 Record Sheet: CAPJEFOS

SOURCE: Greenblat et al. (1987). Reprinted by permission.

Fieldwork Time, and Reporting Period. Field agents may go to Capjefos beginning in 1981; they quickly discover that it is difficult to find a convenient time to talk with villagers, especially during the work and market times when farmers are heavily occupied with the tasks of production and trading.

The village economy is set up so that it operates just above subsistence. Little surplus is available to individual villagers, although there is some differentiation in economic resources. Likewise, on a community level there is little capital available for development. Sickness is rampant, partly due to the drinking of contaminated water, partly due to poor diets, and partly due to regular outbreaks of disease that are not properly treated. Villagers suffer mild, moderate, or severe cases of measles, malaria, worms, and diarrhea on a regular basis; no clinic is available, and treatment is via herbs or care from the traditional doctor. Because of the need for labor in agriculture to meet subsistence needs, and the drain on available time due to sickness, little surplus time is available for villagers to invest in development projects.

"Event cards" are tailored to each role player. They can be given out at random or selected by the operators to introduce particular issues (e.g., demands from Regional Authorities for the agents, the religious leader, and the teacher; requests to farmers for funds from children who are elsewhere in school; visits from relatives, which drain already low time and money resources).

The task of the development agents, then, is made difficult by their lack of familiarity with some of the village customs and by the severe limitations of village resources. In addition, they have the job of obtaining considerable statistical data to file their annual reports in the office, and they must try to learn what type of projects the villagers would like and would support. By Round 3 (in the basic version of the game) they must try to implement those projects they have devised. If 4 or 5 rounds are being played, in Round 3 they are given regional/national mandates for programs; these are likely to conflict with the projects they have developed alone or in conjunction with the Capjefos villagers.

Three types of projects exist in the game. The third type is used only in the full version:

Village Projects. These are the types of activities that villagers might well propose themselves and undertake on their own initiative with little external assistance. Some projects have direct effects on production; others do not. Some of them tend to be stereotyped ways of making Capjefos into a "modern" village. The chief receives information on these during Round 1 (1981).

Local Projects. These are suggested to the field agents at the start of Round 1 (1981). In most cases these projects will require some external assistance to the village in the form of technical advice from the field staff and/or money from the Divisional Officer's discretionary fund. These projects are the type that development staff are more likely than villagers to propose. These projects have mostly been chosen to be simple, labor intensive, and reasonably close to villagers' needs.

Small-Scale Projects (used in full version only). These are proposed by the Minister of Rural Development. In spite of their title, they tend to be capital intensive and to increase economic and technical dependency without necessarily being well-tuned to the specific needs of Capjefos and/or of the smaller farmer. The D.O. is informed of these projects at the start of Round 3 (1983) before the field staff leave for Capjefos.

The rationale of these projects in terms of game play is to introduce a series of events in which "village" and "local" projects will be complementary: (1) if those playing the roles of field staff realize that this is a good tactic; (2) if they attempt to graft the "local" projects onto already existing initiatives in the village; and (3) if they explain them to the villagers. However, whether the field staff does this or not, the "small-scale" projects will tend to conflict with both the "village" and the "local" projects. This will create the contradictory situation in which the field staff often find themselves, squeezed between their knowledge of the village setting and the villagers' problems on the one hand, and the instructions received from higher authorities on the other. However, the field staff see themselves as the carriers of modernity, which is often epitomized to them through the projects proposed by the state. Even though they may at times have a critical position in regard to the higher echelons of their own technical service, this may be because the state does not bring them the benefits and the status they feel they should receive, as their aim is often to climb up the hierarchy or at least to acquire the symbols of status and authority. Their position with regard to the three types of projects will be influenced by this, and the discussion after the game can bring out these contradictions.

As will be obvious from this summary, CAPJEFOS is a complex gaming-simulation with many variables and many materials. The set of information and materials and decisions for any one player, on the other hand, can be mastered readily.

All the game components were designed and subsequently modified as a result of several field tests in Cameroon and in the United States. The first run involved play of the village only (i.e., no development agents) to be sure that little economic change would take place in the village in the absence of outside intervention. The run was very successful, but several components proved too complex. For example, we had included approximately a dozen diseases and three levels of severity; determining the sickness and care needed proved too time-consuming.

The second run involved skeletal development agent roles and a simplified set of villager materials (e.g., sickness was reduced to a set of four diseases and three levels of severity). The players in this field test included both English- and French-speaking participants (and all the materials were in English!), introducing unanticipated problems. The success of this run despite these problems convinced us that the game was well-designed. We also learned that we needed replacements for some of the symbols. For example, we used peanuts (groundnuts) in the shell to represent fish; by the end of the second round, all the "fish" had been eaten, and the villagers had no source of protein! Similarly, the beans we used for food crop proved problematic, as it took too long to count the yield from several cultivated fields, each of which gave the farmer 20 units of food crop.

By the third run of the game we had shifted to more paper components (fish, food, and cash crop), and had elaborated the development roles. Real-life development agents were present for this run and we were thus able to have them review and make suggestions on the development agent instructions and tasks.

The greatest difficulties in design had been with the accounting system. Here several interrelated decisions had to be made. For example, the amount earned by a farmer times the number of farmers, minus subsistence needs for all villagers, minus community needs, would equal community surplus. Production had to be set and cash values assigned to cash crop and food and fish surplus in a manner that would yield limited capital to the community. The costs of commodities and products then had to be set in relation to these potential sources of individual and community assets. These problems seem to have been solved, as the quantitative elements have worked well over a series of approximately 20 runs.

Other "niggling" problems persisted. Operator 1's tasks were deemed too extensive for all but experienced game operators. Hence some elements that worked well for players were changed in order to decrease this operator's activities. Sickness cards were abandoned for a more realistic (and more readily changed) dice throw and consultation of a chart. Subsequently, we returned to the chance cards, realizing the dice throw and chart option once again made more work for the operator. The game has now been run in the United States, Cameroon, France, Canada, and China, with smooth operations and very fruitful discussions each time.

The full set of materials for the game is quite extensive. As of this writing, ways of reducing it are being investigated in order to make the cost of a kit lower. UNESCO's financial difficulties since 1985 have at least temporarily precluded the publication and dissemination activities we and they had originally envisaged, and none of the designers has yet had the time to pursue other options actively. As the game receives more publicity and as more requests for copies appear on our desks, however, the pressure to find a publisher mounts. We thus plan to follow the advice in the latter part of Chapter 11!

THE MARRIAGE GAME
(Cathy Stein Greenblat, Peter J. Stein, and Norman F. Washburne)

THE MARRIAGE GAME may be played by two or more people in any number of settings. The game can be played by small, medium, or large groups of people, and no instructor is necessary for play, though it is easier to get started if there is a coordinator who is familiar with the rules and procedures. The major use of THE MARRIAGE GAME is as a segment of courses or units on Marriage and the Family at the college level. In this context of use, students may learn not only to identify the major elements of the marriage system, but to see their interconnections. They should also better recognize how decisions made in the present affect the shape of life in the future, and, conversely, how visions of the future affect present decision making. The game can also be played outside the classroom as a vehicle to move players into a discussion of their own marital expectations or experiences. In this context of use, the game can be used to provide opportunities for players to get to know one another in a setting that is both educational and enjoyable.

Each player needs a copy of the manual, which contains all the rules of play and materials for one person, as well as a set of related readings. Chapters 1 and 2 should be read prior to the day of play. Each round of play represents one year. The first round requires more time than do subsequent rounds because of the need for preliminary discussion and time to gain familiarity with procedures and materials. About 1-1/2 hours should be allotted to this first round; subsequent rounds can be completed within 50-minute periods. It is best if at least 6 rounds are played, for a number of new decisions will be made in rounds 4 or 5 (e.g., the decision to have a child), and the long-term consequences of some earlier decisions will have been experienced. As with all games, time for postgame discussion is critical. It is possible to change parameters systematically—such as those relating to social class level, sexual permissiveness, and inequality between the sexes—and replay the game, experiencing the effects on the family system of each change. Instructions for making these alterations are given in the manual.

Before play commences, participants are assigned sex roles. Hence it is not essential that there be an equal number of male and female players. There is little for the operator to do besides introducing the game, helping players through the first round, encouraging interaction, and signing Marriage Licenses and Divorce Forms. The operator is thus free to observe interactions among the players.

As noted in the discussion in Chapter 6, there are six types of points players earn and forfeit as a result of their decisions and external events: security points, respect and esteem points, freedom points, enjoyment points, sex-gratification points, marital- and parental-status points, and ego-support points. At the beginning of each round, each player must assign value weights to each of these types of points (see Figure 10.58 for a copy of the form on which these weights are assigned). We believe that these reflect the differential importance people attach to elements of their lives together. The differential importance attached to the whole marital system can be brought in only by the individual player confronted by the need to evaluate and interpret his or her final score. This aspect of the model is conveyed to the players by telling them that

> THE MARRIAGE GAME has no winners or losers because it is a simulation of real life, and in real life the relative contribution of marital rewards to overall satisfaction with life is different for different people. Those whose rewards come primarily from their marriages require higher marital "scores" or greater marital satisfaction than do those whose marriages constitute only one of several sources of satisfaction, and who thus may be willing to sacrifice some marital rewards for rewards in other areas. For example, they may pursue occupational goals at the expense of their family lives. Therefore it is difficult to make direct comparisons between marriages. As you play THE MARRIAGE GAME your goal should be to maximize those rewards you most value rather than to "beat" other players [pp. 3-4].

Players begin as single college graduates at the age at which they are expected to marry and are rewarded for doing so. Many of the major decisions and actions that occur during the six- or seven-year period that follows are presented, including courtship, whether to marry, job decisions, budgeting, leisure time and vacation choices, and family planning. There are a number of steps of play (see Figure 9.3 for a summary) in each round. Each couple will generate a different "marital history" over the course of the 6-7 rounds of play, yielding considerable material for a rich discussion.

THE MARRIAGE GAME is based on a complex model with many elements and linkages. All three designers were sociologists with some familiarity with the literature on the topic. Nonetheless, considerable time was required for the model development, representation, and construction stages. As we developed and refined the model, we engaged in extensive debates about the real-world dimensions of the marital system; for example, we differed in our beliefs about the degree of inequalities in opportunities and economic rewards for men and women in the labor force. Designing the model was extremely heuristic, for most of these debates led us to the library to find studies on the disputed dimension that could be employed to support our arguments. (A few attempts were made to resolve these debates by dunking one another in the pool at Norman's house when we worked over the summer break!)

We were severely constrained in this project by our very limited resources. The endeavor began as an intellectual exercise to be engaged in during our spare time, with no outside funding. It grew like Topsy as a commitment, but our time was minimal, as we were all teaching, doing research, and involved in other professional endeavors. Coordination of time was also difficult. When we began, there were no word processors, so each item had to be typed . . . and retyped and retyped as we made changes. This, too, took time, and each set of changes from field tests necessitated a long wait before we could make up a new kit for another trial.

We were fortunate that we found an editor at Random House who quickly became very enthusiastic about the project when we were midway through the modification stage. He issued a contract and a small advance, which provided us with inspiration to keep going and the funds to speed up the process. When the materials were finally complete, the game went to press. We met with graphics experts at Random House, and changed a few forms. The sales staff was briefed extensively about what this strange product was, and their enthusiasm mounted as initial sales far exceeded expectations. The first edition went to a third printing (total of 20,000 copies) before we agreed a revision was needed. Many of the tables and charts were reloaded with updated figures (e.g., salaries) and we simplified some procedures and forms based on our experience and the advice of others who had used the game. By the time the second edition was published in 1977, the publishing industry (or at least the academic division) was undergoing change, and during the printing stages of the new MARRIAGE GAME, there was high turnover in the editorial office of the college division of Random House. The new volume was marketed with a lower budget, less staff training, and less editorial office support. It sold reasonably well, but by the time a third edition was needed, our lives were occupied with other endeavors and we did not feel the same exuberance from the publisher that we had initially experienced. We chose not to revise the game. I am doubtful that a publisher today would be willing to take on such a product, as they seem less interested in risk-taking and speculative endeavors with market potentials of this size.

POMP AND CIRCUMSTANCE
(Cathy Stein Greenblat, Linda Reich Rosen, and John H. Gagnon)

POMP AND CIRCUMSTANCE is a teaching game. It was designed to achieve two major purposes: to provide information about the costs and benefits of contraception, and to stimulate the players to discuss and think about their own contraceptive choices.

POMP AND CIRCUMSTANCE was designed to be played by adolescents aged about 13 to 17; it is also very useful for play by parents and others who are concerned about these issues, particularly those who argue that they "cannot understand why teenagers fail to contracept."

A kit contains sufficient materials for a group of 30. One operator is sufficient to instruct the players and to run the game. Full instructions on how to run the game are provided in a detailed manual, and no prior experience

---

SUMMARY OF STEPS OF PLAY

1. Assign value weights

2. Determine major statuses and their consequences

    A. Decide marital status for this round and assess effects
    B. Assess effects of parental status this round
    C. Choose a job

3. Make basic financial decisions
    A. Compute total money available for this round
    B. Make basic budget decisions for the round
    C. Purchase goods and services
    D. Draw economic chance card

4. Interact with others
    A. Allocate free time
    B. Go on a vacation
    C. Obtain sexual gratification (optional)
        (1) Exchange of cards
        (2) Conception chance draw (if contraception not used)
        (3) Venereal disease chance draw (if not married)
        (4) Quality of sex relations chance draw (if married)

5. Obtain partner ratings

6. Calculate your final score

Figure 9.3   Steps of Play: THE MARRIAGE GAME

SOURCE: Greenblat, Stein, and Washburne (1977). Reprinted by permission.

with games is required. About two hours are needed to complete both the play and discussion phases of POMP AND CIRCUMSTANCE. It may be run in one consecutive session in a workshop or youth group or school context; if school periods are short, it can be broken into two or three classroom segments. A room large enough to accommodate the players is necessary, but there are no other requirements in terms of room design. The game can be played either on the floor or at tables or desks.

As players arrive, they are divided into two equal-sized groups, labeled as "Inner Track" and "Outer Track" players. They form dyads consisting of one member from each group, and are seated in pairs at the playing boards (one board per dyad). Each board is equipped with chips, a marker, and two dice. Players are also given scoring sheets that indicate the values of the four sets of colored chips. (The chips have different values for Inner and Outer Track players.) Finally, players are given an information sheet that explains how to "Play the Yellows."

The playing board consists of two concentric circles broken into thirty segments. Each contains dots of one or more colors (yellow, green, blue, and red). Dots with an X through them indicate that a chip of that color must be forfeited. Dots without an X indicate that chips of that color should be taken from the appropriate pile of chips on the board (in the four corners). There are also six yellow spaces, broken into sections A, B, C, and D. Figure 9.4 gives a black and white sample of the playing board; shapes have been substituted for the colors for purposes of reproduction here. The actual board is approximately 16" x 20" and is on cardboard.

The players move around the board on the black track between the concentric circles, using a single marker for

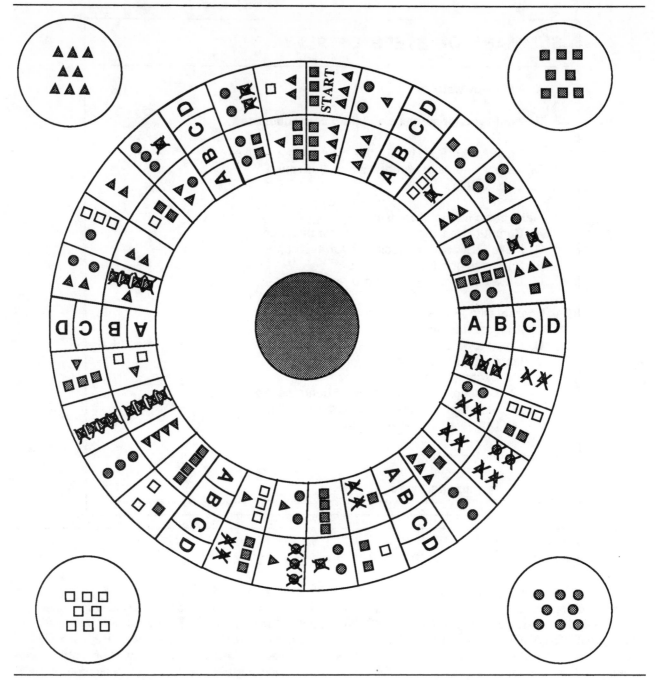

Figure 9.4   Board: POMP AND CIRCUMSTANCE
SOURCE: CSG Enterprises (1978). Reprinted by permission.

the dyad. When they land on a particular space, the Outer Track player gains or loses what is indicated on the outer track, and the Inner Track player gains or loses what is shown on the inner track. If they land on a yellow space, they may play any one of the four options, although they must both play the same option.

To determine the number of spaces to be moved, each player throws one die; then they must decide which of the two throws they will follow. For example, if the Inner Track player throws a 2 and the Outer Track player throws a 4, they must move *either* two or four spaces. The dyad must reach an agreement about the number of spaces to move before the move is made. Since there are more gains than losses on the board, it is usually to the players' advantage to reach an agreement as quickly as possible.

The game is structured such that Outer Track players will not score as high as Inner Track players unless they elect to "play the yellows" when they land on a large yellow space. Playing the yellows will provide higher gains for the Outer Track players because yellow chips are worth more points for them. Some Inner Track players will not realize that they have less to gain and more to lose by playing the yellows. Others will be induced to play the yellows by a partner's offer of red chips. Others will be pressured to do so by their partner's references to "everyone is doing it," or their threats to seek a more compliant partner. Many players in *both* groups will want to play the yellows simply because it makes the game more interesting and exciting.

Playing Yellow A requires simply a decision to do so. Yellow B, C, and D require that players spend some time performing a task that reduces the risk of loss of points from a dice throw that follows. The tasks for C and D are not known as play begins. Many players do not play Yellow C and D during the initial rounds because they do not know what is involved, they are hesitant to pay the cost, or they do not want to take the time to complete these options.

Whichever form of yellow is played, both partners gain chips. Then the Inner Track player must throw the two dice to see whether both players are also to lose points. A high proportion of those who play Yellow A will have a "bad throw," as will many of those who play Yellow B. By the end of the game, many players will have learned that it is most advantageous to play Yellow C or D. A few will decide not to play the yellows at all, while a few will continue to play the high-risk Yellow A or Yellow B, trusting to luck.

After two rounds of play have been completed, all scores are totaled and posted. Inner Track players are instructed to compare their scores with other Inner Track players, and Outer Track players compare with one another. Postgame discussion begins with players revealing how and why they made their decisions. The operator then uses a chart (see Figure 9.5) that shows what the symbols in the game represent and the problems that are simulated. Players and the operator then discuss the parallels between the gaming-simulation and the real-life factors affecting sexual and contraceptive decision making. Depending on the operator's purpose and the context of use, supplementary information and/or a reading list may be provided for the players following the discussion.

The major problems in design stemmed from the decision to treat the phenomenon quite abstractly. Our con-

cern was to model the types of negotiations that take place between dating male and female adolescents, the sexual decisions they must make, the factors that tend to discourage the use of effective contraceptives, and the high risk of pregnancy in noncontracepted sexual behavior.

In our model, adolescent sexual activity was seen as influenced by a wide variety of personal and interpersonal variables. POMP AND CIRCUMSTANCE incorporates some, but not all, of these variables. For instance, we focused on four areas that are of concern to the adolescent: the desire for love and romance, peer approval, adult approval, and sexual gratification. We assumed that these concerns are of differential importance to adolescent males and females. Males, for example, are thought to be most concerned with sexual gratification and peer approval, while females seem most concerned with love and romance, less concerned with peer and adult approval, and least concerned with sexual gratification. Of course, these differential value systems are based on stereotypes of male and female needs, and will not hold true for many adolescents. By making use of these stereotypes, however, we enable adolescents to participate in the game without forcing them to reveal their own personal value systems to the playing group (see the discussion in Chapter 7).

Although the game incorporates the opportunity for players to make use of effective contraceptives (playing Yellow C or D), a great many players will fail to do so, particularly in the early part of the game. The reasons for failure to use contraceptives within the context of the game parallel many of the reasons for contraceptive failure in the real world. For instance, research has shown that many adolescents consistently underestimate the chance of conception from unprotected intercourse. In addition, many adolescents do not use contraceptives because they lack accurate information about when and how to use them, where to get them, and what the "costs"—social as well as economic—are. Teenagers also mention "lack of spontaneity," difficulty in communicating with one's sexual partner, and fear of revealing sexual activity to disapproving peers and adults in their explanations of failure to contracept. (See Gagnon and Greenblat, 1978, for elaboration.)

Based on these ideas, it seemed obvious to us that we should structure the game to be played by multiples of paired partners. All negotiations and decisions should take place within the dyad, with outside influences such as peers and adults represented symbolically. The idea of a game board occurred to us early, but it took some work to decide what the character of the board should be, how to represent the outside influences on it, and what ratios of each colored chip should be available to Inner and Outer Track players. We wanted to assure that, without

Inner Track Players	Adolescent females
Outer Track Players	Adolescent males
Red dots (chips)	Love and romance
Blue dots (chips)	Peer approval
Green dots (chips)	Adult approval
Yellow dots (chips) on white spots	Sexual gratification from necking and petting
"Playing the Yellows"	Sexual intercourse
Yellow chips from playing the yellows	Sexual gratification from intercourse
"Yellow A"	Non-contracepted intercourse: easy; no contraception cost; nothing extra to do; high risk of pregnancy
"Yellow B"	Intercourse with withdrawal: no contraception cost; difficult to do correctly; does not substantially reduce the risks of pregnancy
"Yellow C"	Intercourse with condoms: low regular contraception cost; generally can be done successfully; takes small amount of time; substantially reduces risk of pregnancy
"Yellow D"	Intercourse with the pill: high initial cost for female (who must go to doctor, admit sexual activity, buy pills); then easy (must be taken regularly); reduces risk to very low.
Risks from dice throw	Chances of conception
Loss from "bad" dice throw	Pre-Marital Pregnancy: higher loss for Inner Track (female) Player than for Outer Track (male) player.

Figure 9.5   Symbols in POMP AND CIRCUMSTANCE

SOURCE: CSG Enterprises (1978). Reprinted by permission.

playing the yellows, Inner Track players (females) would gain more points than Outer Track players (males), unless they consciously tried to equalize points. These calibrations took some time, but they were done successfully at an early stage. Very little modification took place on the basis of field tests, which were highly successful from the start.

The resulting format permits game administration and the gaming atmosphere to be simple, with a minimum of movement and noise. Game players need leave their seats only when they have decided to "purchase" effective contraceptives (i.e., to play Yellow C or D). Game players may, however, move about if they find their initial partner to be incompatible in some way and thus attempt to change partners.

This design project was partially funded by a Ford Foundation grant under the Ford and Rockefeller Foundations, Population Policy Research Program. The designers were hired by the recipient of the major grant, Dr. Susan Gustavus Philliber, to design an evaluation instrument for population education courses. The game satisfied that condition, and was successfully used in her research program (see Philliber and Gutterman, 1982). While Susan used a form in which players knew what the game was about and what the symbols represented before they began, she agreed with us that for teaching purposes the "mystery" form was superior.

By prearrangement, copyright rested with CSG Enterprises, a small company in which the three designers were officers. The U.S. Patent Office issued a copyright in 1978, after we were satisfied that we had a complete, working version. We made some early investigations concerning publication. One or two game publishers expressed interest, but we did not believe that they would market the game effectively. All the early efforts suggested this was an excellent tool for school sex-education programs, and hence the game needed to be marketed nationally and to guidance officers and health teachers.

Neither of the game companies were prepared to invest the time or money this would require. We had a few conversations with representatives of action groups concerned with adolescent pregnancy. They were very interested, but as they knew little about games, it would have been necessary for us to spend considerable time briefing their graphics, publicity, and other staff about POMP AND CIRCUMSTANCE if we were to be sure it was correctly produced and sold. John was en route to a visiting appointment at Harvard; Linda had decided to add a Wharton School MBA to her Tufts Ph.D. in psychology; and I had begun a research project on family violence. POMP AND CIRCUMSTANCE took a back seat to these other endeavors.

We answered most letters of inquiry with a promise of information in the future; we provided a few kits to people who were adamant about their immediate need and enthusiastic about the use of the game. On the whole, the game sat on our shelves. As of this writing, there appears to be a major impetus in the United States to increase and improve sex education, and we plan to return more effectively to the tasks of publication and dissemination in the coming months.

10

Construction and Modification

At last you are ready for the stage at which many unsuccessful would-be designers begin: constructing the game. Following the statements you developed in Stage III, you now must select materials, draft forms, assemble pieces, and construct the scenario, roles, procedures and rules, external factors, visual imagery and symbols, and the accounting system. You will find some general guidelines in your decisions about design style, particularly those concerning the appropriate level of abstraction. Begin by reviewing the examples offered in prior chapters, which illustrate different approaches and different levels of complexity.

To create a successfully running gaming-simulation, you should do the following:

(1) assemble a set of possibly useful materials;
(2) decide whether to use a computer for aid in construction and/or for game operation; if so, have the computer and needed programs at hand;
(3) following the guidelines in this chapter, make a prototype (note: it is not necessary to make the components in the order they are discussed here—rather, you will go back and forth a great deal);
(4) field test the game;
(5) make modifications in the game based on the field tests;
(6) repeat 4 and 5 until you have had several fully successful runs.

This stage requires time and ingenuity. The particular things you need to do will be very game specific, but some general guidelines are offered here, and a rich array of examples from existing games are used as illustrations.

ASSEMBLING A SET OF MATERIALS

As you prepare to work, gather some general materials you may need. You can, of course, obtain some of these later, but it is helpful to have many of them available as you start:

- standard size paper in several colors (you will find it easier to keep track of what you have done if you use a different color paper for each set of materials—roles, scenario,

rules and procedures, external factors, visual imagery and symbols, accounting system)
- graph paper
- index cards
- glue, scotch tape, rubber cement, paper clips
- scissors
- colored pencils and colored markers
- colored construction paper or cardboard
- stencils, a compass, a ruler, and other materials for drawing
- you may also want to have items such as stick-on coding dots, a timer, dice, some items that can be used as markers, some form of chips, coins, wood blocks or Lego blocks, plastic miniatures, a word puzzle book, 1 or 2 decks of playing cards, play money, name tags or badges, press-on wax letters or designs

When I began to design gaming-simulations, I was given excellent advice by Fred Goodman, who said "Before you actually select materials, spend a few hours walking through a stationary store, a toy store, and a hardware store." I have regularly done this, and I find that these casual visits always yield good results. I have often been alerted to existing materials that I had not considered, but that could easily and cheaply be incorporated into my gaming-simulations. When I offer design workshops in other countries, I always make an early visit to the local markets to see what materials can be readily obtained. As a result, I have learned that buttons, safety pins, paper clips, beans, and other such items are as useful as paper chips and paper materials that are often in short supply outside the West. These materials not only "work" well, but make it much easier to ask users to assemble their own kits.

You should also think about whether there are any simple games or materials already familiar to players that you can utilize. We used a dart game in BLOOD MONEY, assuming that our adult male players would know how to throw darts and would feel comfortable doing so. Simple card games can often be built into a more complex game with ease. Look for other smaller games that might be incorporated in your larger one.

BUILDING A PROTOTYPE

A. Scenario

As indicated in Chapter 8, the scenario introduces players to where they are and to the problem with which they will be coping. It should also indicate what they will be doing and what the major roles are.

In CAPJEFOS all players are originally introduced to the game through a script read by the main operator. Players are first told something about

- what a gaming-simulation is

  this is a two paragraph description that includes some of the information presented in Chapter 2 of this volume

- what CAPJEFOS is about

  this gives some information about the subject matter of the game, and explains what the title means

- our purposes in running it

  this is taken from the specifications (see Chapter 9)

- what will happen

  here players are told that they will be divided into two groups—villagers and development agents—and that they will receive separate information following the division

They are then given information about the operators' roles and about special rules: These sections read as follows.

[Operators' roles:] _____ and I will be playing the roles of Operators 1 and 2. Our job is to keep the game running smoothly. We will mostly be following and enforcing the rules of the game, but we are willing to entertain requests from players about doing things not specified in the game materials. Our decisions about whether to let you do something will be based on whether or not we believe it is realistic. That is, would your real-world counterparts be able to do that?

In addition, we will represent various services, persons, and institutions you will *not* play, such as the postal services, the bank, relatives and friends elsewhere, and national government agencies. We will transmit messages to our institutions on your behalf, and inform you of their decisions.

[Special rules:] You will be given a number of rules in the game, and these should be followed. You are encouraged, however, to use your imagination in playing your role, and there are many ways for you to do so. There are three things that I must mention about the rules given to you, however:

First, some of the rules represent laws of nature. These cannot be defied. For example, you cannot shorten the distance between Capjefos and Somnas, and hence travel between them easily. Likewise, you will be told that one cash crop field or one food crop field produces 20 units; you cannot decide that yours produces 40! On the other hand, if we tell you that you have 5 cash crop fields, that is a social

fact, not a law of nature. If you are able to convince someone to sell or lend you more fields, you may do so and inform me.

Second, _____ and I have many things to do to make the game a valuable experience for you. We do not want to spend our time serving as policemen and guards. THUS YOU MUST NOT STEAL MONEY, COMMODITIES, FOOD OR CASH CROP UNITS, FISH, OR ANYTHING ELSE FROM OUR TABLES!!! SIMILARLY, YOU MUST RESPECT NATURE AND NOT TAKE MORE THAN THE CORRECT NUMBER OF UNITS FROM THE FIELDS OR FISH FROM THE STREAM!

Third, occasionally a group of players decide they wish to eject someone from a meeting or other event. We do not wish to have physical force used by players. If you are asked to leave, you may verbally protest, but if you are told again that you are ejected, please leave peacefully by yourself.

Finally, they are told about the expectability of confusion at first and that play should be fun. Once they have been divided into villagers and development agents, separate scenario scripts are read to each group. The villagers, for example, are told about the steps in each round, the time allotted for play of a round and of each step, how they will know when we change from one step to another, and about the symbols used in the game. At that point, roles are allocated. Information on the village itself is included with their role profiles.

Play of CALAGRANDE and of ST. PHILIP begins with players being told about the hypothetical countries within which they are to "live," as illustrated in Figures 10.1 and 10.2.

It is possible to give different scenarios to different groups. In addition, one may have these scenarios offer *conflicting* information. This is not typical, but there are situations in which it should be considered. (For elaboration of this idea, see Greenblat, 1974.)

B. Roles

In determining the roles to be created, there are numerous decisions the designer must make. The degree of *role specificity* is one such dimension. Who participants are asked to play can take a number of forms:

(1) Where players are experts in some subject matter field, they should be asked to play themselves, bringing to bear on the gaming problem the values, knowledge, interest, and political stakes they have in reality, and considering the impact of a proposed action on their sector as a whole (e.g., THE HEMOPHILIA CARE PLANNING GAME).

(2) Participants may be told to play as themselves (i.e., use their own skills and values) but to assume another occupational role (city planner in CLUG, journalist in RADIO COVINGHAM); another age and marital status (person about to get married in THE MARRIAGE

Background:

Calagrande is a coastal state bounded by three neighbors - Castel Atlantic, Vabien and Alidar. The borders with these countries are characterized by mountainous areas except for narrow coastal strips. Three great rivers divide the country and concentrate communications on the capital - Calagrande City.

The country is divided into five states - Cancanouche, Tropicana, Bassa Niger, Montaneto and Delibre. The first and the last are predominantly French speaking, while the rest are predominantly Spanish speaking. The states furthest from the capital city are culturally more different from the more central states. This has led historically to a feeling of political isolation in Cancanouche and Delibre, both of which feel culturally more connected to the neighboring countries of Alidar and Vabien (see the descriptions of the individual states).

The country has a long and turbulent history of colonization by the French, Spanish, and British, followed by decolonization and civil war. For the past fifty years, Calagrande has been under regular periods of military rule with intermittent periods of civilian government. The present government has just come to power following elections which the military had hoped would establish a right-wing civilian government. In the event, the electorate backed by big business and the unions have returned a reformist government which is dedicated to land reform, a decentralized Federal state and a radical approach to the problems of the big cities. It is generally thought that the military are only waiting for these policies to fail and step in again and seize power. The large landowners, who control most of Caligrande's productive land, are also bitterly opposed to the programme of reform and the concentration on the cities.

Calagrande is rich in natural resources, although these have not, as yet, been exploited. These consist of minerals in the mountainous areas, vast areas of hardwood forest and as yet unproved oil bearing strata off the coast of Tropicana in an area of the continental shelf which is disputed by Castel Atlantica. The country generally lacks the technical skills with which to approach the exploitation of resources and it is by no means certain that the population as a whole would welcome a transition from an agrarian to an industrial society.

Calagrande's neighbors vary considerably in political complexion. Castel Atlantica is a right-wing military dictatorship which, before the advent of the present government, could rely on Calagrande to suppress dissident exile groups. Vabien is a very poor but democratic country which relies desperately on the rail link to the coast through Calagrande for its export trade. Alidar is an aggressive left-wing republic which has historic claims to Cancanouche and parts of Delibre. Both Castel Atlantica and Alidar hope to see the present government fail in its policies so that it may be replaced by one of more extreme policies.

Figure 10.1   Scenario: CALAGRANDE

SOURCE: Mackie. Reprinted by permission.

GAME); or another national identity and occupation (island fisherman in CARIBBEAN FISHERMAN, Indian rice-farmer in THE GREEN REVOLUTION GAME).

(3) Players may be given a set of general values in the form of rules of their culture or group. Alpha society members in BAFA-BAFA are told they are easy going, friendly, sexist, and enjoy contact with others who obey the rules of their culture; Beta society members are told they are concerned with bargaining and making money.

(4) Players may be given very detailed information about who they are and what positions they are to take on various issues. For example, in THE ACADEMIC

St. Philip: Background Information

St. Philip is one of those small Caribbean islands that somehow always seems difficult to place, exactly...(see map).

It is situated between the Windward and Leeward island groups, but not really part of either. Sixty square miles (155 square kilometers) in area, it has a population of just over 30,000. As an Associated State, it relies on Britain for external policy and aid but controls its own internal affairs through a twelve person legislature. 16,000 of the population live in and around Queenstown, the capital and most historic city of the island, also the seat of Parliament. The only other major settlement on the island is the smaller port of Purple River.

The northern sector of the island is low and flat and is joined to the main part by a narrow peninsula. North Bay is a rather strange place, and people who live there are peripheral to the mainstream of island activity. In the south, there are two extinct volcanic peaks, from which several small rivers flow. The best soils are in Mid-Island, but nowhere is there really first class agricultural land, and the rather thin and stony soils have usually to be farmed with care and ingenuity to produce good results. The beaches are pleasant, but the sand is the less popular brown color.

St. Philip was first visited by Europeans in 1622 when Thomas Warner dropped anchor in Anchorage Bay on his way back from Guiana and St. Kitts. Later, British colonists arrived, and by the eighteenth century sugar plantations were established, but the decline in cane agriculture began in the early nineteenth century.

In the twentieth century, increasing costs of production made sugar cultivation uneconomic, and unrest about labor conditions eventually led to the collapse of the sugar estates in the 1950s. Samuel Wells led the St. Philip Friendly Society, a trade union in essence, into opposition against the planters. All the planters left the island save one, Evelyn Talbot, who later became a friend of Wells. Wells came into political power and has been Prime Minister ever since, except for the years 1976-79, when Francis Smythe and the United Party were briefly in power. The two political parties on the island seem divided by pragmatic rather than doctrinaire differences.

Under Wells, the sugar lands were divided amongst Philippians into plots of between one and four acres (0.4 to 1.6 hectares) and the development of banana growing encouraged. Bananas can exist on a wide range of cultivable land, even on stony and marginal soils; they need little labor, no processing, and produce a first fruit within twelve months of planting, and so were admirable as a replacement crop for sugar. Thus small banana farms grew up in the 1950s and 1960s to replace the old sugar estates. An agreement was reached with the E.B.G., a big European importing firm, but the banana industry in St. Philip has suffered troubles recently from competition from Jamaica and West Africa, and from bad weather conditions. Bananas are now exported in boxes rather than on the stem, but the future of the industry is unclear, and many growers are becoming frustrated and unhappy.

There are two banana boxing plants on the island, but no other industry of export significance. There are few vegetable farmers, some coconut and lime groves, and some shell fishing from coastal villages. Bananas are ninety percent of the exports.

St. Philip faces population pressure, rising unemployment, and the vulnerability of a one crop economy. Recently the idea of tourism has been talked about in guarded terms, but Philippians have seen its disruptive influence on other islands and are unsure about what effect large-scale development would have.

Tourists have arrived via the cruise ships and ferries which call at Queenstown in increasing numbers in the summer. But the island has only a small airstrip, north of Queenstown, and no airport as yet capable of handling medium or long-range jets—the likely carriers of the "package holiday" market.

A Map of the Island of St. Philip

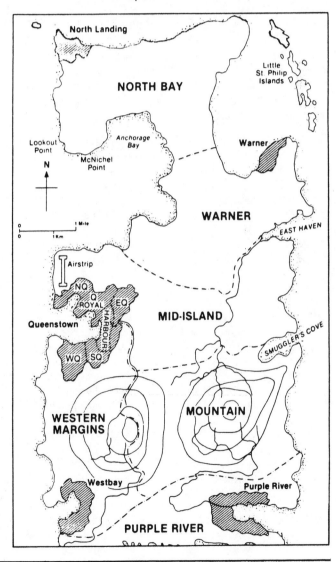

Figure 10.2 Scenario: ST. PHILIP

SOURCE: Walford. Published by CPS, Oatlands, High St., Carington, Cambridge, England, CB3 8LT. Reprinted by permission.

GAME, one player is told he or she is very concerned with his or her own work and is disinterested in spending time talking with others, while another is told he or she enjoys giving advice to students and colleagues.

(5) Finally, players may be given real-life persons to play—a specific political leader, corporate executive, or other individual whose personal values and style are to be simulated.

Many experienced game designers advise that players not be given specific instructions (option 5 above) about playing a particular person (President Reagan, the actual mayor of the city), as it is too easy for them to later deny responsibility for their actions, saying "I didn't think that was the right thing to do, but it's what I thought Ronald Reagan would do." It is better to make the person "The Mayor," giving him or her the resources and constraints that are available to a mayor. Similarly, it is generally accepted that assignment of attitudes and values along with the role (option 4) should be avoided or minimized, although some very good games (such as THE ACADEMIC GAME) violate this principle.

There are several options in terms of the number and type of roles that can be provided, and the resultant form of player organization:

(1) All players can be given the same role and goal and activity. In THE COMMONS GAME each player is told to try to maximize his or her earnings; in CARIBBEAN FISHERMAN, all players are fishermen trying to maximize their catch.

(2) Players can be told they are members of parallel teams, with each team given a common goal and common resources (CLUG; THE FISH GAME; THE CONFERENCE GAME), leaving it to individuals to make collective decisions or to allocate responsibilities and coordinate their activities.

(3) Players can be divided into two or three (or more) different teams with different instructions and resources. In the HEX game, for example, most of the players are local administrators, some are regional administrators, and some are national leaders. Each member of each role set has common goals and activities, although their resources vary. In BAFA-BAFA, half the players are members of the Alpha Culture and half are members of the Beta Culture.

(4) There can be several role sets, each broken down into several different specific roles, each with their own characterizations. In BLOOD MONEY, most players are hemophiliacs (with different resources and disabilities, but with common goals and activities); others are M.D.s, blood bankers, employers, and welfare agents. In CAPJEFOS, different role descriptions are written for the chief, the traditional doctor, the priest, the village men, the village women, and the development agents. In CLASSROOM EXPERIENCING, one person is the teacher, six are students, and seven are "talliers." Each of the students receives a different role description and a different goal.

In considering the initial disadvantage of one group's resources relative to another, Allen Feldt and Fred Goodman (1975, pp. 174-175) note that this can be accomplished through the allocation of different distributions of wealth and property, but they add some other manners of creating such disadvantage:

More significant and long term disadvantages may be developed in some cases however by simply requiring one group of players to wear gloves when the game requires some degree of manual dexterity, making them write or shoot left-handed, not allowing them pencils or erasers for keeping records, and so on. Another variation which offers promise on some occasions is to have some players enter the game an hour or two after others have begun with no opportunity to have the rules explained to them. In such cases a group of new immigrants or a younger generation is created which becomes quite dependent upon the older inhabitants for information and socialization into the mechanics of play. Coupling these innovations with aging and removal of older players raises an entire new set of concerns over intergenerational conflicts and educational processes, all within a game whose initial design may have been directed toward some other subject.

In keeping with the above elements, role descriptions can be very simple or quite complex, as the examples of role descriptions in the next figures indicate. Figure 10.3 gives a sample role from ST. PHILIP. Figure 10.4 gives a somewhat longer example, taken from CLASSROOM EXPERIENCING. In Figure 10.5, the chief's role in CAPJEFOS is offered; this is followed by a page of instructions about activities each round, which is shown in Figure 10.6. Figure 10.7 illustrates a role card from YOUR NUMBER IS UP. A somewhat unusual format is used in WHAT'S NEWS for the players who play the "source" roles (each player has several source roles to play during the course of a full run of the game). All these source roles are realistically drawn from the actual news events of the late 1970s that are employed in the game. One of these sets of role instructions is presented in Figure 10.8. Finally, Figure 10.9 illustrates one of the 5 roles in STRATEGEM-1. This sheet is supplemented by a few pages headed "Useful Information," which give the player general principles and data to use in making his or her decisions.

Two unusual examples will also be mentioned here. The URBAN POLICY GAME role descriptions are quite long, and embody considerable surrounding information about the role. For example, a general section of text that precedes the descriptions of the mayor's and city council members' roles includes ideas about elected officials. Players are told about general tasks and expectations of elected officials, and about how officials vary in terms of background, career ambitions, personality, and political philosophy. The mayor's role is then described in a 2½ page discussion of career types and how they differentially

> **Bob Ballinger**   **M.P. for Mountain**   **United Party**
>
> Your constituency includes many of the poorest banana farms, and many are on the verge of economic ruin. You want help for the banana farmers, but you also see the need for the island to diversify into other forms of agriculture. Smuggler's Cove in your constituency is a small rocky inlet that might have tourist potential, but it could only be on a small-scale and certainly not as big as Anchorage Bay.
>
> Q. Do you support tourism as a way of making the island prosperous? Or is the best way forward to stay with traditional rural occupations?

Figure 10.3   Sample Role: ST. PHILIP
SOURCE: Walford. Published by CPS, Oatlands, High St., Carington, Cambridge, England CB3 8LT. Reprinted by permission.

You are Mark (Mary) Taylor. Make and wear a name tag using the appropriate name. You are seven years old. This is your first year in Mr. Fisher's class, and you like him because he is kind to you.

Your parents argue and fight a lot. Because of this, you like to shut yourself in your room and read. Your favorite stories are about princes and princesses who look like plain people at first, but during the story discover who they are and perform some miraculous deed to save the country. You often dream that you are such a prince (princess).

At school you like to read, but you don't like to do math because you never seem to get the right answer even when you try. You find counting especially hard when the numbers are bigger than five, getting a different number each time you count. You get especially flustered if the teacher takes away your counting sticks because when you count on your fingers you can never remember whether you counted your thumb or not.

Your goal for the game is to escape the attention of the teacher and the other members of the class. Since you like the teacher, if he makes an effort to attract your attention, you will try to give it to him for a few minutes.

Daydreaming will be defined as drawing six-pointed stars. You will receive 1 point for each star drawn. You may not talk while you are drawing stars.

Like most boys and girls you want to be liked. You will receive 5 points each time another student smiles at you and 5 points each time the teacher smiles at you. If you are able to do the math, you will receive 2 points for each correct answer.

Figure 10.4   Sample Role: CLASSROOM EXPERIENCING
SOURCE: Jackson. Reprinted by permission.

CAPJEFOS: CHIEF'S ROLE CARD

As Chief of Capjefos, you have very important responsibilities to maintain the cohesion of your community. Your goals are to receive the loyalty and obedience of your subjects, to maintain peace and village stability, and to assure that the traditions of many generations of citizens of Tesluscu are respected. Wear your chief's hat at all times with pride.

Your responsibilities include collecting levies for community use, receiving visitors, representing the villagers to the government, presiding over cases which require adjudication, and making ceremonial speeches. You are also the custodian of the village lands. Your subjects will reward you with gifts in appreciation of good work and in respect of your position.

As Chief you are the head of the Traditional Council. You must diligently watch for threats to the community's traditions. Visitors to Capjefos should receive your approval before meeting with others. If you give them such approval, pin a star on their nametags.

You will need to collect donations for your own subsistence needs of 10 food units, 2 fish, and 1 basic necessity. In addition, you must collect funds for development projects, and get villagers to agree to donate some of their work and leisure time to community projects. (You will be given estimates of the time and funds needed for various projects.)

You must complete a record sheet and give it to Operator 1 each year. In addition, you have a small notebook in which you may wish to keep private notes about people's activities and contributions, write speech notes, etc.

At the community meeting you will be expected to distribute awards to those few persons who have been outstanding members of the community that year; thus you must identify these people during the course of play.

Figure 10.5 **Sample Role: CAPJEFOS Chief**
SOURCE: Greenblat et al. (1987). Reprinted by permission.

operate as mayor, the powers of the office, the mayor's objectives, and how the mayor may wield power and attempt to attain objectives. (See pp. 29-33 of the URBAN POLICY GAME Manual for details.)

The second example comes from INTO AGING. What is unusual about this is that the *operators* are given descriptions of how they should act vis-à-vis players. These instructions are not offered in role cards, but they

Your activities during each step of a round are as follows:

A. Work Time:

1. Collect levies (see enclosed information about existing rates).

2. Receive gifts for your personal needs and for community projects.

3. Observe and regulate village life.

4. Greet visitors.

5. Prepare for Traditional Council and Community meetings.

6. Convince villagers of the importance of donating time and OCSENU to development projects you support.

B. Market Time:

1. Make sure you have 10 food units and 2 fish for your family's survival needs.

2. If it has not been given you as a gift, buy at least one basic necessity.

3. Turn in your survival needs to Operator 1.

4. Buy any special goods you desire from a trader if your subjects have not provided as much as you feel is necessary for you to have a standard of living appropriate to your important position in the community.

5. Continue with activities listed under work time.

C. Group Meetings:

Chair a meeting of the village Traditional Council. *Remember this can only last ten (10) minutes.*

D. Community Meeting:

Lead the meeting; give a speech; listen to villagers' suggestions and complaints; make awards. You may present visitors and allow them to make speeches if you wish. Ask the schoolteacher to serve as secretary.

Again, remember that this meeting only lasts ten (10) minutes. Make your speeches and those of others brief.

At the first meeting (in 1980), allow the Traditional Doctor, the Religious Leader, and the Teacher to make brief speeches. In subssequent years, create your own agenda.

E. Social Life:

Before going to celebrate, turn in this year's record sheet to Operator 1.

Foster community spirit.

Figure 10.6 CAPJEFOS: Chief's Activities Each Round
SOURCE: Greenblat et al. (1987). Reprinted by permission.

Patient

1 Your aim is to be discharged in good health within the 30 minute duration of the game. Discharge is shown by your holding a No. 10 Health Card and payment of all hospital bills. To attain this goal you may need to see the notes on your condition, including your daily record chart. These are held at the nurses' station. Seeing these notes will allow you to ask relevant questions of the VMO. Only the VMO can give you a different Health Card number to show your health has improved, and only the VMO can order your discharge.

2 The RMO will tell you how mobile you are. This depends on your Health Card number. While waiting for the RMO, you must remain seated in your allotted area. You must be seen by as many hospital staff as possible, so you should try to maintain constant contact with them. If you are not attended to for any length of time your Health Card number may be reduced by GOD.

3 The fewer the patients there are in your bay the greater the opportunity for the VMO to see you.

4 Your total financial resources are in your envelope. If you get into financial difficulties you may:
(a) apply to the Social Worker for relief,
(b) ask the Chaplain for help,
(c) ask the Trolley Lady for credit, or
(d) try to get a discharged patient to visit you and give you a loan.

5 The Health Cards run in the following sequence:
1 (death)   2   3   4   5   6   7   8   9   10 (discharge).

6 You may move from your chair *only* with the permission of the RMO, otherwise your health will deteriorate.

7 If you are mobile try to read your condition information notes on the nurses' station table.

8 When you want attention ring your bell.

Figure 10.7   Sample Role: YOUR NUMBER IS UP

SOURCE: Reprinted with permission from Hope and McAra, 1984, Pergamon Books, Ltd.

function as the equivalent of them, and hence are reproduced in this section as Figure 10.10. (Another gaming-simulation that gives this type of instructions to operators is ME, THE SLOW LEARNER.)

C. Procedures and Rules

The most critical general advice about designing the procedures and rules is that, to the extent possible, these

Round #2   Happening #5   *Moro Assassination*

Source 5a: ITALIAN GOVERNMENT SPOKESPERSON

What is known: Italian police have discovered the body of former premier Aldo Moro. Earlier Moro had been kidnapped by the Red Brigade, a left-wing terrorist group. The Red Brigade opposes the coalition government of the Communist Party and the Christian Democratic Party.

Complaint power: Yes

Agenda: To show the determination of the government to stamp out terrorism in general and the Red Brigade in particular; to show that the government will not allow its policies to be influenced in any way by terrorism

Your general line:

(1) Moro's body was discovered after someone—presumably a Red Brigade member—phoned the police and tipped them off. The body was found in a parked car on a street midway between the headquarters of the Communist Party and the Christian Democratic Party.

(2) The Communist Party had no responsibility for what happened, and the coalition government will continue.

(3) The terrorists demanded release of their comrades arrested for various crimes of violence. The government couldn't possibly meet these demands, and there was no guarantee that they wouldn't have killed Moro anyway.

(4) Aldo Moro's death is a real tragedy for Italy and the world. He was a great man. The government will increase its efforts to stop this brutal terrorism.

Off the record: The Red Brigades are a bunch of swine. Boiling in oil would be too good for them. It's embarrassing, and very hard to explain to the world, how the Red Brigades have been able to avoid the intensive police search for them over such a long period.

Figure 10.8 Sample Role: WHAT'S NEWS
SOURCE: Gamson (1984). Reprinted with permission.

should reflect real-life options and limitations. In addition, Glazier (1970, p. 7) urges that they should be worded in real-life terms, giving the following examples:

... if the corridor is a railway, a player must have a ticket to ride. Another example would be a case of a language barrier between representatives of two nations. One would forbid these two players to talk to one another, except through a specific third party as interpreter. In a game with a monetary structure, you would want to set prices or give the terms (usually mutual agreement) on which players can set their own. While some decision-making is an individual matter, other decisions must be made by a group according to a rule (majority, plurality, unanimity).

As indicated in Chapter 8, you must first be concerned with the overall rules and procedures. Where the structure of the game is linear or radial, each step may have separate instructions. Examples of some of the general rules of play have already been given in the CAPJEFOS scenario segment earlier in this chapter. Clear and succinct overall rules are found in all of Ken Jones's games, and are illustrated here with his "Notes for Participants" in RADIO COVINGHAM in Figure 10.11. A somewhat different format is used in presenting the overall procedures and rules for INTO AGING, which are shown in Figure 10.12. Where the simulation is a long and complex one, the overall schedule may need to be presented, supplemented by separate instructions as each stage is reached. Figure 10.13 gives a sample of such a schedule of procedures for SIMCORP, and Figure 10.14 gives a portion of the explanation of how to fulfill one of the tasks in that schedule: preparing a resume. Consistent with J. T. Low's (1979, p. 267) advice that trial runs at the start of the game are crucial to gaming effectiveness, THE EXECUTIVE SIMULATION's overall schedule includes play of a trial run and then a return to the beginning for actual play.

In cases in which the gaming-simulation has an interactive structure with play taking place in rounds, procedures and rules will also have to be presented for play of a cycle or round. Again, it is helpful to have an overview of what is being done by any given player during the round, and an example from THE HEXAGON GAME is

Industry & Social Services Minister Role Description

GOAL

Your principal objective is to produce sufficient goods to satisfy the material consumption needs of the population, the investment needs of the economy, and the requirements for export income from goods. You should also invest in human services capital. This will raise the health and education standards of the population ,and thereby help reduce the birth rate, by capital.

INITIAL CONDITIONS

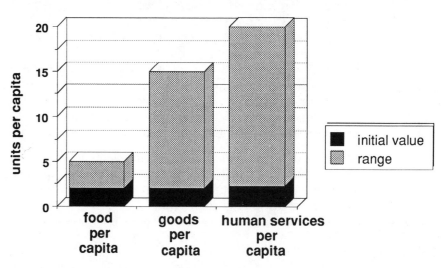

Productivity of the labor force is low, about 1/10th of what could be attained by maximum investment in goods production capital and human services capital. Your region's population is not receiving a very high standard of living - that is, the goods allocated for the population during the previous cycle were low. They equalled only 2 per person per year (15 is the maximum possible). Similarly, human services (health and education) are also low. Presently the ratio of human services capital to population is only 2.25; a maximum of 20 is possible.

DECISIONS

STEP OF PLAY	INDIRECT EFFECTS
#5 Allocate some portion of the Goods Available for Investment to: • Goods Production Capital Under Construction • Human Services Capital Under Construction	Availability of goods for investment in the other physical capital stocks; regional energy requirements; quality of the environment; labor productivity; birth rate.

Figure 10.9   Portion of Sample Role: STRATEGEM-1

SOURCE: Meadows (1985). Reprinted by permission.

Operator's Instructions:

...Part of the effect of the game is accomplished by the sarcasm and humor of the table operators. It is their role to intervene at the appropriate times to enhance the effect of certain messages. For example, some of the circumstances are meant to illustrate the double standards applied to the elderly. If a younger person forgets the date or day of the week, the fact passes unnoticed, whereas an older person will be thought to be "going senile" for the same slip. This myth may be reinforced by the operators whenever the opportunity arises. The operator may attempt to draw in other players to substantiate the evidence by saying (in a stage whisper),"...did you notice how so-and-so has been slipping ever since retirement?"

The operator's role is played differently at each level. At table one, the tone of the game is set. Norms are established and the player begins to realize the extent of discrimination. This operator is subtle in the presentation of agism. In comparison to the other two operators, operator one is the most positive. This person makes statements which emphasize myths about aging, e.g., "You really need to rest now that you're 65" and "You can't teach an old dog a new trick." When a player goes to the next table, you might say this can be expected at old age. Reinforce the "joys" of retirement and leisure time. These are only a few examples, but in general, this operator is dealing with a bunch of nice old folks!

At table two, the operator and experiences of the players are somewhat more negative. The operator should be unsure of the participant's abilities and always maintain a questioning attitude. When a choice is available, the operator should strongly encourage one choice and also emphasize the role of the family and how they are concerned with the player's safety and that "they know best."

At table three, the operator and experiences are the most negative. The player is made dependent upon the operator who maintains a condescending attitude toward the players. Any act of independence is discouraged. When in doubt, the operator assumes the worst. No choices are extended but rather everything is done for the player. Assume that health problems need not be treated since they are old and treat the players as children. Do not allow players to get up once they sit down to further emphasize their dependence.

In general, the players experience more negative attitudes from the table operators as they move from table one to three. They increasingly lose control of their situation, are less involved in decision making, and are rendered powerless. It should become more apparent that the players are reacted to as one of many old people who must be sick, senile and dependent and, therefore, must have things done for them. Aren't all old people like that? The player is not viewed as an individual with strengths and weaknesses. Only negative aspects are viewed and reinforced...

Throughout the game, table operators should be observing players for feelings and behaviors displayed in response to the condition of the game. Then, when play is finished, they can assist the game director in the debriefing season. For example, they might ask a player at their table how they felt when they faced a certain situation or were responded to in a certain way. Review the myths you tried to convey and discuss their relevancy and effects.

Figure 10.10   Operator's Role: INTO AGING
SOURCE: Hoffman and Reif (1978). Reprinted by permission.

given in Figure 10.15. The instructions for the CAPJEFOS chief presented earlier (in Figure 10.5) show how individual players can be informed about their procedures and rules for cycle play. Figure 10.16 shows the set of rules given the person who plays the mayor in the URBAN POLICY GAME.

In addition, particular sets of decisions or actions may necessitate the description of other sets of rules, as, for example, the rules for operation of the basic industry (BASIN) in SIMSOC, given in Figure 10.17.

Rules for terminating play have already been discussed in Chapter 8. Rules for scoring will be discussed in Section F of this chapter (Accounting Systems).

NOTES FOR PARTICIPANTS   *RADIO COVINGHAM*

What it's about

You produce and broadcast a ten minute programme on Radio Covingham called *News and Views at 7.* You'll find most of the information about how to do it in the Station Manager's Memo. Read it very carefully. When it starts you'll get a pile of listeners' letters and handouts. These came in the morning mail. But the news items will come in one by one, gradually, right up to the time you go on the air. The organiser will brief you, and tell you the exact time you go on the air.

What you can do, and what you can't do

You can rewrite the material, but you can't invent news.

You can interview members of your own team in various roles, say as someone who wrote a letter, or is connected with a handout or the news items, but only in connection with the material.

You can, if you have a tape recorder, use it to see what an item sounds like, but you cannot use taped inserts in the broadcast itself. The broadcast itself should be recorded on tape, but it must be completely live, with no pre-recordings fed into it.

If you have time you can have a rehearsal, but this will not stop news flowing in.

Advice

Ten minutes is longer than you think! So aim for at least 2 interviews, preferably 3 or 4, and possibly 5 or 6.

Before the simulation begins, decide on how you are going to handle the material — perhaps with three groups dealing with letters, handouts and news.

If you are the producer, don't get bogged down in individual items, particularly if you have a large team. Make sure that someone is in charge of the timing — perhaps using hand signals for slowing down or speeding up, or putting up fingers to show the number of seconds or minutes remaining.

Before you begin, decide on the general shape of the programme. Should news be bunched together at the beginning, in the middle, or at the end, or should it be scattered throughout the programme? Will you have news headlines at the beginning? Will you have news headlines at the end? Will you have a special section or spot on a particular subject – such as entertainment, business and industry, etc? But you'll have to wait until you get the materials to decide the subjects. And remember the programme must contain 'views' – this means you can comment on items.

If you've finished your particular job then don't just sit around — ask the producer what else you can do.

Figure 10.11   "Notes for Participants": **RADIO COVINGHAM**

SOURCE: Ken Jones, Nine Graded Simulations from: Simulations I "Radio Covingham," Max Hueber, Munich, 1984. Sales rights for non-German-speaking countries: Filmscan/Lingual House, Esher, Surrey.

D. External Factors

External factors may be introduced in several fashions.

(1) They may be predetermined. That is, the operator is told to introduce event A at a specific point, and event B at a later time. Figure 10.18 shows an event introduced

Method of Play

The game consists of three playing areas. Area One is representative of independent life styles of the elderly. This could be one's own home, apartment, condominium or independent life style in a retirement village.

Each player will begin play in this area with their "full deck" of identity cards. Players will take turns choosing a consequence card from the *Game Overall Director* who is in charge of this area. The player must then follow the directions on the card. Each player who remains in this area is permitted to go to the income area after the turn to try to improve his economic resources.

Area Two represents semi-dependent life styles. In real life this might mean living in the house of a family member, a retirement village with some services provided or attendance at a day care facility for a portion of the day.

Entrance into Area Two occurs when circumstances occur through a consequence card which no longer permits the player to remain at the independent level. The player will continue play in Area Two until changing circumstances require that a return to Area One or go to Area Three.

Unfortunately, upon entering Area Two, each player must forfeit the Residence Card, occupation symbol, one favorite possession and one half self-image chips, as well as half of the income chips.

Area Three represents a nursing home or similar place with nearly total dependence. The mode of entry is the same as level two. Upon entering the area, each player will forfeit all but one income chip and one self-image chip. If you have already lost these, DON'T WORRY—You can't re-lose something you don't have.

If a player dies in the course of play, that player is out of the game and moves to the cemetery. Points should be totaled according to what is possessed at this time which will be the player's ALL TIME SCORE, and represents the social value placed on the individual. At the end of play, the player with the highest ALL TIME SCORE is the winner.

Figure 10.12 Procedures and Rules: Overall—INTO AGING

SOURCE: Hoffman and Reif (1978). Reprinted by permission.

about halfway through THE HEMOPHILIA CARE PLANNING GAME. Figure 10.19 gives examples of "Happenings" in WHAT'S NEWS?, in this case to be introduced during Round 2.

(2) They may be selected by the operator, depending upon his or her judgment of the dynamics of the run and of important issues with which players should have to grapple. In SIMSOC, for example, the operator can choose between several "special events" such as the one in Figure 10.20.

(3) Events may be introduced in response to players' actions. For example, the operator may be told to introduce a particular event if the state of the economy reaches a particular (low or high) point. In CAPJEFOS, if a lineage or individual does not obtain enough protein during a round, an event card is given by the operator the next round informing the player of reduced work capacity (see Figure 10.21).

(4) External factors may be introduced by *chance*. Too often, gaming-simulation designers think only of introducing chance events in the form in which they appear in a game such as MONOPOLY—a form that should generally be avoided. (Reread the cautions about reliance on chance in Chapter 8.)

Chance events, however, can be introduced in more complex ways. They can be based upon *probabilities*. For example, if the model specifies the probabilities of drought, a die can be rolled each "year" to see if there is a drought (as in THE GREEN REVOLUTION GAME). If weather conditions affect the success of different strategies, these can likewise be introduced through chance related to the probabilities. In some parts of the Caribbean, for example, weather conditions turn bad approximately once every six days, and when they turn bad they often stay bad for two to three days. Thus designer Rex

DAILY WORK SCHEDULE

DAY/DATE/WEEK	CLASS ACTIVITY	ASSIGNMENTS
_____ 1 _____	Introduction Overview of SIMCORP	Read Manual
_____ 2 _____	Instructions for resume writing Instructions for application to SIMCORP	
_____ 3 _____	ONE DAY IN AN ORGANIZATION: Mini-simulation Job Placement and Orientation to SIMCORP	* Hand in Resumes, Job Applications, Employment Preference Forms, and Acceptance Letter Form * Complete "Characteristics" page * Acceptance letter returned
_____ 4 _____	Client presentation and group interview Concurrent Departmental Worktime	* Give Employee Attendance Record and Employee Data Sheet to Accounting Division
_____ 5 _____	Concurrent Departmental Worktime Concurrent Departmental Worktime	* Submit Participation Diary: Applying to the Organization
_____ 6 _____	Concurrent Departmental Worktime Concurrent Departmental Worktime	* Submit Participation Diary: Resume Writing ** Status Report #1 due * Give 2 copies of Employee Performance Appraisal Form to immediate supervisor
_____ 7 _____	Concurrent Departmental Worktime	* Performance Appraisal due; complete Supervisory Performance Appraisal Form and give 2 copies to Executive Vice President of Internal Operations

Figure 10.13 SIMCORP: Overall Schedule

SOURCE: Lederman and Stewart (1983). Reprinted by permission.

DAILY WORK SCHEDULE

DAY/DATE/WEEK	CLASS ACTIVITY	ASSIGNMENTS
_____ 8	Concurrent Departmental Worktime	** Status Report #2 due PAPER #1 due
_____	Concurrent Departmental Worktime	* WRITTEN REPORT TO CLIENT
_____ 9	Formal Presentation to Client	
_____	Concurrent Departmental Worktime	
_____ 10	Concurrent Departmental Worktime	Submit Participation Diary: Working in the Organization
_____	Concurrent Departmental Worktime	** Status Report #3 due
_____ 11	Concurrent Departmental Worktime	* Submit SIMCORP Networking Diary
_____	Concurrent Departmental Worktime	
_____ 12	Concurrent Departmental Worktime	** Status Report #4 due
_____	Concurrent Departmental Worktime	* Submit "Characteristics" (Later Reflections)
		* Give 2 copies of Employee Performance Appraisal Form to immediate supervisor
_____ 13	Concurrent Departmental Worktime	* Performance Appaisal due; complete Supervisory Performance Appraisal Form and give 2 copies to Executive Vice President of Internal Operations
_____	Concurrent Departmental Worktime	* Written Report to Client
_____ 14	Final Presentation to Client	** Status Report #5 due
_____	Final Debriefing Session and Office Party	** PAPER #2 due
		* Complete Course Evaluation Form

Figure 10.13 Continued

ENTERING THE ORGANIZATION

How to Apply for a Job

Applicants for jobs with SIMCORP must submit two copies of the completed Application Form (SC01), two copies of their resume, a copy of the Employment Preference Form (SC02) and a copy of the Acceptance Letter (SC03) to the President of SIMCORP on the day indicated on the Daily Work Schedule.

The President of SIMCORP in consultation with the External Consultant will review all resumes and application forms. Wherever possible, applicants will be assigned to their first preference for jobs providing that they are qualified for those jobs. From past experiences with SIMCORP, it is clear, however, that some jobs have more qualified applicants than can be accommodated in an organization of this size. In such cases, the President and External Consultant will determine which applicants are best qualified for these positions. Every effort is made to insure that the SIMCORP SIMULATION is a valuable learning experience for every student. Often students who do not get their first job preference find that they learn more about the functioning of organizations than students who receive their first preference. As in all simulations, the key to successful learning is what the student is willing to invest in the experience.

Resume Writing

Writing a resume is often the most difficult part of applying for a job. Before attempting to write a resume, you should take some time to think about what you have done for the past three or four years. Write down all of the jobs you have had, the extracurricular activities you have participated in, any special skills you have, and anything else that comes to mind. Serious thinking at this stage will save time later on.

Resumes serve two basic functions. First, a resume is a brief description of your employment and educational experiences. It gives an employer a concise summary of your background. Second, a resume is a sample of your work. Your resume shows a potential employer what kind of work you do. A sloppy, ungrammatical resume tells an employer a great deal about the kind of work you do. A well-done, well-printed resume shows an employer that you are capable of neat, accurate, well-written, and appropriately presented work.

To make your resume as professional as possible, start with good quality paper. Eraseable bond typing paper is fine for term papers, but not for resumes. Your resume should be done on high quality bond paper. Look at the different types of paper available in the bookstore (or at a printer) and pick a heavy-weight paper with a high rag content. (The higher the rag content the better the paper "feels.") The paper should be white or a very light shade of grey or beige. You cannot go wrong with white paper. If you are applying to a conservative company stick to white paper. For more up-to-date companies such as advertising agencies you might try other colors if you think they will show you in a favorable light.

Your resume should be typed on an electric typewriter with a carbon ribbon (the one that looks almost like printing) or typeset by a printer. Again, the emphasis is on professional. Make your resume appealing to the eye by leaving

Figure 10.14   Rules for Preparing a Resume: **SIMCORP**

SOURCE: Lederman and Stewart (1983). Reprinted by permission.

adequate margins and white space.   Type your resume in several different forms to see which form looks best. Experiment with spacing to provide the best visual look. The objective is to design a resume that includes all of the vital information about you and can be read quickly. Employers are busy people; a resume which can be quickly skimmed and understood is more likely to be looked at than one which takes hours to read.

Your resume should include:

Your <u>name</u>

Your <u>current address</u> (If you have a school address and a home address, in-
                 dicate when you can be reached at each one.)

Your <u>phone number</u> (Be sure to include area codes)

Your <u>career objective</u> (A brief statement of the position you desire -- for the
                 SIMCORP SIMULATION, your career objective is "A position
                 as _____ with SIMCORP.")

Your <u>education</u> (Include high school only if you did something outstanding such
                 as winning a major award.)

Your <u>extracurricular activities</u>

Your <u>employment experience</u> (In chronological order starting with the most
                 recent experience.)

<u>Awards</u> and <u>honors</u> you have received

Special <u>skills</u> you have (such as computer knowledge)

<u>Fluency</u> in any language

A statement such as <u>"References available upon request"</u>

Notice that this list does not include things such as age, weight, health, marital status, and religion. Those things are not bona fide occupational qualifications. In other words, an employer is prohibited by law from making hiring decisions on the basis of those things. Thus, an applicant who in-cludes that information on his or her resume is showing that he or she does not understand current business practices.

The most successful resumes (in terms of leading to interviews) that your instructors have seen emphasize education as opposed to employment experience. Most college students do not have much career-related employment experience, and most employers understand that. Employers are looking for college grad-uates who have a solid undergraduate education. Thus, whenever possible, emphasize your education. If your employment experience is mainly jobs such as store clerk, waiter, or life guard, you might want to include a statement such as: "Summer employment as a clerk, Jones Hardware, Somerset, New Jersey and life guard at New Brunswick Pool was used to provide a ____ percent your college expenses."

No two resumes are ever alike because no two people are exactly alike. Design your resume to put your education and your employment experiences in the best possible light. The following resumes were done by members of past SIMCORP SIMULATIONS. Use them as guides in developing your resume. But remember, your resume will be as unique as you are.

Figure 10.14 Continued

LOCAL	REGIONAL	NATIONAL	BANKER	OPERATOR
				Introduction to the game
Production of foods	Receive event cards.	Receive event cards	Hand production to local players. Respond to regional and national events.	Hand out regional & national event cards
Receive event cards			Respond to local events.	Hand out local event cards
Pay taxes	Collect taxes	Receive taxes		
Trade	Trade	Discuss policy		
Form policy. Make requests	Form policy. Make requests. Allocate resources	Receive requests. International trade. Allocate resources	International trade	
				Signal end of cycle

END OF CYCLE

Fill out accounting form	Collect accounting forms		Tally accounting forms	
			Announce local deficiencies	Consumption of all goods. Population increase.
Report on cycle	Report on cycle	Report on cycle		

Figure 10.15   Cycle Activities: THE HEXAGON GAME

SOURCE: The Hexagon Game, copyright 1987, Richard D. Duke & Associates, Inc. Reprinted by permission.

Mayor rules

1. The Mayor must submit a proposed budget (Form 4) to the City Council at least one-half hour before the end of the fiscal year. The Mayor is not bound by any request from the bureaucracy, but cannot submit his or her proposal to the Council before receiving the Finance Agency and Planning Agency requests.

2. The Mayor must submit any proposals for fee and tax rate changes (Form 5) to the Council. The Mayor is not bound by Finance Agency requests, but cannot submit requests to the Council before receiving a proposal from the Finance Agency.

3. The Mayor must sign all requests for federal assistance and all other forms originating in the office for them to be official.

4. The Mayor may veto any City Council budget, tax rate, or fee rate. Any veto may be overridden by two-thirds of those voting in the Council. The Mayor does not have an item veto over the budget; the entire Council proposal must be either approved or vetoed.

5. The Mayor may overrule Finance Agency time deadlines, or try to enforce deadlines with his powers of removal.

6. The Mayor may remove any department head (Form 3), but must offer another bureaucratic position to the deposed head. Replacement heads may be appointed from any role in the game except the City Council.

Figure 10.16   Mayor Rules: URBAN POLICY GAME
SOURCE: Henderson and Foster (1978). Reprinted by permission.

Walford introduced a die throw into CARIBBEAN FISHERMAN. If a 6 is thrown, the weather turns bad; in the round following a 6, either 4, 5, or 6 means it stays bad; and in the next round a 5 or 6 keeps it bad. Otherwise the weather is fair. In BLOOD MONEY, there is a 25% chance of a player having an attack each time the "grim reaper" comes, and about a 25% chance that the attack will be a "serious" one. This is simulated by the player's cutting a deck of standard playing cards. If a spade is turned up, he or she has had an attack of bleeding; if it is a jack, queen, or king of spades, it is a serious attack; if it is the ace of spades it is a catastrophic attack. A standard deck of playing cards is easy to use for chance events where these events are based on probabilities. In addition, the deck of cards can be changed during the course of the game as new conditions arise and the probabilities change.

Spinners are generally unreliable, as they are rarely balanced, and hence I do not recommend them. If you do use one, however, note that it can be fairly sophisticated. For example, it can reflect different probabilities of events transpiring given different levels of investment, as shown in the sample spinner in Figure 10.22, or other contingent probabilities.

A set of 10 cards, numbered "0" through "9" are included in each player's set of materials for THE MARRIAGE GAME. When a player is to learn about external events, he or she is told how to draw cards to yield a 2-digit number, and then is referred to a chart to see what that number indicates. The probabilities of positive and negative events, and of particular possibilities, have been set by the designers (see Figure 10.23).

Chance cards can also be *variant* for those playing different roles or engaged in different activities. Separate decks of chance cards are provided for those in school, at work, and engaged in hustling in GHETTO (see the examples in Chapter 2). Separate chance cards are provided for graduate students and professors in THE ACADEMIC GAME (see examples in Figure 10.24) and for local, regional, and national administrators in THE HEXAGON GAME (see examples in Figure 10.25). Different chance cards are given to different players in COMPACTS; an example is given in Figure 10.26.

As you will note from an examination of these samples, the events can be simple or complex. The players must be told what the action or pay-off consequences are: for example, "speak to the doctor about this," or "decide what you will do in response to this news," or "lose 10 points."

E. Visual Imagery and Symbols

A board may provide considerable orientation for players, by serving as a place for storing goods and

(Basic Industry)

Overall Objective: To Expand Its Assets and Income as Much as Possible.
BASIN represents a basic extractive industry such as mining. Its raw material
is words, from which it extracts the vowels *a, e, i, o,* and *u.* In each session,
BASIN may purchase from the coordinator any number of verbal passages up to
five. These passages need not all be purchased at the same time; they may be
purchased any time during the session. BASIN's work on the passage consists of
making a list of the correct number for each type of vowel that appears in the
passage.

All purchases of passages must be authorized by the head of BASIN, using
Form H. The passages purchased will vary in length, and hence in the labor
involved in determining the correct number of vowels. The exact cost of a passage
and the payment for a completed one vary depending on the size level of the
society; they are summarized in Table 1. This Table shows that BASIN receives
a 25% profit on its investment for extracting the vowels correctly.

The return which BASIN receives for a completed passage is reduced if
there are errors in the solution. Each number that BASIN is off from the correct
solution counts as an error. Thus, if a solution has the correct number of *a*'s, *e*'s,
and *i*'s, but has two fewer *o*'s than the correct answer and one more *u* than the
correct answer, this constitutes three errors. Each error reduces the payment or
credit to BASIN for a completed passage by 10% of the purchase price. For
example, in a Size Level Two society, BASIN would pay $60 for a passage. If the
solution had four errors, instead of receiving the full payment of $75 it would
receive $75 − (4 × $6) = $51. BASIN receives zero payment for solutions in
which there are six or more errors.

To receive credit for a passage, the solution must be turned in to the coordinator (using Form H) *during the same session in which the passage was
purchased.* Passages purchased in one session cannot be held over to be completed
in later sessions. Payment or credit for a completed passage is not received until
the session is over. In other words, if BASIN completes a passage early in the
session, it cannot use the payment for this product immediately, since it does not
receive it until the session is over. The coordinator will keep track of BASIN's
assets, and the head of BASIN will receive 10% interest on its assets at the
begining of each new session, including the value of work completed by the end
of the previous session. The head of BASIN can withdraw part or all of its assets
from the bank at any time by filling out Form I and giving it to the coordinator.

BASIN can purchase passages by using its assets in the bank and its income
from these assets. In the beginning of the society, however, BASIN assets and
income are not high enough to purchase five passages. Therefore, if BASIN
wishes to buy the greatest possible number of passages, it will need to raise
Simbucks from other individuals and groups in the society. It may do this by
promising others some return on their money, by persuading them that this will
help the society, or by offering other inducements, arguments or even threats to
get people to lend their money to BASIN.

Figure 10.17   BASIN Rules: SIMSOC

SOURCE: Gamson (1978). Reprinted by permission.

News Bulletin:

As a result of the new coverage offered hemophiliacs in the
Catastrophic Disease National Health Insurance Act, a large number of
hemophiliacs previously unknown to the hemophilia system have
appeared. In a period of about two years, some 12 or 13 thousand new
patients came for treatment. These patients were divided between mild
sufferers who were seeking more adequate and frequent treatment and
those more severe cases suffering from chronic effects of hemophilia.
This latter group was older, had more severe disabilities, and were
poorer, less skilled, rural persons who are now seeking adequate health
care. These persons stress the system in very particular ways since they
need a good deal of orthopedic surgery, dental care, and psychological
and vocational rehabilitation in order to take their place in society. All of
the new patients, regardless of the severity of disease, require full
diagnostic work-ups and the usual tests that are given to the
hemophiliacs. You will find the current hemophiliac population
described in the accompanying tables.

Figure 10.18   Sample External Event: HEMOPHILIA PLANNING GAMES
SOURCE: Greenblat and Gagnon (1976). Reprinted by permission.

recording success. The board in GHETTO, for example, shows the options available and the amount of time each player has invested in each of the possible activities. The boards in THE HEXAGON GAME show the general character of the areas and the differential population and resources in each. In CUSTOD-E, the board represents different stages of adjustment of the adolescent players to their parents' divorce, and measures progress toward successful coping strategies. Ken Jones has creatively made a board that players see piece by piece as they make decisions on where to go when they have crashed in SHIPWRECKED.

The POMP AND CIRCUMSTANCE board has already been shown in Chapter 9; several other boards are illustrated in the pages that follow. Figure 10.27 gives an example of a map-type board, in this case from CALA-GRANDE. This board provides information and orientation during play. The next two examples, from STRATE-GEM-1 and PLANAFAM (in Figures 10.28 and 10.29) are boards around which players sit and on which they move tokens or place cards.

Boards can also be divided in pieces and placed in different locations. In CAPJEFOS, one board is a grid representing food crop fields; another represents cash crop fields; and a third represents the river (including the fishing spot); these are placed in different parts of the "village" room. In FISH BANKS LTD., separate small boards, such as the one in Figure 10.30, represent Fishing Areas 1 and 2, and the harbor. The board for THE HEXAGON GAME (Figure 10.31) is in three parts that are placed one above the other, representing the local

areas (on the bottom), the regional areas (in the middle), and the nation (on the top).

There are numerous other ways to design creative boards; I hope these examples will spark your imagination and yield fruitful results. (A fine description of types of boards is found in Thatcher and Robinson, 1980; instructions for designing simple board games are offered in Ellington, Addinall, and Percival, 1983.)

If you are using a board in your gaming-simulation, do not spend too much time making the first prototype, as you will undoubtedly make several more versions before you are satisfied with it and consider it final. Use pencil to sketch the early forms on paper. As you get closer to a satisfactory design, switch to sturdier cardboard. Felt-tip markers are far preferable to crayons or paints for coloring, as they give much more stable and permanent color. You can cover the boards with self-adhesive transparent film. While multicolored boards are very pretty, you should also keep in mind that they are both difficult and expensive to reproduce. Thus I recommend that you keep your artistic expressiveness (and particularly the use of colors) to the essentials unless you anticipate having considerable funds for commercial reproduction and sale! In making early versions of role cards, charts, and cards, the same advice pertains: make them neat, but do not spend too much time making them elaborate and beautiful, as you are likely to find that they will require several modifications.

Large charts are also sometimes helpful. In INTO AGING, a large chart is placed at Table 3 (see Figure 10.32). In CAPJEFOS, a large sign is placed over the

Title: *Moro Assassination*

Round #2   Happening #5

Location: Rome   Location costs: 15

What is known: Italian police have discovered the body of former premier Aldo Moro. Earlier, Moro had been kidnapped by the Red Brigade, a left-wing terrorist group. The Red Brigade opposes the coalition government of the Communist Party and Christian Democratic Party.

Visuals: Action footage

Prior coverage: Twice a week (updates)

Sources: a. Italian government spokesperson
          b. Italian Communist Party leader
          c. Red Brigade leader

————————————————————————————————————

Title: *European Unemployment Demonstrations*

Round #2   Happening #7

Location: Rome   Location costs: 15

What is known: There were demonstrations over unemployment in several European countries.

Visuals: Action footage

Prior coverage: None

Sources: a. Union leader in Italy
          b. European Common Market official

Figure 10.19 "Happening": WHAT'S NEWS
SOURCE: Gamson (1978). Reprinted by permission.

refreshment area (see Figure 10. 33). A very useful chart is the Scoreboard for THE ACADEMIC GAME (Figure 10.34) on which the occupational position of each player at any point during the game is shown.

One important decision you will have to make concerns the use of tokens versus paper-and-pencil counts (or some combination of the two). Samuel Livingston (1972, p. 2) briefly describes the relative advantages as follows:

> Tokens have the advantage of being something tangible that the players can handle and exchange. They also help to keep errors from going unnoticed. On the other hand, the use of tokens requires that quantities be expressed in small whole numbers, which often is not realistic. Pencil-and-paper calculations permit the use of large numbers or small fractions. Which method you use will depend on the type of items you're trying to represent and the age, interests, and abilities of the players you are designing the game for.

Other construction decisions will also entail choices between paper-and-pencil forms and concrete symbols. Feldt and Goodman (1975, p. 172), as indicated in Chapter 7, advocate considerable use of the latter:

> The utility and power of any game is significantly enhanced if the designer makes creative and imaginative use of graphic

Special Event # _____   Session # _____

Epidemic in the Red Region

A highly contagious disease, called Red Fever, has broken out in the Red Region. Anyone exposed to this disease who is not immunized by the end of the session, has a 1 in 5 chance of dying.

Exposure. Everyone in the Red Region is exposed. In addition, anyone visiting the Red Region is exposed. Any exposed person who has not been immunized exposes everyone in any other region he enters. Thus, if someone visits Red from Yellow, then returns to Yellow without being immunized, everyone in Yellow is now exposed.

Immunization. Immunization can be obtained from the coordinator at any time during the session at a cost of $10 for each person immunized.

Deaths have the usual effect on the National Indicators. The epidemic lasts only for this session.

Figure 10.20 Sample External Event: SIMSOC
SOURCE: Gamson (1978). Reprinted by permission.

<u>Instructions to Operator 1 re: Special Event Card #2:</u>

If any lineage gave 5 or fewer fish last round,
give them "special event card #2" at the beginning of
the next round. If any individual gave no fish,
also give this card.

SPECIAL EVENT CARD #2:

Each lineage/family member: spend 2 more
units in sickness this round than is indicated
on your health chance card.

Figure 10.21 CAPJEFOS: Special Event Card #2
SOURCE: Greenblat et al. (1987). Reprinted by permission.

display and mnemonic materials. Game boards, counters, color coding of objects, creation of two dimensional and three dimensional composite representations of game components and their status, pins, strings, badges, and hats are all important parts of the creative and utilitarian design of games. Such objects are not simply "gimmicks" to amuse and engross potential players, however. Chosen and used effectively, they are important assets to the understanding and insight of the players as to ways in which the game is progressing and useful accounting mechanisms for keeping track of various accounting processes operating within the game.

The key words here are "chosen and used effectively," for when adopted indiscriminately or excessively such materials can distract players from the lessons of the gaming-simulation. You must thus try to avoid having too many roles, cards, or other paraphernalia.

The next set of figures illustrate some of the kinds of symbols that can be used. The scoreboard for THE MARRIAGE GAME (see Figure 10.35) is a cardboard form included in the player's manual. It is used with a set of paper clips. A large clip is used to hold the financial decisions form (the cardboard provides a stiff back to

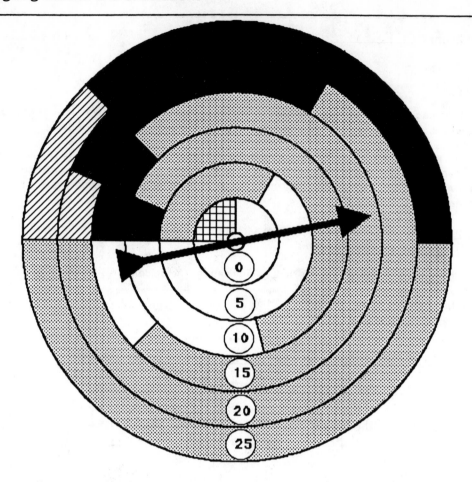

HOW TO READ THE SPINNER
Read the ring corresponding to the chips you've invested

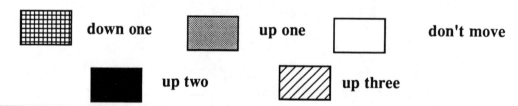

Figure 10.22   Spinner

make the paper-and-pencil record-keeping easier). Small paper clips are then used to encircle the numbers for the four types of points that are regularly accumulated and spent during a round: Free Time Units, Social Esteem Points, Enjoyment Points, and Strokes and Zaps. This saves the players from considerable pencil-and-paper calculating.

The next three figures give illustrations of some cards that have been created for games: SIMSOC (Figure 10.36), CAPJEFOS (Figure 10.37), THE FARMING GAME (Figure 10.38), and GENERATION GAP (Figure 10.39).

Finally, Figure 10.40 shows how Richard Duke and his colleagues were able to use inexpensive materials as symbols in THE HEXAGON GAME, and Figure 10.41 indicates some of the handicaps used in ME, THE SLOW LEARNER.

In concluding this section, I have a last piece of advice. If you wish to produce a kit (or to instruct others to do so), consider the possibilities of making as many materials

Chart 9: Effects of Economic Chance Card Drawing

If you draw:	Effects:
00, 01, 02 03, 04, 05	If you have a full-time job, you have lost it. You must spend six months seeking a new one, receiving half pay as unemployment insurance. Therefore, reduce your income from your full-time job by 25 percent. Increase your free-time units by 25. Social esteem points are reduced for men by 50, for single women by 10, and for married women by 5.
06, 07, 08, 09, 10	You are sick in bed for a week. Pay $200 medical costs. Free-time units reduced by 1. Forfeit 5 sex gratification cards.
11, 12, 13	You become quite ill for two weeks. Pay $200 medical costs. Free-time units reduced by 2, forfeit 10 sex gratification cards.
14, 15	You must go to the hospital for an operation. Pay $500 medical costs not covered by health insurance. Free-time units reduced by 3; forfeit 15 sex gratification cards.
16, 17, 18, 19, 20, 21, 22, 23, 24, 25	If you have children, a child is sick for a week. Pay $50 medical costs. One parent loses 1 free-time unit. If you don't have children, there is no effect this drawing.
26, 27, 28, 29, 30	If you have children, a child is sick for two weeks. Pay $150 medical costs. One parent loses two free-time units; the other parent loses one. If you have no children, there is no effect this drawing.
31, 32, 33	If you have children, a child is sick for three weeks and must be hospitalized. Pay $500 medical costs not covered by health insurance. One parent loses 3 free-time units; the other loses two. If you have no children, there is no effect this drawing.
34	Congratulations! You've won a contest. Gain $400.
35, 36	Extraordinary housing opportunity. Gain 10 social esteem points at no additional expense.
37, 38, 39	You receive $100 in cash as a gift.
40, 41, 42, 43, 44	Extraordinary job opportunity. Basic salary for your full-time job is increased by 10 percent from this round on. Note this on the job options chart.
45	Fire! You and your family lose all your goods and clothing, and if you own a house, you lose that as well. Insurance pays ½ the original cost of goods, and 90 percent the cost of your home. You lose 2 free-time units in order to purchase replacements and you lose any social esteem points and enjoyment points the lost goods and clothing would have given you.
46, 47	Automobile accident! If you own a car, pay $100. Whether or not you own a car, lose 1 free-time unit to process claims, visit doctors, lawyers, and insurance people.
48, 49, 50, 51, 52, 53, 54, 55, 56, 57	Your parents report that one of them is seriously ill. Pay $200 in travel costs and lose 2 free-time units.
58, 59	You are robbed! Lose $300.
60, 61, 62, 63, 64, 65, 66, 67, 68, 69	Tax increase. If you live in Neighborhood A pay additional $200 this round and every round thereafter; if you live in Neighborhood B pay additional $150 this round and every round thereafter, and if you live in Neighborhood C pay an additional $100 this round and every round thereafter.
70–99	No effects this round.

Figure 10.23 THE MARRIAGE GAME: External Events

SOURCE: Greenblat, Stein, and Washburne (1977). Reprinted by permission.

as possible in *reusable* form. Scoresheets, for example, can be laminated, and players can write on them with water-soluble pens; they can be easily "erased" and used again. Boards produced on oilcloth can be rolled up and are less easily damaged than paper or cardboard ones. If, on the other hand, you want a *book* format, hoping to find a book publisher to produce participant's manuals, *consumable* materials are desirable (book publishers do not welcome a resale market!), and paper-and-pencil operations should usually be selected over symbols that are expensive to produce.

F. Accounting System

In constructing the accounting system, you will need to start with the list you made in the design stage of all the places at which there are quantifications (see Chapter 8). Now your task is to make charts, tables, and graphs with numbers in them. Some of these will be used for making information available to players and some will be used for making information available to the operator. In addition,

you will probably need forms for them to record units gained, spent, or transferred, and for calculation of outcomes.

Many of the quantifications will entail *players' resources.* Some of these may be simple to determine: For example, you may choose to make players' "salaries" realistic by consulting current figures for that type of worker. Others may require that you attach numbers to something more abstract, such as influence or prestige. The key in such cases is to make the *relative amounts* given each player realistic. To ascertain the linkages among player resources and other elements, you may find it helpful to consider the following questions (the more complex the game, the more such questions there will be):

(a) *What type* of resources do each of the players have (e.g., money, land, time, votes)?

(b) *How much* of each resource does each player or set of players have initially (at this stage of design you can just indicate high, medium, low)?

Graduate student:
Your paper is accepted
for publication.

Male   **Female**

Reward: +6

                              Reward: +3
                              (in women's
                              journal)

Junior Faculty:

You are being socially isolated
in the department.

Male   **Female**

Cost: -1   Cost: -2

Senior Faculty:
You lost your lease on your
apartment and must search for
a new one. If you are:

Single male/female:
                              Cost = -1

Married male: Get your wife to
                      do it. No penalty

Married female: Your husband
                      is too busy. Do
                      it alone. Cost= -2

Figure 10.24   Sample Chance Cards: THE ACADEMIC GAME
SOURCE: Bredemeier. Reprinted by permission.

NATIONAL

Border disputes require
allocation of 30 units for arms
at once.

Give 30 cash units to
Operator or agriculture
in Region 1 will be lost.

Region 1:

Region offered matching grant
of 5 housing units.

Take this card to banker with 5
of your own housing units
to receive additional 5 units.

Allocate units to settlements.

Urban 1:

Drought in neighboring country
results in the immigration of
five population units
in the urban settlement.

Hand in this card to banker
to receive 5 population units.

Figure 10.25 THE HEXAGON GAME: Sample Chance Cards

SOURCE: The Hexagon Game, copyright 1987, Richard D. Duke & Associates, Inc. Reprinted by permission.

UNANTICIPATED
CONSEQUENCES

Your activities have added to your sense of
self-confidence, but your demands have
elicited hostility from others.

Add 1 unit of personal energy,
but subtract 1 of legitimacy and legality
if appropriate.

Figure 10.26 Sample Chance Cards: COMPACTS

SOURCE: Lauffer (1984). Reprinted by permission.

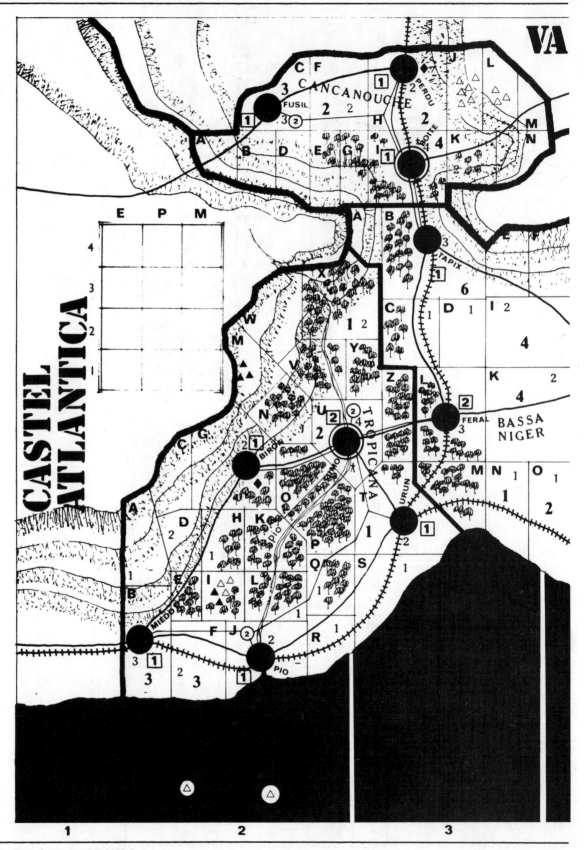

Figure 10.27   Board: CALAGRANDE
SOURCE: Mackie (1980). Reprinted with permission.

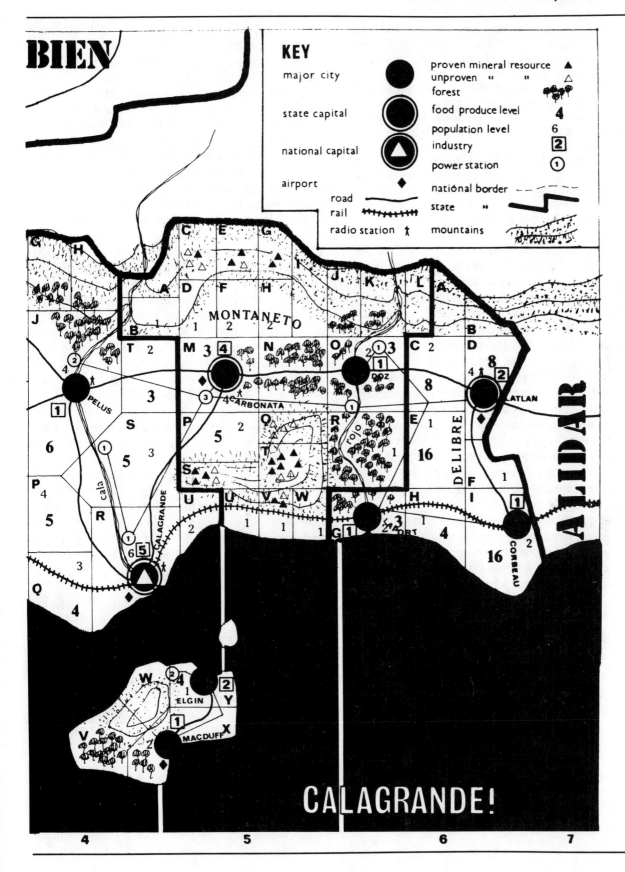

CALAGRANDE!

(c) How, if at all, can such resources be *transferred* (e.g., players can give one another money; they can promise to cast their votes in a particular way, but cannot give another player the votes)?

(d) How can more of these resources be *gained* (e.g., each round spent "at work" gains N units of money; successful passage of a bill that one's constituents support in one round gains additional influence for the legislator in the next round)?

(e) What might each resource be *spent* on? That is, what costs are there that have to be paid with these resources (e.g., minimum subsistence needs; taxes; prestige that must be maintained; medical care costs per unit; minimum time to be spent at work)?

In many games you will also have to calculate the impact of external factors. A table should thus be made indicating the types of external factors that are to be included, and the *types* of costs or rewards they entail (e.g., flood destroys houses; inflation increases production costs; too little time studying requires repeat of a school year; being caught by police carries a chance of being sent to prison). This will have to be done for external factors and for all role players who are not represented by participants, but whose actions are built into the model or into the operator's actions.

If there is a board, indicate what types of units are to be represented (e.g., number of houses that are in a given area, cost of land in an area, degree of deterioration of property in that area, chances of a boat being lost if it fishes in a given area, number of barrels of rice produced per hectare).

Another quantitative element in many gaming-simulations is a mode of calculating final scores. Scores most frequently emphasize competition between players, but cooperation can be emphasized (as in THE MARRIAGE GAME) by making players' scores interdependent. Furthermore, you may wish to suggest that players compare their scores *only* with others in similar roles (e.g., parents compare with other parents, children compare with other children, as in GENERATION GAP; "Inner Track players" compare with other "Inner Track players" and "Outer Track players" compare with other "Outer Track players" in POMP AND CIRCUMSTANCE).

This delineation of places in which you will have to insert figures will alert you to data that are needed for accurate calibration. It will also be helpful if you begin by making "dummy" tables in which you indicate the factors that have to be interrelated. Figure 10.42, for example, shows a dummy table for BLOOD MONEY, indicating that we wanted to make the costs of medical care dependent upon two factors: (1) the degree of disability the player already had and (2) the severity of the current attack.

Let me give some examples of pay-off matrices first. POLICY NEGOTIATIONS is a game of the allocation of limited resources type; the resource is influence. Each of six constituencies begins the game with a specific amount of prestige and a specific amount of influence. The prestige levels relate to the odds of being reelected through the roll of a die. The six players negotiate on 24 possible issues. Each influence level on the board (and in the table in Figure 10.43) is worth four lego blocks, so the player at level 3 receives 12 blocks to allocate during the round. These can be allocated toward passage or failure of the issue on the floor that round, or toward or against bringing another issue to the floor the next round. In addition, passage or failure of any issue may effect the constituencies' allotments of influence and levels of prestige the next round (players do not know the impacts until after an issue has passed or failed). Some of these impacts are shown in Figure 10.43. Play of the school board version (referred to as the "priming game") of POLICY NEGOTIATIONS is meant to be a preliminary step before players engage in redesign of the game to simulate another system (see the discussion of POLICY NEGOTIATIONS in Chapter 2). Working through the tasks of redesigning this frame game is a very useful exercise for would-be designers to learn how to set up an accounting system.

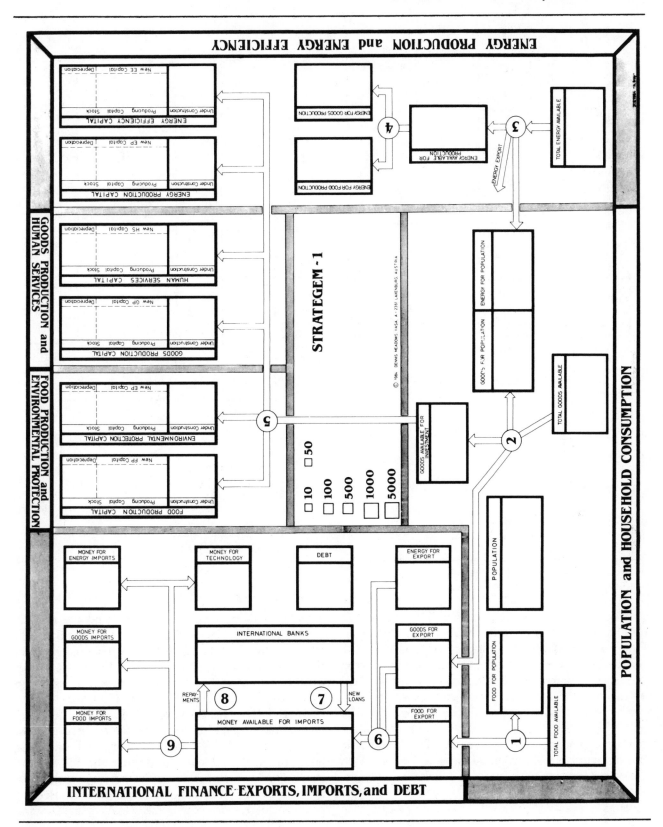

Figure 10.28 Board: STRATEGEM-1

SOURCE: Meadows (1985). Reprinted by permission.

S

| 5 CARDS AT -0.7 EACH |
| 5 CARDS AT -0.9 EACH |
| 5 CARDS AT -1.05 EACH |
| 5 CARDS AT -1.6 EACH |
| ANY # OF CARDS AT -2.2 EACH |

A

| 1ST -4 |
| 2ND -6 |
| 3RD -8 |
| 4TH -12 |
| 5TH -16 |
| 6TH, ETC. -20 |

C

-0.2 PER CARD

A, 2= PREGNANCY

U I

NO COST

A,2,3,4,5 = PREGNANCY

B

| 1ST +13 |
| 2ND +9 |
| 3RD +4 |
| 4TH -3 |
| 5TH -13 |
| 6TH, ETC. -26 |

G

| 1ST +9 |
| 2ND +4 |
| 3RD -3 |
| 4TH -13 |
| 5TH -26 |
| 6TH, ETC. -42 |

D

| 1ST -1 |
| 2ND -1 |
| 3RD -1 |
| 4TH -1 |
| 5TH -1 |
| 6TH, ETC. -1 |

Fate Deck

JACK, QUEEN, KING
OF SPADES = DEATH

Figure 10.29   Board: PLAN-A-FAM
SOURCE: Finseth. Reprinted with permission.

A simple pay-off matrix is used in THE FARMING GAME (formerly called THE POVERTY GAME) (see Figure 10.44). Male and female farmers in CAPJEFOS must allocate work time units to the fields (cash crop production for men and food crop production for women) and spend time at the river (men may choose to fish and women must obtain water). Figure 10.45 shows the Yields Sign which indicates their pay-offs for expenditure of time units spent in these places. In COMPACTS, the pay-off matrices were made by the designers and then divided up into different players' materials. For example, the "Voluntary Associations and Organized Consumer Groups" players are given initial resource allocations in terms of personal energy, social standing and political influence, and legitimacy and legality. They are then told how to increase these resources and what may deplete them, in the form of the materials in Figure 10.46. Yet another example is drawn from the matrices presented to THE GREEN REVOLUTION GAME players on the "Seasonal Record Sheet," presented in Figure 10.47.

The final illustration to be presented here is quite different. INTO AGING has an "income grid" on poster board on the floor. Figure 10.48 shows the grid and the instructions to the operator for having players generate income through the toss of chips onto it. Related examples of this idea of a "game within a game" are the

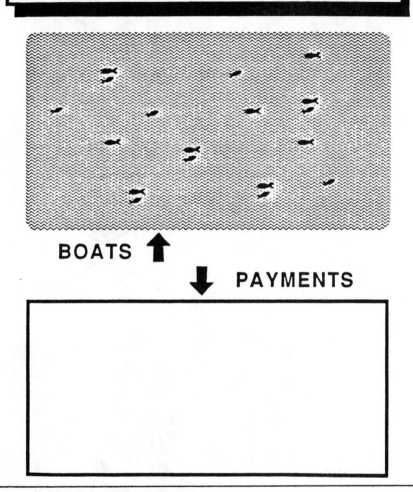

Figure 10.30 Portion of Board: FISH BANKS LTD.

SOURCE: Meadows (1985). Reprinted by permission.

use of the darts games in the employment sector of **BLOOD MONEY** and the regularly changing pay-off matrices in **END OF THE LINE**.

Once you have made pay-off matrices, you will have to decide how to communicate the information. Sometimes this is given to players on their role cards or related materials; sometimes it is embedded in the procedures and rules; and yet other times it is at least partially offered in the external factors.

Almost all games will also require some forms for players to record their decisions. These, of course, are game specific. The following examples from GENERATION GAP (Figure 10.49), PRODUCTION LINE, INC. (Figure 10.50), FISH BANKS LTD. (Figure 10. 51), THE MARRIAGE GAME (Figure 10.52), THE FARMING GAME (Figure 10.53), and THE GREEN REVOLUTION GAME (Figure 10.54) should suffice to start you on designing the forms you need.

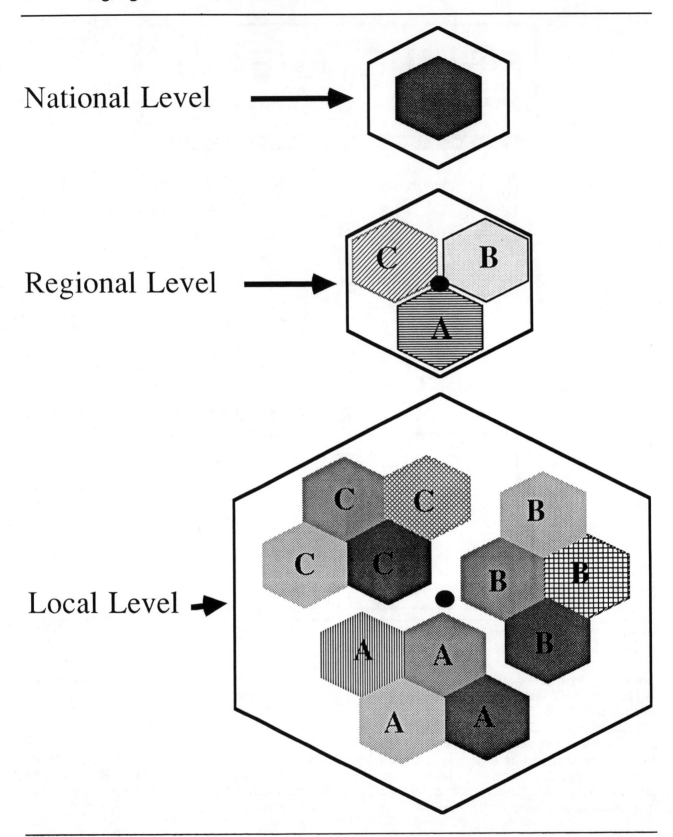

Figure 10.31   THE HEXAGON GAME Board

Table 3.
DEPENDENT LIFE STYLE
RULES ARE STRICTLY ENFORCED

Forfeit:
--Residence   No smoking
--Occupation   You must be in bed by 8:00 PM
--One favorite   Showers only on Tuesday
   possession
--All but one income
   and self-image chip
MAKE YOURSELF AT HOME!

Figure 10.32 INTO AGING: Table 3 Chart
SOURCE: Hoffman and Reif (1978). Reprinted by permission.

BAR- RESTAURANT
"NO WOMAN, NO CRY"

Cost of palm wine=
5 OCSENU per glass

Customers please note:
King Credit is dead--
(he killed himself)

Figure 10.33 CAPJEFOS: Chart for "No Woman, No Cry Bar"
SOURCE: Greenblat et al. (1987). Reprinted by permission.

Finally, you may need forms for the operator and/or players to compute end-of-cycle and end-of-game scores. A simple mode of calculating end-of-cycle scores is employed in THE HEXAGON GAME. The banker receives all accounting forms and tallies the results on the indicator chart shown in Figure 10.55. In SIMSOC, many player actions and decisions affect four "national indicators": Food and Energy Supply (FES), Standard of Living (SL), Social Cohesion (SC), and Public Commitment (PC). Each of these begins at 100 in the first session. Figure 10.56 presents designer William Gamson's instructions for calculating changes in the national indicators, and Figure 10.57 shows the form used for these calculations.

In THE MARRIAGE GAME, players use a Summary Form (Figure 10.58) to calculate their marital (overall) score for the round by multiplying the number of each of six types of points they have gained by the value weights assigned to each.

If there is to be a "winner" of the game, you will have to decide how that person or group is to be determined. Ray Glazier (1970, p. 8) offers some options:

I. A player wins when he achieves his objectives in the game. If only one winner is desirable, it can be the one who achieves his goals first.

II. The winner can be the individual or team which most fully satisfied its objectives (has the highest score).

III. It is possible, in a role-play simulation, to have the winner be he who best plays his role, in the opinion of all the players. In the classroom, however, this may easily turn into a popularity contest in which non-game factors are paramount.

IV. The main object in most games should be efficiency in

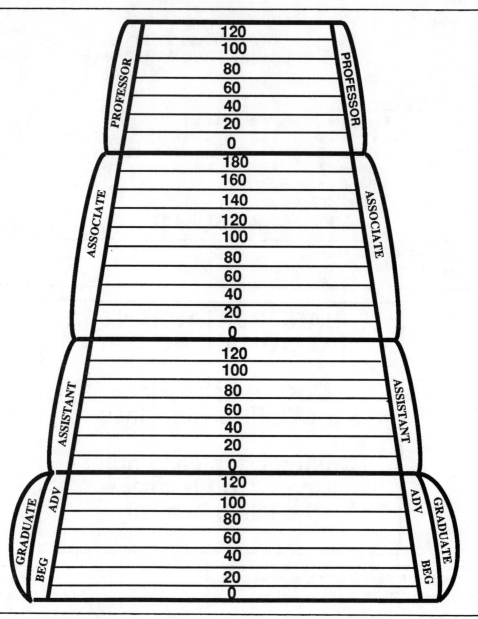

Figure 10.34   Scoreboard: THE ACADEMIC GAME
SOURCE: Bredemeier et al. Reprinted by permission.

a very abstract sense, that is, what one gains on investment. For this to be so, the basic resources and chances must either

(a) be equal for all players
(b) be equalized in the final scoring (e.g., subtracting different resources held at the outset from the players' scores, or, more fairly, dividing final scores by initial resources, if there is a multiplier effect somewhere in the game).

If several kinds of resources are acquired in the game, you may find it impossible to work out a formula to equalize them (on the order of: 1 cow = 3 goats), so you may wish to have several sorts of winners (player with the largest farm, player

with best combination of land and workers, player with the most livestock).

FIELD TESTING AND MODIFYING THE GAMING-SIMULATION

When you have assembled the materials for the prototype, you are ready to find a group to field test it. In general, you should attempt to run the game with players as much like those for whom it is designed as possible. If you need only a few players, you may wish to ask a few friends to play through the game with you the first time. Even if they are unlike the players for whom the game is

	Hundreds	Tens	Units
	2 1 0	9 8 7 6 5 4 3 2 1 0	9 8 7 6 5 4 3 2 1 0

FREE TIME UNITS

Use of this scoresheet requires 13 regular size paper clips, 2 large clips, and a Financial Decisions Sheet for each round.

Put 3 paper clips on each of the 4 score sections. Set all at 000 as follows:

Hundreds	Tens	Units
3 2 1 0	9 8 7 6 5 4 3 2 1 0	9 8 7 6 5 4 3 2 1 0

As you acquire or lose points during the round, adjust the appropriate clips to keep a *cumulative* total for the round. For example, "75" should be recorded as:

Hundreds	Tens	Units
3 2 1 0	9 8 7 6 5 4 3 2 1 0	9 8 7 6 5 4 3 2 1 0

Money costs and rewards need to be written. For each round use a Financial Decisions Sheet. Fold it in half as indicated. Use a large clip to attach it to this sheet in the spot indicated (covering these instructions). Follow the instructions in the manual, recording the financial effects of your decisions.

Clip the Summary Form to the back with the same large clip.

Clip folded Financial Decisions Sheet here.

SCOREBOARD

SOCIAL ESTEEM POINTS

Hundreds	Tens	Units
3 2 1 0	9 8 7 6 5 4 3 2 1 0	9 8 7 6 5 4 3 2 1 0

ENJOYMENT POINTS

Hundreds	Tens	Units
3 2 1 0	9 8 7 6 5 4 3 2 1 0	9 8 7 6 5 4 3 2 1 0

STROKES		*ZAPS*	
Tens	Units	Tens	Units
6 5 4 3 2 1 0	9 8 7 6 5 4 3 2 1 0	6 5 4 3 2 1 0	9 8 7 6 5 4 3 2 1 0

Figure 10.35   Player's Scoreboard: THE MARRIAGE GAME

SOURCE: Greenblat, Stein, and Washburne (1977). Reprinted by permission.

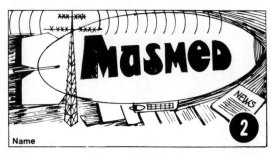

Individual Goal Declaration

Name _____ Session #3
Are you satisfied with how well you are
meeting your individual goals? (check one)

_____ Yes, I'm satisfied.

_____ No, I'm not satisfied.

_____ I've changed my individual goals:

from _____ to _____

Figure 10.36   Cards: SIMSOC
SOURCE: Gamson (1978). Reprinted by permission.

ultimately designed, the most obvious problems will be revealed and you can modify those aspects before moving to strangers. Sometimes you may deliberately reject this policy, particularly in the earliest trials; for example, if you are designing a game for business persons or other practitioners who have very scarce time and whom you cannot readily assemble for a trial run, you may find it is better to assemble a group of business students for the earliest runs, waiting until you think you have a version that is more "finished" before you try it with professionals.

During or immediately after each run, take notes about problems that arose. What instructions were not clear? What strategies did players employ that you did not expect (or that you do not want to be possible)? What outcomes were generated that were not realistic? Were

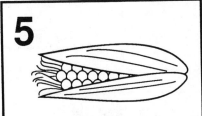

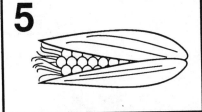

PUSHCART

PRICE: 500 OCSENU

USE: Can be used by 4 people-- men or women farmers

BENEFIT: Increases crop cultivation efficiency. Each user gains 1 work time each round after purchase.

(Show card to Operator 1 to collect time benefits.)

PROTEIN DEFICIENCY

You did not have enough fish last year. Each lineage member: spend one more unit in sickness this round than is indicated on your sickness card.

SICKNESS CARD

MODERATE SEVERITY MALARIA in your lineage this year.

Time lost to sickness:
Women: three time units
Men: two time units

Pay 100 OCSENU to the Traditional Doctor for treatment, or each spend one more time unit in sickness

WATER

Very Important Person

Figure 10.37 Cards: CAPJEFOS
SOURCE: Greenblat et al. (1987). Reprinted by permission.

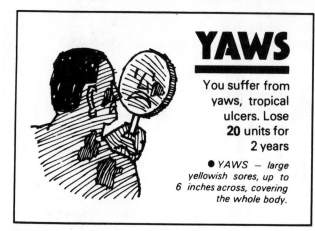

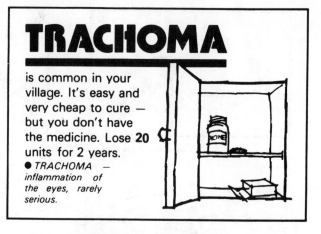

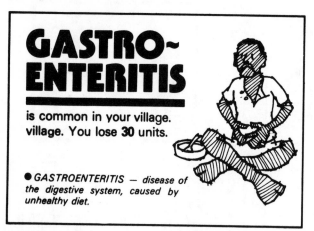

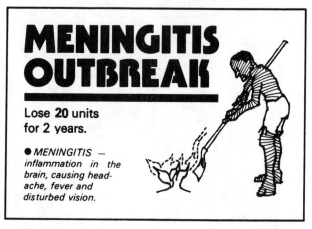

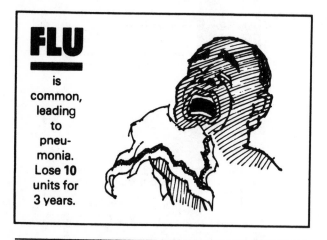

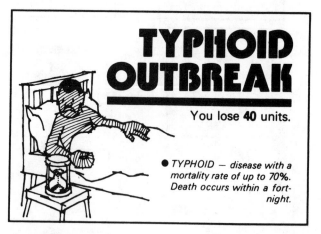

Figure 10.38 Cards: THE FARMING GAME

SOURCE: The Farming Game, published by Oxfam UK, 274 Banbury Road, Oxford OX2 7D2, UK. Reprinted by permission.

players sufficiently interested? Was the tempo of play satisfactory? It is also useful to ask students for comments and criticisms. If you have a colleague who is interested in the subject matter or your project, invite him or her to watch a run. Be sure to note what things players do that you had not anticipated, and what they do not do that you wanted them to do. Seeing how they "cheat" or beat your rules is also instructive.

As you consider the "success" of the product you have constructed, there are several criteria to employ, which have been implied by the above questions. While the grossest violations should have been obvious by looking

P   You will do all of your homework this week.

T   You won't do much homework this week.

P   Your child will do all of his homework this week.

T   Your child won't do all of his homework this week.

P   You will get your hair cut (girls' won't wear make-up) this week.

T   You will let your hair grow (girls will wear make-up) this week.

P   Your Son will get his hair cut (Daughter: will not wear make-up) this week.

T   Your Son will let his hair grow (Daughter: will wear make-up) this week.

P   You will spend most of this weekend working around the house.

T   You won't help much around the house this weekend.

P   Your child will spend most of this weekend helping around the house.

T   Your child won't help much around the house this weekend.

SATISFACTION IF I CHOOSE BEHAVIOR **T 8**

SATISFACTION IF MY CHILD CHOOSES BEHAVIOR **P 6**

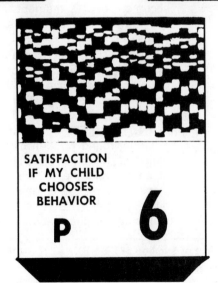

Figure 10.39   Cards: GENERATION GAP
SOURCE: Boocock. Reprinted by permission.

To simplify the accounting of symbols in the game, two rules have been made. First, the value of these seven symbols are the same, i.e., one unit of food is equal to a single unit of housing, etc. (An exception is made for international trade exchanges, and will be explained later.) All symbols are either white or red or plain in color. The white symbols equal one unit, and the red symbols equal ten units. Gaming symbols are explained as follows:

CASH Cash is represented by green and red bingo chips. Cash represents any type of internal currency. No cash is to be used on the local level; the local level has a purely barter economy

COMMODITIES Commodities are represented by white and red buttons. Commodities represent items produced for sale in the market place. This would include such items as cash crops or food, clothing, baskets, or any item not used by the producer.

FOOD Food is represented by white and red corn. Food represents any food crop produced for domestic consumption; it would not include cash crop food produced for export.

HOUSING Housing is represented by white and red wooden blocks. Housing represents all housing forms, whether it be shanty town, government, or middle class in design.

INFRASTRUCTURE Infrastructure is represented by white and red pebbles. Infrastructure represents physical human settlement infrastructure (i.e., water systems, sewage systems, roads, communications), the physical means of production (i.e., factories, mines, harbors), plus energy that is used in all production operations.

POPULATION Population is represented by white and red dowels that are placed on plastic lego strips on each occupied local settlement. Population represents all components of the nation's population, including all ages, sexes, and origins

SERVICES Services are represented by white and red paper clips. Services represent all non-physical forms of assistance, including health services, pest control, all government aid, education, police and fire protection, and national security forces.

INSTABILITY Instability of the country is symbolized by large, round wooden blocks. Each block represents a deficit of 10 required symbols on the local level. At the end of each cycle the banker totals these instability blocks and places one on top of another in the center of the national board. The height of the blocks represents the degree of instability of the national government.

Figure 10.40   List of Symbols: THE HEXAGON GAME

SOURCE: The Hexagon Game, copyright 1987, Richard D. Duke & Associates, Inc. Reprinted by permission.

Handicaps Used

(1) Spectacles prepared to give the effect of tunnel vision (simulating tunnel vision and making it difficult to focus).

(2) Spectacles prepared to give the effect of blurred vision (opaque spectacles to give the effects of cataracts).

(3) Colored eye shades which give the effect of certain types of color blindness (simulating color blindness).

(4) Eye patch covering one eye completely (simulating partial blindness).

(5) A back plaster over the elobw and upper and lower arms to produce very restricted arm and hand movement). This could be exacerbated with the use of finger splints on the hand.

(6) A neck restraint used with another handicap, e.g. finger strapping or an eye patch (simulating the restricted movement of the upper trunk).

(7) Finger restraints with the use of finger splints and strapping to join two or more fingers together (simulating deformed hands).

(8) An arm fixed in a sling attached to the neck to prevent ease of movement (simulating a different form of restricted movement in the trunk and limbs).

(9) Wax ear plugs (simulating partial hearing).

(10) A block of wood strapped to one foot (simulating a foot condition leading to a permanent limp).

(11) The use of a neck and collar to immobilise one arm behind the participant's back (simulating the loss of a limb).

The handicaps can be repeated and some participants can be given more than one if desired. It can have an interesting emotional effect if an additional handicap is given after the first with a comment like `Oh, you are not very badly handicapped, you had better have this as well'. In addition to the handicaps, all the participants must have the dominant hand marked at the same time as they receive the handicap so that the dominant hand is easily visible throughout the simulation game. (Experience of using the simulation suggests that eye and ear handicaps are the most effective.)

Figure 10.41 Symbols Handicaps Used in ME, THE SLOW LEARNER

SOURCE: Donald Thatcher and June Robinson (1984) Me–The Slow Learner. Revised and Reprinted (1987) Solent Simulations, 80 Miller Drive, Fareham, Hants, PO16 7LL, England. Reprinted by permission.

at the materials, careful evaluation requires that you judge these aspects by examining the gaming-simulation *in operation*:

(1) *Validity.* Here the question is, does the content of the gaming-simulation accurately represent the real-world situation it is designed to simulate? You may wish to ask a subject-matter expert (such as a colleague who is knowledgeable about the topic) to help you assess how successfully you have translated the conceptual model into a gaming-simulation and about ways the validity might be improved.

(2) *Verisimilitude.* Do the players have a *sense* of being in the real situation? Validity and verisimilitude do not necessarily go together. The game may be valid, but players may not *feel* it to be realistic. Alternatively, they may feel it is realistic, but more expert examination may reveal many inaccurate representations. Obviously, you must strive for both validity and verisimilitude!

(3) *Playability.* This refers to the timing, clarity of instructions, and similar issues. If players become very confused or bored, they will not play, even though the model is

MINIMUM COSTS OF CARE AND BLOOD
All costs indicated in white chips

MEDICAL HISTORY: 0-2 DOTS

TYPE OF CARE:

Type of attack:	Minimal		Moderate		Optimal	
	Cost of treatment	Cost of blood	Cost of treatment	Cost of blood	Cost of treatment	Cost of blood
Moderate						
Severe						
Catastrophic						

MEDICAL HISTORY: 3-4 DOTS

TYPE OF CARE:

Type of attack:	Minimal		Moderate		Optimal	
	Cost of treatment	Cost of blood	Cost of treatment	Cost of blood	Cost of treatment	Cost of blood
Moderate						
Severe						
Catastrophic						

MEDICAL HISTORY :5-7 DOTS

TYPE OF CARE:

Type of attack:	Minimal		Moderate		Optimal	
	Cost of treatment	Cost of blood	Cost of treatment	Cost of blood	Cost of treatment	Cost of blood
Moderate						
Severe						
Catastrophic						

Figure 10.42 "Dummy" Table for BLOOD MONEY
SOURCE: Greenblat and Gagnon (1976). Reprinted by permission.

			ISSUE 1		ISSUE 2		ISSUE 3	
			Pass	Fail	Pass	Fail	Pass	Fail
School Board								
Inner City School Board	Influence	4						
	Prestige	6				-1	+1	
Conservative School Board	Influence	3						
	Prestige	9	-1	+1	-1	+1	+1	
Suburban School Board	Influence	4						
	Prestige	7						
Teachers:								
Young Teachers	Influence	4					+1	
	Prestige	8	+2	-1	+1	-1	+2	-2
Specialists	Influence	5					+1	
	Prestige	7	+1		+1	-1		
Old Teachers	Influence	4					+1	
	Prestige	8	+1	-1	+1	-1	+1	-1

Figure 10.43 Starting Resources and Some Pay-Offs in POLICY NEGOTIATIONS
SOURCE: Goodman (1970). Reprinted by permission.

valid. It may take considerably longer to reach desired states (e.g., running out of fish, budgetary problems) or to complete play of the game than you wish.

(4) *Operability*. In a similar fashion, the game must be manageable without the operator being a magician! If the full design team is needed to run the game, beware! Usually a limited number of assistants can be obtained by an operator, and so the tasks of running the game must be manageable by one or two persons.

(5) *Pedagogically Sound*. Does the game do what you, the designer, intended? That is, does it meet your initial objectives as spelled out in Stage I? If so, you will obviously be pleased; if not, you need to make further modifications. Alternatively, you may have the flexibility to *alter* the objectives (e.g., to decide it is a good gaming-simulation for a younger group of players than you intended), although this "luxury" is generally not available to those working on contract for a client or designing for their own training programs.

As long as problems arise in any of these domains, you must follow the field tests with modification of the

Crop Card

Crop	*Wet*	*Dry*	
ROOT	Yams	70	20
	Cassava	40	60
CEREAL	Maize	60	30
	Millet	30	50
PROTEIN	Groundnuts	50	30
	Peas	40	40

Your village has 10 small fields. In these you must grow at least 3 different crops for variety in diet. You must grow at least 2 fields of protein crops.

If your agricultural produce falls below 450, your village will suffer malnutrition and possibly from outbreaks of illness. This will mean you cannot work well in the fields and therefore your crops the next year will not be so good.

If you produce more than 500 units, you may store up to 50 units for the next year.

If the food supply falls below 200 for two years, people starve to death.

Figure 10.44   Crop Card: THE FARMING GAME

SOURCE: The Farming Game, published by Oxfam UK, 274 Banbury Road, Oxford OX2 7D2, UK. Reprinted by permission.

materials, and then retest. You may also have the pleasant experience of finding that some elements work better than you anticipated, or that the game has utility for a broader audience than you initially conceived.

CONCLUDING NOTES: ON BUGS AND SKIS

If you worked carefully through the prior stages, you should find that the basic gaming-simulation is sound,

CAPJEFOS YIELDS

1 man's work time unit —— **7 fish**

 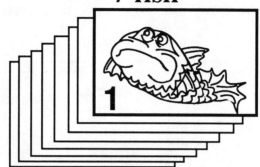

1 man's work time unit —— **20 cash crop units**

 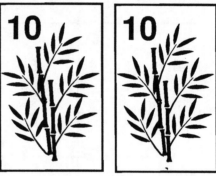

1 woman's work time unit —— **20 food crop units**

 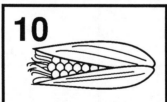 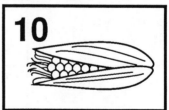

1 woman's work time unit —— **1 water unit**

Figure 10.45 CAPJEFOS: Pay-Off Matrix—Time Spent in Fields and at River

RESOURCES: Voluntary associations and organized consumer groups may have to rely almost exclusively on personal energy to work towards the defeat or enactment of a proposal. Most consumers, however, have some access to social standing, political influence, and legitimacy. At the start of the first round of play, these resources are allocated as follows:

RESOURCES / CONSUMER	Personal energy	Social standing & political influence	Legitimacy & legality
	Blue	Black	Transparent
Black Community	8	6	5
Senior Citizens	6	4	
Neighborhood Associations	6	4	2
Physically and Mentally III or Handicapped	6		
Concerned Citizens	6	6	3
Welfare Rights	6	3	1

Figure 10.46 COMPACTS: Voluntary Associations' and Organized Consumer Groups' Initial Resources
SOURCE: Lauffer (1984). Reprinted by permission.

though it has "bugs" to be worked out. Each "bug" leads the designer back to a reexamination of the conceptual model and the game model in search of a missing element or one inaccurately linked to others. I am reminded of a "Hagar the Horrible" cartoon, in which the first frame shows only the heads of Hagar and a friend, with the captions, "What's that?" and "Skis—I just invented them." The second frame shows full bodies. Hagar is staring at his friend's feet, which are strapped onto backwards skis (i.e., the curved end is in the back). The

Fields/Acres

	1	2	3	4	5	6	7	8	9	10
Write 'W' for well										
Write 'F' for fertilizer										
Write 'H' for HYV										

Germination

	1	2	3	4	5	6	7	8	9	10
Write rain or Drought										
Write 'P' for pest										
Write 'S' for pesticide spray / Write 'I' for irrigate from well										
Crop state										

Middle Growth

	1	2	3	4	5	6	7	8	9	10
Write rain or Drought										
Write 'P' for pest										
Write 'S' for pesticide spray / Write 'I' for irrigate from well										
Crop state										

Flowering

	1	2	3	4	5	6	7	8	9	10
Write rain or Drought										
Write 'P' for pest										
Write 'S' for pesticide spray / Write 'I' for irrigate from well										
Final crop state										
Yield										

Transitional Matrices   h=high, m=medium, l=low

Environment

Germination (from → to)	Rain No Pests	Rain Pests	Drought No Pests	Drought Pests
Do nothing	h → h	h → l	h → m	h → l
Only spray	h → h	h → m	h → h	h → l
Only irrigate	h → h	h → l	h → h	h → m
Irrigate + spray	h → h	h → m	h → h	h → m

Middle Growth (from → to)	Rain No Pests	Rain Pests	Drought No Pests	Drought Pests
(from)	h m l	h m l	h m l	h m l
Do nothing	h m l	m l l	h m l	m l l
Only spray	h m l	h m l	h m l	h m l
Only irrigate	h m l	m l l	h m l	h m l
Irrigate + spray	h m l	m m l	h m l	m m l

Flowering (from → to)	Rain No Pests	Rain Pests	Drought No Pests	Drought Pests
(from)	h m l	h m l	h m l	h m l
Do nothing	h m l	l l l	h m l	l l l
Only spray	h m l	h m l	h m l	l l l
Only irrigate	h m l	l l l	h m l	h m l
Irrigate + spray	h m l	h m l	h m l	m m l

Table of yields per acre

Crop state	Ordinary rice	Ordinary rice + fertilizer*	HYV rice	HYV rice + fertilizer*
h	33	40*	36	46*
m	22	26*	24	31*
l	13	16*	10	15*

*NB Fertilizer bonus applies only if there was no drought in Germination or Middle Growth – but using a well will save your bonus. A drought in Flowering only does not lose the bonus.

Total yield	Consumption	Rice surplus or deficit

Farm Name

Year

Figure 10.47   THE GREEN REVOLUTION GAME: "Seasonal Record Sheet"

SOURCE: Chapman. Published by The Green Revolution Partnership, 2A Green End Road, Cambridge CB4 IRX, U.K. Reprinted by permission.

INCOME GRID

An area of the room about 12 feet in length is necessary to accomodate the income grid which is run by the game director. An income grid should be made on poster board according to Figure 3 and taped to the floor.

Bonus: Double your original income. (6 chips)	Gain one chip.
Lose all income and go to next table.	Double what you presently have.
Increase income to original amount. (3 chips)	No Gain.

Figure 3
Income grid.

A tape line is placed approximately 12 feet from the grid. Players attempt to gain income here at designated times during the game. Players at table one are allowed a chance at the grid after each turn or drawing of a life event card unless the card denies this privilege. Players at table two go to the income grid only when the life event card they pick indicates they may do so. Players at table three are not permitted to go to the income grid. Upon direction, a player at a table goes to the income grid, stands at the tape line and throws one of the income chips toward the grid trying to land on the square that will provide more income on which to subsist. Penalty squares are also on the grid and the player should try to avoid these. The income chips (poker chips) are light and it is difficult to land on the grid let alone on the income space. If a player does not land on the grid on the first throw, allow one more chance. The game director should point out that this is understandable since age has made these things difficult. If on the second throw the grid is again missed, the director might say that perhaps this is an indication that money is hard to handle at this age and send the player to the next table. If a player lands on a square that provides some income, the director presents that player with more chips but again questions the player's ability to handle money since the player is "old" and offers to take care of it for him. A player may return to table one and take an appropriate turn when income is gained. If a square is landed on that indicates going to another table, the player is to go there. The game director maintains a questioning attitude about each player's ability to obtain and handle money because of age. This role may be as simple or complex as the director wishes to make it. It may be quite creative. The director may pay off each player the exact amount for the first few times, then approach a player to make a "deal". It could be an offer to the player of a chance to toss all of the acquired chips at the board and being paid off for each one that lands on a paying square--providing that the player throws with the non-dominant hand. The task of tossing the light poker chip and getting it to land on the board is difficult and most players have little control over where the chip lands. The player, in effect, usually throws the chips away. Observe for those who are skeptical and suspicious, and point out these reactions to them. Any kind of combination of throws may be offered, not necessarily to each player. Another option is to offer the player the opportunity of throwing either all the self-image chips or all the income chips. This makes the player think about which is more important to exist. This area, which is intended to be a chance to earn money, may turn out to be a confidence game.

Figure 10.48 Income Grid and Operator Instructions from INTO AGING

SOURCE: Hoffman and Reif (1978). Reprinted by permission.

PARENT'S Score Sheet

ISSUES	PRACTICE ROUND	ROUNDS				
		1	2	3	4	5
Doing homework						
Helping around house						
Going to a show						
Letting hair grow						
Going on a date Saturday						
TOTAL						

TEENAGER'S Score Sheet

ISSUES	PRACTICE ROUND		ROUNDS								
	Satis-faction	Punish-ment	1 +	1 −	2 +	2 −	3 +	3 −	4 +	4 −	5 +	5 −
Doing homework											
Helping around house											
Going to a show											
Letting hair grow											
Going on a date Saturday											
TOTALS											
GRAND TOTAL											

Figure 10.49 GENERATION GAP: Score Sheets for Parents and Teenagers
SOURCE: Boocock. Reprinted by permission.

friend adds "Of course I don't have all the bugs worked out." The basic idea of your game may be there, but the "twist" needed to make the game work effectively may be elusive. On the other hand, you may be carried through this stage by the satisfaction you will derive from the realization that you are close to success!

PRODUCTION LINE, INC.				TEAM # _____	

⑤ PRODUCTION SCHEDULE REPORT
WEEK # _____

MACHINE #1		MACHINE #2		MACHINE #3	
PRODUCT	HOURS	PRODUCT	HOURS	PRODUCT	HOURS

Figure 10.50 **PRODUCTION LINE, INC.: Production Schedule Report**
SOURCE: Meadows (1985). Reprinted by permission.

THE FISH GAME   COUNTRY NAME _____   # _____

DECISION SHEET

Annual Report

	Year	1	2	3	4	5	6	7	8	9	10
AO:1	Deep Sea Bank Catch (# fish last year)										
AO:2	Coastal Bank Catch (# fish last year)										
AO:3	Price of Fish ($ / fish last year)										
AO:4	Total Fish Sales ($ last year)										
AO:5	Interest ($ last year)										
AO:6	Initial Bank Balance ($ this year)										
AO:7	Ship Fleet Before Auctions and Trades										

Auction, Trades, & Orders

	Year	1	2	3	4	5	6	7	8	9	10
AI:1	Ships Purchased in Auction										
AI:2	Money Spent on Auction Purchases										
AI:3	Ships Purchased In Trades										
AI:4	Money Spent on Trade Purchases										
AI:5	Ships Sold in Trade										
AI:6	Money from Trade Sales										
AI:7	New Ships Ordered										

Ship Allocations

	Year	1	2	3	4	5	6	7	8	9	10
AI:8	Ship Fleet after Auctions & Trades										
AI:9	Ships Sent to Deep Sea Bank										
AI:10	Ships Sent to Coastal Bank										
AI:11	Ships Remaining in Harbor										

Figure 10.51 FISH BANKS LTD.: Decision Sheet

SOURCE: Meadows (1985). Reprinted by permission.

Name of person being rated: _____   Sex Role: M   F

Round No. _____

Answer each question using the scale so that 1 indicates a rating of very little and a rating of 10 indicates very much. If you do not have enough information to rate your partner, circle 0.

1. How satisfied are you with your partner's attitudes and decisions about work?   0   1   2   3   4   5   6   7   8   9   10

2. How satisfied are you with your partner's attitudes and decisions about budget allocations?   0   1   2   3   4   5   6   7   8   9   10

3. How satisfied are you with your partner's attitudes and decisions about leisure-time activities? 0   1   2   3   4   5   6   7   8   9   10

4. How satisfied are you with your partner's attitudes and decisions about marriage?   0   1   2   3   4   5   6   7   8   9   10

5. How satisfied are you with your partner's attitudes and decisions about sex?   0   1   2   3   4   5   6   7   8   9   10

6. How satisfied are you with your partner's attitudes and decisions about parenthood?   0   1   2   3   4   5   6   7   8   9   10

7. How sensitive was your partner to your needs and desires this round?   0   1   2   3   4   5   6   7   8   9   10

8. How responsive was your partner to your needs and desires?   0   1   2   3   4   5   6   7   8   9   10

9. How well were the two of you able to communicate this round?   0   1   2   3   4   5   6   7   8   9   10

10. Overall, how interesting and enjoyable was this round with this partner?   0   1   2   3   4   5   6   7   8   9   10

WHEN THIS FORM HAS BEEN COMPLETED BY THE PERSON(S) YOU HAVE ASKED FOR RATINGS, ADD THE NUMBER CIRCLED AND ENTER HERE: _____

ADD THE TOTAL NUMBER OF STROKES
  RECEIVED THIS ROUND   + _____

SUBTRACT THE TOTAL NUMBER OF ZAPS
  RECEIVED THIS ROUND   − _____

TOTAL EGO SUPPORT FOR THE ROUND
  (enter on Summary Form)   = _____

Figure 10.52   THE MARRIAGE GAME: Partner Rating Form
SOURCE: Greenblat, Stein, and Washburne (1977). Reprinted by permission.

Year No.

	Fields	Yields
Yams		
Maize		
Cassava		
Millet		
Groundnuts		
Peas		

Food -total possible production _____

Loss from illness and malnutrition
     LAST YEAR   _____

Loss due to DISASTER   _____

Plus food stored from last year   =========

SO...

ACTUAL FOOD PRODUCTION =   _____

```
NEXT YEAR
Malnutrition loss (if  any) _ _ _ _ _ _ _ _
Disease loss (if any) _ _ _ _ _ _ _ _ _ _ _
Total loss (deduct NEXT YEAR ) _ _ _ _ _ _
```

Figure 10.53 THE FARMING GAME: Player's Record
SOURCE: The Farming Game, published by Oxfam UK., 274 Banbury Road, Oxford OX2 7D2, UK. Reprinted by permission.

INCOME

_____ maunds of rice @ _____ Rupees per maund

_____ maunds of late rice @ _____ % of market price

Interest on Rupees _____ Bonds at _____ %

_____ bonds surrendered to bank

_____ acres of land at _____ Rupees per acre

TOTAL

BALANCE IF DEFICIT

EXPENDITURE

_____ Loan repaid + interest at _____ % total

_____ acres of fertilizer at _____ Rupees per acre

_____ acres of pesticide at _____ Rupees per acre

_____ acres of well at _____ Rupees per acre

_____ maunds of ordinary rice at _____ Rupees per maund

_____ maunds of HYV at _____ Rupees per maund

_____ acres of land at _____ Rupees per acre

_____ industrial bonds at face value

TOTAL

BALANCE IF SURPLUS

Farm Name

Year

RECONCILIATION

Cash to bank

Or

Cash from bank

Loan

Accounts Certified

This form is solely for recording transactions with the bank. Private deals should not be included.

Figure 10.54 THE GREEN REVOLUTION GAME: Balance Sheet

SOURCE: Chapman. Published by The Green Revolution Partnership, 2A Green End Road, Cambridge CB4 1RX, U.K. Reprinted by permission.

Region / Land Use		Housing			Services			Infra-structure			Food			Com-modities		
Resources / Round		1	2	3	1	2	3	1	2	3	1	2	3	1	2	3
A	Agriculture 1															
	Agriculture 2															
	Urban 1															
	Forest															
B	Mining															
	Urban 2															
	Savannah															
	Agriculture 3															
C	Urban 3															
	Fishing 1															
	Fishing 2															
	Ocean															
TOTAL																

Figure 10.55 THE HEXAGON GAME: Indicators Chart

SOURCE: The Hexagon Game, copyright 1987, Richard D. Duke & Associates, Inc. Reprinted by permission.

Each National Indicator begins at 100 for the first session. Many of the things that influence different indicators will be discussed further below. The effects are summarized here and in Table 3.

1. *Spontaneous decline.* Each indicator automatically declines by 10% between sessions to represent a spontaneous decay factor.

2. *Public Programs.* Simbucks invested in the two programs described above raise the National Indicators; however, these programs have "administrative costs," so that a Simbuck invested in them does not bring an equivalent rise in the National Indicators.

    a.   *Research and Conservation.* This program raises the Food and Energy Supply (FES) by 40% of the value of all new money invested in it and the Standard of Living (SL) by 10% of the value of all new money invested in it.

    b.   *Welfare Services.* This program raises the Standard of Living (SL) by 10% of the value of all new money invested in it and Social Cohesion (SC) and Public Commitment (PC) by 20% of the value of all new money invested in it.

3. *Industrial Production.* Each passage purchased by BASIN lowers FES by two units, but each passage completed raises SL by 1 unit. Each anagram invested in by RETSIN raises SL by 1 unit but lowers PC by 1 unit.

4. *Absenteeism.* Each absentee lowers SL and PC both by 2 units.

5. *Unemployment.* Each unemployed person lowers SL and SC by 3 units and PC by 1 unit.

6. *Riots.* Each rioter lowers PC by 2 units and SC by the amounts indicated in Table 4 (page 29). Each guard post lowers Social Cohesion by 5 units.

7. *Arrests.* Each arrest lowers SC and PC by 3 units.

8. *Deaths.* Each death lowers SL, SC, and PC by 5 units.

9. *Individual Goal Declarations.* Every *four* positive individual goal declarations ("Yes, I'm satisfied") raise PC by 1 unit; each negative declaration ("No, I'm not satisfied") lowers PC by one unit. Any declaration of change in individual goals leaves PC unaffected.

Figure 10.56 SIMSOC: Changes in National Indicators
SOURCE: Gamson (1978). Reprinted by permission.

Table 1. Summary of BASIN Assets, Income, Investment Costs, and Returns

	Starting Assets in Bank	Income in First Session	Cost per Passage	Payment for Completed Passage	Error Deduction[a]
Size Level One	$100	$10	$40	$ 50	$4
Size Level Two	$150	15	60	75	6
Size Level Three	$200	20	80	100	8

[a] BASIN receives no payment if there are six or more errors.

Table 3. Effects of Investment and Other Actions on National Indicators

	FES	SL	SC	PC
Research and Conservation	+40%[a]	+10%	0	0
Welfare Services	0	+10%	+20%	+20%
BASIN	—2 units	+1 unit	0	0
RETSIN	0	+1	0	—1
Absentees	0	—2	0	—2
Unemployed	0	—3	—3	—1
Rioters	0	0	—[b]	—2
Arrested	0	0	—3	—3
Dead	0	—5	—5	—5
Individual Goal Declaration	0	0	0	±1[c]

[a] This means that if, for example, $10 were invested in Research and Conservation, FES would rise by 40% of this or by four units. Similarly, SL would go up by 10% while SC and PC would not be affected.
[b] See Table 4 (p. 29) for exact effects. Note that guard posts each lower SC by —5.
[c] Plus 1 for every four positive declarations; minus 1 for each negative declaration.

Figure 10.56 Continued

National Indicator Calculations

Form W

Session # _____

National Indicators

	FES	SL	SC	PC
1. Initial value (at beginning of session)	____	____	____	____
2. Natural decline (10% of line 1)	– ____	– ____	– ____	– ____
3. Research and Conservation = _____ (FES = +40%; SL = +10%)	+ ____	+ ____	0 ____	0 ____
4. Welfare Services = _____ (SL = +10%; SC, PC = +20%)	0 ____	+ ____	+ ____	+ ____
5. BASIN passages bought = _____ (FES = –2; SL = +1)	– ____	+ ____	0 ____	0 ____
6. RETSIN anagrams bought = _____ (SL = +1; PC = –1)	0 ____	+ ____	0 ____	– ____
7. Number of absentees (Ab) = _____ (SL, PC = –2Ab)	0 ____	– ____	0 ____	– ____
8. Number of unemployed (U) = _____ (SL, SC = –3U; PC = –1U)	0 ____	– ____	– ____	– ____
9. Number of rioters (R) = _____ (For SC, see Form P; PC = –2R)	0 ____	0 ____	– ____	– ____
10. Number of arrests (Ar) = _____ (SC, PC = –3Ar)	0 ____	0 ____	– ____	– ____
11. Number of deaths (D) = _____ (SL, SC, PC = –5D)	0 ____	– ____	– ____	– ____
12. Individual goal declarations: Positive (P) = _____; Negative (N) = _____ (PC = .25P–N)	0 ____	0 ____	0 ____	± ____
13. Special events	____	____	____	____
14. Total of all pluses	____	____	____	____
15. Total of all minuses	____	____	____	____
16. Net change (add lines 14 & 15)	____	____	____	____
17. Final value (add lines 1 & 16)	____	____	____	____

Figure 10.57 SIMSOC: National Indicators Calculations
SOURCE: Gamson (1978). Reprinted by permission.

Name:_____   Sex Role M F   Round No._____

This form is used in Step 1 and again in Step 6.

STEP 1: Assign a weight of no less than 1 nor more than 5 to each of the six types of points. The more important the value, the greater the weight you should assign it. **The six value weights must total 20.**

STEP 6: When you have finished computing the number of points you have gained in each area, enter them in the points column here. Then multiply the value weight you assigned by the points you gained to determine the weighted totals for each area and enter in the total points column. Add these and divide by 20 to determine your Marital Score for the round.

TYPES OF POINTS	Value Weight	Points	Weighted Total Points
1. Financial Assets (income, savings, homeownership)	_____ ×	_____ =	_____
2. Enjoyment (from current consumption, leisure activities and goods)	_____ ×	_____ =	_____
3. Social Esteem	_____ ×	_____ =	_____
4. Sex Gratification	_____ ×	_____ =	_____
5. Ego Support	_____ ×	_____ =	_____
6. Parental Status	_____ ×	_____ =	_____
TOTALS	20		_____

÷ 20

Marital Score for the Round _____

Total savings accumulated in previous rounds:_____

Total indebtedness from previous rounds: _____

Figure 10.58 THE MARRIAGE GAME: Summary Form
SOURCE: Greenblat, Stein, and Washburne (1977). Reprinted by permission.

11

Preparing Your
Gaming-Simulation
for Use by Others

When you are satisfied that the game has successfully run at least 10 times, you should turn your attention to making it accessible to others. The players' materials will now be complete, but you will need to prepare a thorough guide for the operator. As you will see in a moment, much of the work for this will already be completed, but some new tasks remain to be done. Then there are the difficult tasks of arranging for publication and dissemination.

WRITING THE OPERATOR'S MODEL

The following is a list of topics that should be treated in the operator's manual:

(1) Technical Overview

    Subject matter and purpose
    Players
    Number of players
    Personnel needed to run the game
    Time requirement
    Space requirement
    Materials requirement

(2) The Conceptual Model

(3) Description of the Game in Operation

(4) Running the Game

    Pregame preparations (kit, materials, room set-up, assigning roles)
    Introducing the game
    Running the game
    Ending the game

(5) Guide for postplay discussion

Even a cursory review of the list of topics will reveal that the writing you did in Stages I and II of the design process can be used with some editing to make up the bulk of Sections 1 and 2 of the operator's manual. The technical overview should be clear and succinct, for many potential users will read only that section to ascertain whether the game is suitable for their usage. Where there are options for any of the dimensions (number of players, time needed), spell them out in detail. For example, it may be possible to run the game in several different time formats; this should be presented in a manner similar to that illustrated in Figure 11.1, which is taken from the coordinator's manual for WHAT'S NEWS.

It is unfortunate that very few game designers offer much information to users about the conceptual model that underlies the gaming-simulation. This leaves the operator to infer the model from watching the game operation, which is difficult and sometimes risky. I strongly urge, therefore, that you present a serious discussion of your conceptualization, highlighting the elements, linkages, and principles of primary importance. If you have followed the recommendations in Chapter 6 and have prepared a written and graphic statement of the model as part of the design process, much of your work for Section 2 is already done. You must turn this statement into language that will be clear to the operator, who may lack the expertise to read a complex or highly technical document. You may want to supplement the information on the model that you give to the operator, with a somewhat parallel discussion for the participants. Again, a fine example appears in the long essay in the participants' manual for WHAT'S NEWS. In this manual, designer William Gamson has written a lengthy conceptual essay on "Making the News," an outline of which is provided in Figure 11.2.

It is very useful to the first-time user of your game if you provide a brief description of the game in operation in Section 3 of the operator's manual. Some of the text in Chapter 9 of this book is taken from such descriptions in the manuals of the four games that constitute the case studies. Check the prose you prepare for this section with someone who has not seen the game in operation;

A. *50-Minute Class*[a]

1. Review rules; first part of Step 1 (Camera Crew Assignments)
2. Rest of Step 1 and Step 2
3. Step 3
4. Step 4
5. Round 2: Steps 1 and 2
6. Round 2: Steps 3 and 4
7. Round 3: Steps 1 and 2
8. Round 3: Steps 3 and 4
9. Debriefing and discussion

B. *75-Minute Class*[a]

1. Review rules; Step 1
2. Steps 2 and 3
3. Step 4 and Round 2, Step 1
4. Round 2, Steps 2 and 3
5. Round 2, Step 4 and Round 3, Step 1
6. Round 3, Steps 2 and 3
7. Round 3, Step 4; debriefing and discussion

C. *Two-Hour Class*[a]

1. Review rules; Steps 1 and 2
2. Steps 3 and 4; Round 2, Step 1
3. Round 2, Steps 2, 3, and 4
4. Round 3, Steps 1, 2, and 3
5. Round 3, Step 4; debriefing and discussion

D. *Evening and All-Day Workshop*[b]

7:00–8:00 P.M. Review rules
8:00–9:00 Step 1
9:00–9:30 Step 2
(following day)
9:00-10:00 A.M. Step 3
10:00–10:30 Step 4
10:30–11:00 Round 2, Step 1
11:00–11:30 Round 2, Step 2
11:30–noon Round 2, Step 3
(luncheon break)
1:00–1:30 Round 2, Step 4
1:30–3:30 Round 3, all steps
3:30–4:30 Debriefing and discussion

E. *All-Day Workshop*[b] (2 rounds)

9:00–10:00 A.M. Review rules
10:00–11:00 Step 1
11:00–11:30 Step 2
11:30–12:30 Step 3
(luncheon break)
1:30–2:00 Step 4
2:00–4:00 Round 2, all steps
4:00–5:00 Debriefing and discussion

F. *Half-Day Workshop*[b] (1 round)

1:00–2:00 Review rules
2:00–3:00 Step 1
3:00–3:30 Step 2
3:30–4:15 Step 3
4:15–4:45 Step 4
4:45–5:00 Discussion

[a]Schedule assumes that students have read rules in advance of first session and a class of twenty or more with at least five source players. Smaller classes where rules have not been read in advance will need longer, as discussed in text.

[b]Schedule assumes that participants have not read rules in advance. The first part of the workshop will be shorter if they already have this preparation. Note that Step 2 is doubled in length in games of less than twenty, with only three source players.

Figure 11.1 Time Formats for WHAT'S NEWS
SOURCE: Gamson (1984). Reprinted by permission.

ask whether your description yields the desired general sense of what to expect. Then check it with someone who has seen or participated in the game; ask if it conveys the general character and the "flavor" of the experience reasonably well. Section 4 necessitates that you make explicit some of the things that you, as the designer, know about how to run the game. Provide a checklist of materials that should be in your kit and of supplementary materials that the operator must provide. A diagram of the room set-up should also be included. Then make a detailed account of what should be done as general preparation, what should be done prior to the first session, and what should be done during each cycle. Fine

examples of such a checklist and of instructions can be found in the WHAT'S NEWS manual (see Figures 11.3 and 11.4). A much more elaborate set of instructions is required for operators of SIMSOC, and the manual for that game is a superb model of how to write detailed instructions. Operators of THE EXECUTIVE SIMULATION are also given excellent instructions about how to integrate the game into a class, including student assignments and preparation for game play, scheduling decisions for teams, how presentations should be made, criteria for evaluation of team performance, and follow-up exercises (see pp. 3-11 of the operator's manual for THE EXECUTIVE SIMULATION).

I. News as a Social Construction
   A. The Career of a Happening
   B. Social Construction in WHAT'S NEWS
II. The Nature of Sources
   A. Sources as Professionals
   B. Sources as Organizations
   C. Sources as Part of News Routines
   D. Sources and Journalists in WHAT'S NEWS
III. Journalistic Practice
   A. Before the Idea of Objectivity
   B. The Nature of Social Facts
   C. Objectivity as a Set of Practices
   D. Objectivity in WHAT'S NEWS
IV. The Nature of News Assemblers
   A. News Assemblers as Businesses
   B. Advertisers and Pressure Groups
   C. The Social Organization of the Broadcasting Industry
   D. Special Constraints of the Television Medium
   E. Economic and Organizational Considerations in WHAT'S NEWS
V. The Political Interests of News Organizations
   A. Direct Pressure
   B. Official Bias
   C. Political Pressures in WHAT'S NEWS
VI. Audience Considerations
   A. Attracting a News Audience
   B. Audience Irrelevance for News Content
   C. Audience Considerations in WHAT'S NEWS
VII. News Frames
   A. Interpretive Packages
   B. Condensing Symbols
   C. The Framing Opposition Movements
   D. Framing in WHAT'S NEWS
VIII. Conclusion

Figure 11.2   Outline of Essay on "Making the News": WHAT'S NEWS
SOURCE: Gamson (1984). Reprinted by permission.

In my game manuals I have regularly provided a "script" for the operator to use in introducing the game. Sometimes I also offer an outline of this script for the person who has run the game several times. To prepare this, I tape record myself or a codesigner as we run the game with several groups; then the transcripts of these introductory remarks can be edited to prepare a general purpose script for use by others. It has proven an easy and effective way to be sure that all points are covered. Some designers have found it useful to provide tape cassette introductions. (For example, in BAFA-BAFA the scripts in the manual are repeated on two separate tapes, one for the Alpha Culture and one for the Beta Culture.) Other designers have prepared sets of slides or overhead transparencies for the operator to use in getting play started. (There are fine sets of overheads available for operators of STRATEGEM-1 and FISH BANKS LTD.) At this point I ask a colleague or friend who has never seen the game to review Section 3 and to offer suggestions for revision. Next I find someone to run the game; I offer to be present as a back-up to the operator's manual should anything in it not be clear. Such a person should be able to provide you with many insights into points that require elaboration or clarification. In your observer role you will see what kind of supplementary information is needed by people who are not familiar with the game. You may need to repeat this procedure several times as you revise the manual. Since the postgame discussion is one of the most important elements of the successful use of your game, you should spend considerable time generating the guide for debriefing to be presented in Section 5 of the operator's manual. It should include the needed ingredients to make the debriefing a structured, guided experience, which will, in

Form K: Coordinator's Checklist

Preparation

_____ Clip board

_____ Name tags

_____ Timer

_____ Envelopes

_____ Happening cards

_____ Source forms

_____ Coordinator forms

Step One

_____ Distribute sets of source roles to source players

_____ Record source player names on Form C: Sources' Order of Appearance.

_____ Fill out Roster (Form H)

_____ Collect Form B: Camera Crew Allocation, from networks (reminding them to keep a copy).

_____ Distribute happening cards

_____ Announce names of source players for Form C

Step Two

_____ Announce beginning of each interviewing phase

_____ Set timer

_____ Collect Form D: Budget

_____ (optional) Check budget calculations for accuracy

Step Three

_____ Check with networks for questions on task

_____ Check with sources for questions on use of Form G

_____ Collect Form E: Broadcast Allocation

Step Four

_____ Time broadcasts

_____ Copy broadcast allocations (Form E) on blackboard

_____ Collect Form G and announce source complaints (deduct point from network if two or more against it)

_____ Award bonus point for winning the quality rating

_____ Add news values from Form I to blackboard tally

_____ Calculate final audience scores for networks (including bonus point for picking the lead) and record results on Form J

_____ Replace producers who exceeded budget or finished last (and record changes on Roster)

Figure 11.3 Operator's Checklist: WHAT'S NEWS
SOURCE: Gamson (1984). Reprinted by permission.

turn, make the game play meaningful. The debriefing should include descriptions of what transpired, analysis of the game elements, comparison of the game model with "reality," and consideration of the real-world issues that participants should address. Figures 11.5 and 11.6 present some samples of brief debriefing guidelines from THE TRADING GAME and from CLASSROOM EXPERIENCING.

Summary of Team Game

Objective: To score as many audience points as possible.

Each round has twelve possible happenings to be used in a 24-minute broadcast.

A complete game is three rounds.

Audience points are gained by:

1. Allocating the same time to happenings that they received by the median network in the real world
2. One bonus point for picking the "correct" lead
3. One bonus point for winning the quality rating

Costs of covering news:

1. Camera crews
   a. 5 Newsbucks for a regular crew; must be paid whether crew is used or not
   b. 20 Newsbucks for a special crew (if one must be hired to cover a happening)
2. Location costs: 0, 5, 10 or 15 Newsbucks, depending on how far the location of the story is from network headquarters in New York or Washington.

Summary of Individual Game

Step	Producers	Reporters	Sources
1. Preparations and assignments	a. Use Form B to assign up to 16 regular camera crews. b. Use Form D to assign reporters to happenings.	a. Advise producers on where to assign camera crews and which happenings to cover. b. Plan questions for sources.	a. Study source forms. b. Practice interviews with other sources.
2. Completing the story	a. Use Form D to calculate the costs of coverage. b. (if time) Monitor the reporter interviewing.	a. Use Form C to locate and interview relevant sources. b. (if time) Draft 60–70-word leads for possible broadcast.	a. Answer reporters' questions.
3. Preparing the broadcast	a. Use Form E to allocate broadcast time to happenings. b. (Asst. Producer) Use Form F to record reporter points.	a. Finish preparing 60–70-word leads on stories. b. Advise producer on broadcast time allocation. c. Decide how to present broadcast.	a. Allocate time to happenings as if preparing a broadcast. b. Prepare Form G for use during next step.
4. Broadcast	a. Observe and plan improvements for next round.	a. Present broadcast.	Use Form G to: a. Rate quality of broadcasts. b. Decide whether to use complaint power (when applicable).

Producers lose their jobs if

1. their network finishes last in audience points, *or*
2. they fail to stay within their budget (with a leeway of 20 Newsbucks for the leading network).

Figure 11.4   Summary of Team Game and Individual Game: WHAT'S NEWS
SOURCE: Gamson (1984). Reprinted by permission.

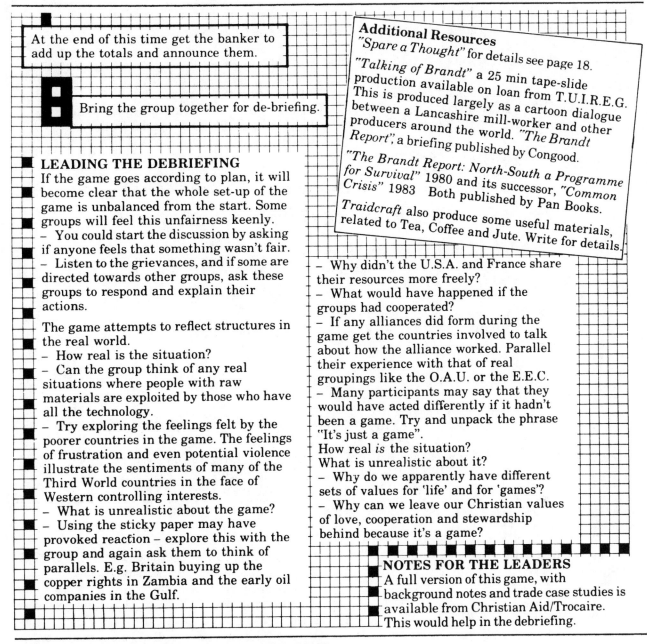

At the end of this time get the banker to add up the totals and announce them.

Bring the group together for de-briefing.

LEADING THE DEBRIEFING

If the game goes according to plan, it will become clear that the whole set-up of the game is unbalanced from the start. Some groups will feel this unfairness keenly.
- You could start the discussion by asking if anyone feels that something wasn't fair.
- Listen to the grievances, and if some are directed towards other groups, ask these groups to respond and explain their actions.

The game attempts to reflect structures in the real world.
- How real is the situation?
- Can the group think of any real situations where people with raw materials are exploited by those who have all the technology.
- Try exploring the feelings felt by the poorer countries in the game. The feelings of frustration and even potential violence illustrate the sentiments of many of the Third World countries in the face of Western controlling interests.
- What is unrealistic about the game?
- Using the sticky paper may have provoked reaction – explore this with the group and again ask them to think of parallels. E.g. Britain buying up the copper rights in Zambia and the early oil companies in the Gulf.

Additional Resources
"*Spare a Thought*" for details see page 18.
"*Talking of Brandt*" a 25 min tape-slide production available on loan from T.U.I.R.E.G. This is produced largely as a cartoon dialogue between a Lancashire mill-worker and other producers around the world. "*The Brandt Report*", a briefing published by Congood.
"*The Brandt Report: North-South a Programme for Survival*" 1980 and its successor, "*Common Crisis*" 1983   Both published by Pan Books.
Traidcraft also produce some useful materials, related to Tea, Coffee and Jute. Write for details.

- Why didn't the U.S.A. and France share their resources more freely?
- What would have happened if the groups had cooperated?
- If any alliances did form during the game get the countries involved to talk about how the alliance worked. Parallel their experience with that of real groupings like the O.A.U. or the E.E.C.
- Many participants may say that they would have acted differently if it hadn't been a game. Try and unpack the phrase "It's just a game".
How real *is* the situation?
What is unrealistic about it?
- Why do we apparently have different sets of values for 'life' and for 'games'?
- Why can we leave our Christian values of love, cooperation and stewardship behind because it's a game?

NOTES FOR THE LEADERS
A full version of this game, with background notes and trade case studies is available from Christian Aid/Trocaire. This would help in the debriefing.

Figure 11.5   Debriefing Guidelines: **THE TRADING GAME**
SOURCE: Elliott and McKeown (1985). Reprinted from The Trading Game, copyright Christian Aid. Reprinted by permission.

Some games have more extensive guidelines for debriefing. For example, the manual for THE MARBLE COMPANY presents a set of generic questions that flow from the three criteria that Lederman and Steward suggest should create the framework for debriefing: validity, reliability, and utility. Their framework is as follows:

Questions dealing with *validity* (face validity—the counterparts to the experience; construct validity—the connections with the world being modeled) include:

What was this about?
What is it like in the real world?
What did you do?
How does it compare with real world behaviors?
What are the implications?
What are the concepts being modeled?

Questions dealing with *reliability* (the replicability of the experience—either the predictability of the product or the experience or of the process in which participants engage) include:

Debriefing provides members of the group with an opportunity to discuss what has happened. A suggested procedure for debriefing is as follows:

1. Description by the group of what happened in the game.

   List the names of the students on the blackboard or a chart --
   Mary (Mark) Taylor, Donald (Darlene) Phillips, Shelton (Sally) Moran, Bob (Barbara) Waters, Charles (Carol) Lane, Frank (Francis) Butler

   Discussion of each student role:
   First, ask the teacher(s):
   DESCRIBE IN ONE OR TWO WORDS THE BEHAVIOR OF
   _____ (Mark, etc.)
   WHAT DO YOU THINK THIS STUDENT'S GOAL WAS?

   Then ask the student playing the role:
   WHAT DID YOU KNOW ABOUT YOURSELF? WHAT WERE YOU WORKING FOR?

   Then ask the group as a whole:
   WHAT COULD BE DONE TO HELP THIS STUDENT IN THE CLASSROOM?

2. Description by the group of the game itself.

   Ask the group as a whole:
   HOW DO YOU FEEL THIS GAME COMPARES WITH A REAL CLASSROOM?
   HOW IS IT LIKE A REAL CLASSROOM? HOW IS IT DIFFERENT?
   IS IT HELPFUL EVEN THOUGH IT IS DIFFERENT?
   WHAT CHANGES WOULD YOU MAKE IN THE GAME?

Figure 11.6 Debriefing Guidelines: CLASSROOM EXPERIENCING
SOURCE: Jakson. Reprinted by permission.

What occurred, and how was it predictable?
How did it unfold?
Why did it happen?
What did you do?
What are the implications of your behavior?

Questions dealing with *utility* (the cost/benefit analysis: what did the participants get from the experience compared to what they had to invest in terms of time, money and/or energy) include:

What did you get out of the experience?
What did you pay for the experience?
How worthwhile was the experience?
How else might you have learned about these concepts?
[THE MARBLE COMPANY, p. 20]

THE MARBLE COMPANY manual also contains an excellent discussion of experience-guidance skills for game directors. Some of this discussion can also be found in Lederman (1984). Bredemeier, Rotter, and Stadsklev (1981) also provide good general guidelines for debriefing; and the entire December 1986 issue of

Simulation/Games for Learning (SAGSET, 1986) is devoted to debriefing issues and strategies.

Some designers have also provided guidance to the user in the form of suggestions for related exercises, such as papers, diaries, interviews with people who, in real life, play the roles simulated in the gaming-simulation, or redesign of some of the elements. A simple set of suggestions is provided in YOUR NUMBER IS UP (Figure 11.7). Once again, the manuals for SIMSOC and WHAT'S NEWS provide first-class examples of such suggestions. Figure 11.8 shows the written work suggestions given players of SIMSOC.

Some of the games that are produced in the form of a book/manual to be purchased by each player include a set of readings that parallel the game play. Readings accompanying THE MARRIAGE GAME materials and the SIMSOC materials, for example, were selected by the designers from published literature on the topic; they are meant to guide players in analysis of what transpired. WHAT'S NEWS and THE EXECUTIVE SIMULATION

1. List the factors which may extend a patient's stay in hospital.
2. Describe how a patient's behavior may change according to his/her length of stay in hospital
3. What control do you think the patient has over his/her own health care in the hospital environment?
4. Describe the avenues of social and emotional help available to the patient in the hospital.
5. Here is a list of roles which have been used in the game. Rank them in order of importance (1-9) from the perspective of the role you played:

___ Patient	___ Nurse	___ Hospital Chaplain
___ Charge Nurse	___ VMO	___ RMO
___ Team Leader	___ Social Worker	___ Trolley Lady

6. Rank in order of importance the members of a ward team in real life. Explain why you have put them in this order.

Figure 11.7   Suggestions for Follow-Up: YOUR NUMBER IS UP
SOURCE: Reprinted with permission from Hope and McAra, 1984, Pergamon Books, Ltd.

players receive related readings developed especially for those manuals; some of the readings offer helpful hints to players on strategies they can employ during the run.

DISSEMINATION

If you wish the gaming-simulation you developed to be used by others outside your institution, you must investigate copyright, publication, and dissemination possibilities. These are very variable from one location to another, so no specific advice can be offered here. If you know others who have published similar materials, consult them. It is also wise to discuss copyright regulations and procedures with a lawyer (solicitor) to be sure your rights are protected, particularly at the stages at which you send out samples and sign contracts.

You might begin by preparing a 1-2 page summary of the completed gaming-simulation. Send this to colleagues in your discipline, and to the heads of the professional gaming organizations listed in the back of this volume. They may be able to pass information about the game to others, and perhaps they can put you in touch with people who share your interests and activities and who can offer advice. If you can arrange to attend the annual meetings of one or more of these organizations, you may receive further assistance and ideas about how to proceed.

The next step should be getting the game reviewed, both informally and formally. Arrange to run it at your own and other institutions first. Collect evaluation data and anecdotal reports; if some participants or operators are particularly enthusiastic, ask if they would be willing to put some of their thoughts into a letter to you. Next, try to arrange to run the gaming-simulation at a profes-

sional meeting in your discipline. Follow the same procedures about evaluation and endorsements. If it is possible to do so, arrange for newspaper coverage of one or more runs. Finally, if you can make a few copies available to other people to run, obtain similar written endorsements from them.

The point of the activities suggested in the preceding paragraph is to compile a portfolio of *written confirmation of the effectiveness of the gaming-simulation*. This will prove more impressive when you solicit publication and dissemination outlets than your word that the product is a fine one. You should also do some solid marketing analysis and develop a clear statement of the nature and size of the potential groups of users. If you know of channels of communication to these groups, such as professional journals or newsletters, document this as well.

Now you are ready to look for a publisher. This is not an easy enterprise. Short games with few materials might lend themselves to publication in a magazine or a journal. CARIBBEAN FISHERMAN, for example, first appeared in a geography journal, and STRATEGEM-2 materials, including the computer program, were completely reproduced in *Simulation and Games*. If there are limited materials, you may find it feasible to reproduce kits yourself, with little capital investment and an effective marketing strategy. Likewise, it may be possible to produce do-it-yourself manuals that explain how the user can make his or her own kit. The manual should be an inexpensive item to produce and market; consider preparing it on a word processor with a high-quality printer to make it look appealing.

Many of the products you create will not be amenable to such simple publication solutions. Then there are a few

The post-game discussion is an important step in turning the experience of playing SIMSOC into a learning experience. A second step involves written work or other projects based on SIMSOC. Some suggestions follow:

1. Have the participants write papers addressing issues that are made more vivid by their participation in SIMSOC. Assignment one in the *Participant's Manual* suggests a series of questions that players should be stimulated to think about by participating in SIMSOC. You will undoubtedly think of others based on what happened in a particular SIMSOC. The objective of these questions is to move the focus from SIMSOC to the processes in the real world that the game attempts to simulate. These questions can be used for further class discussions as well as for written work.

2. Ask the participants to become simulators. Playing a game may be a more active experience than listening to a lecture, but developing a game is more active still. Assignments two and three in the *Participant's Manual* are attempts to have students make the jump from player to simulator. As players, they accept certain constraints which are given in the rules and use resources to achieve objectives specified or suggested by the rules. When they act as simulators, the rules themselves become the resources, and they can manipulate these—hypothetically or actually—to see whether the resulting process will take the form that they believe it will. Depending on the emphasis you wish to give this aspect of your course or program, you may wish to assign some of the readings listed in the brief game-simulation bibliography included in this manual (p. 67).

3. Ask participants to keep a diary while they are playing. If the focus in using SIMSOC is on interpersonal behavior, these diaries may be a rich source of material to use later, especially if you ask people to record their feelings about what is going on rather than simply to describe events. The diaries can help the participants to recall reactions that may have become distorted and "corrected" by hindsight. Clovis R. Shepherd and colleagues at the Department of Sociology, University of Cincinnati, Cincinnati, Ohio, have developed a form for such a diary.

4. Have participants do research on SIMSOC. Lawrence Alschuler at the University of Hawaii has developed a research exercise based on SIMSOC. Some students, instead of playing, carry on systematic research and evaluation, developing questionnaires or special observation techniques, interviewing participants, and analyzing and reporting results. It is possible to carry out replications of existing studies (for example, surveys about attitudes toward government and politics) using SIMSOC's government and politics as the reference point. Questions and attitude scales used in other studies can be reworded for this purpose. Alschuler discusses this idea more fully in an unpublished paper, "Simulating Politics and Simulating Research: A Teaching Idea" (1969).

Figure 11.8   Written Work: SIMSOC

SOURCE: Gamson (1978). Reprinted by permission.

types of outlets that you should consider.

First, it may be possible to make the game available through one of the professional gaming associations. At this moment, NASAGA has a newly developed publication program; by the time you read these pages, other organizations may have followed that lead.

MAXIMASIA
A MAXIM MANAGEMENT GAME

OUTMANOEUVRE YOUR MARKET COMPETITORS

Experience the excitement of a tendering market. Small differences in bids can greatly affect your profits.

MAXIMASIA is a tendering game which examines effects of competition on decision making and explores a range of market strategies. Each team's decisions affect the performance and market position of others in this cut and thrust business game.

MAXIMASIA: INTRODUCTION

Teams make and supply the same basic product, and compete for:

— Market share of finished goods
— Purchases of raw materials.

Teams must develop strategies to beat their competitors on selling price, outbid them for supplies of raw materials and organise production in two sites.

OPERATION

MAXIMASIA operates over several decision periods. Game organisers announce the size of finished goods markets and quantities of raw materials available one period in advance. Teams decide:

— Raw materials : amount required and bid price.
— Finished goods : quantity offered for sale and selling price.
— Production levels on two sites

Decisions are processed on a computer by game organisers to produce trading statements.

GAME MODEL

MAXIMASIA simulates the instability of markets when tendering dominates. The computer allocates raw materials and sales of finished goods according to bids received. Since market size and raw material supplies rarely match total requirements, teams must develop sophisticated market strategies to succeed.

GAME FACTS

- TIME TO PLAY .... 2 hours
- NUMBER OF PARTICIPANTS .... 2-6 teams, each with 3-6 players
- PRICE .... £95 plus VAT.

PACK CONTENTS

- Organisers Handbook, including straightforward computer operating instructions, guidelines for game presentation and feedback.
- Computer disk (IBM PC and Compatibles)
- Participants' Handbooks
- Differing Economic Scenarios

MAXIM TRAINING SYSTEMS LTD
6 MARLBOROUGH PLACE   BRIGHTON   SUSSEX BN1 1UB   TEL BRIGHTON (0273) 672920

Figure 11.9   Advertisement: MAXIMASIA

SOURCE: Brand. Reprinted by permission.

What happens in Relocation?

What should be done with the headquarters building of Ace Manufacturing? Should it remain in North City, be relocated in the beautiful countryside of surburban Pine Hills or follow the flight of other corporations to the Sun Belt? These are the questions which face the students in their roles as president or vice president of legal, personnel, finance and public relations of the Ace Manufacturing Company. At the beginning of the game, each person studies the problem from the perspective of his or her role. For example, the legal vice president examines the legal problems associated with relocating the company, the personnel vice president from the personnel point of view, and so forth. They then form executive teams and attempt to reach a decision.

As they make their decision, the full complexity of the problem gradually reveals itself. It becomes apparent that making such a move will not only affect the profit and loss column of the corporation but has the potential of dramatically altering every aspect of the business including ways of thinking and acting which have always been taken for granted. These reasons are listed on the board, ranked and discussed as a possible list of priorities for all companies which are faced with a similar problem. It is during the discussion that the students are confronted with the question of the corporation's moral responsibility to North City and the employees who live there.

What do they learn?

Participants become aware of the full range of outside pressures affecting a corporate decision to relocate: the effect on the city which they are leaving, the community to which they are moving, the employees, management, the organizational structure and the financial health of the corporation.

Who is it for?

RELOCATION was designed to be used by two groups: College students enrolled in any course concerned with the impact of the corporation on America and managers or employees who might benefit from being exposed to the problems and issues facing a corporation which is anticipating such a move. It requires a minimum of six students and no more than thirty. The optimum is twenty-five.

How long does it take?

The game can be played and discussed in one fifty minute period.

How much preparation time is required?

Ten to thirty minutes, depending on one's experience with educational simulations.

What is included in the kits?

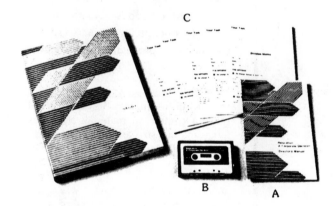

A = Directors Manual
B = Cassette Recording: Participants Instructions
C = Instructions for: President, Legal Vice President, Personnel Vice President, Financial Vice President, Public Relations Vice President

Figure 11.10   Advertisement: RELOCATION
SOURCE: Shirts. Out of print. Reprinted by permission.

Second, if the format you have used is amenable to this possibility, it might be possible to convince a book publisher to produce the game. (If you followed the advice in Chapter 1 and read through this manual before you started to work, you may have deliberately tailored your product toward this outlet.) CLUG, SIMSOC, THE URBAN POLICY GAME, and WHAT'S NEWS were all published by The Free Press; THE MARRIAGE GAME was published by Random House; a series of business games, such as THE BUSINESS POLICY GAME, MODERN BUSINESS DECISIONS, and STRATPLAN were published by Prentice-Hall. These are all large book publishing houses, and will consider only products that promise large markets. If you intend to approach a company of this sort, be sure to follow the preceding advice about preparation of a portfolio and of market analysis before you make initial contact with a representative. There are also smaller publishing companies that might be willing to consider publication of your gaming-simulation. They often require a smaller printing to make a profit, but will nonetheless want assurance that there are potential users who can be identified and reached through a marketing program.

Third, there are a handful of companies that specialize in the production of games. I doubt that you will have much success with companies that produce the popular commercial games; one friend reported to me that a representative of one of the well-known companies of this sort said he wouldn't consider a product that promised to sell fewer than 500,000 copies! Look at some of the listings in the back of this manual and at some of the producers of games on your shelf. You might wish to contact the designers who have used these companies as publication outlets to ascertain whether they have been satisfied with what was done with their games; if you get positive reports, make contact by mail or telephone, and indicate the bases of your contention that this is a fine product for which there is a demand.

Fourth, you might contact special interest groups that are concerned with the substantive areas dealt with in your gaming-simulation. For example, contact groups concerned with energy for an energy game; contact groups concerned with environmental protection for a game on that subject; contact groups concerned with civil rights for a game on prejudice and discrimination.

Whatever outlet you find, make sure that the publicity for the game is accurate and attractive. Figures 11.9 and 11.10 show good one-page advertisements for two games, MAXIMASIA and RELOCATION.

EPILOGUE

It is now three weeks since I wrote the last word of this manuscript. I am struck with the realization of how difficult it is to "let go," to decide one is finished with a piece of writing or with a game-design project. Of course, in a sense one is *never* finished with either one—if they have caught the writer or designer intellectually, they continue to rise to consciousness for a long time after the "official completion," as new ideas emerge. And then one thinks "but I must add that . . ."

Nonetheless, one must eventually reach a satisfactory conclusion, a stopping point, no matter what new thoughts can be expected to come after the manuscript has gone to press or appeared in print. The book then becomes the property of others—readers who will sift the grain and the chaff, find what is worth noting, and develop the ideas in fuller form as they put them to use. So, too, with a gaming-simulation—one provides only the initial ideas. The players must grab these, lay them out, examine them, and turn them into useful starting points for their own investigations.

These, then, are some guidelines for developing your own projects. They offer a systematic way to convert your intentions to develop a gaming-simulation into a final product that will be realistic and useful. You must add the substantive ideas, the other skills you possess, the "music" that will make both the design process and the game you develop more than a mechanical exercise. To do so, you will not only have to read and to write, but you will have to dream, to idle, to speculate, to loiter over thoughts, to contemplate ambiguous connections, and, mostly, to engage in that most challenging of enterprises: to create.

REFERENCES

Abt, Clark. 1974. *Serious Games*. New York: Viking.

Armstrong, Robert and Margaret Hobson. 1969. "Games and Urban Planning." *Surveyor* 31(October):32-34.

Becker, Henk A. and Alan L. Porter, eds. 1986a. *Impact Assessment Today*. 2 Vol. Utrecht, Netherlands: Uitgeverij Jan van Arkel.

Becker, Henk A. and Alan L. Porter, eds. 1986b. *Methods and Experiences in Impact Assessment*. Dordrecht, Netherlands, and Boston/Lancaster/Tokyo: D. Reidel.

Barthes, Roland. 1964. *Elements of Semiology*. London: Jonathan Cape.

Biggs, William D. 1986. "Computerized Business Management Simulations for Tyros." In *Developments in Business Simulation and Experiential Exercises*, Vol. 13, edited by Alvin C. Burns and Lane Kelly. Little Rock: ABSEL, University of Arkansas.

Boocock, Sarane S. and E. O. Schild. 1968. *Simulation Games in Learning*. Newbury Park, CA: Sage.

Branwyn, Gareth. 1986. "Gaming: Simulating Future Realities." *Futurist* (January-February):29-35.

Bredemeier, Mary E. and Cathy Stein Greenblat. 1981. "The Educational Effectiveness of Simulation Games: A Synthesis of Recent Findings." *Simulation and Games* 12 (September).

Bredemeier, Mary E., Naomi G. Rotter, and Ron Stadsklev. 1981. "'The Academic Game' as a Frame Game." *Journal of Experiential Learning and Simulation (JELS)* 3(2):73-83.

Bruin, Klaas, Jan de Haan, Cees Teijken, and Wijbren Veeman. 1979. *How to Build a Simulation/Game: Proceedings of the 10th ISAGA Conference*. Leeuwarden, Netherlands: Ubbo Emmius Teacher Training Institute.

Burns, Alvin C. and Lane Kelley. 1986. *Developments in Business Simulation and Experiential Exercises*. Vol. 13. Stillwater: Oklahoma State University.

Crookall, David, Allan Martin, Danny Saunders, and Alan Coote. 1986. "Human and Computer Involvement in Simulation." *Simulation and Games* 17(3):345-375.

Crookall, David and Rebecca Oxford. 1987. "Gaming Context, Communication, Reality and Future: An Introduction." In *Simulation/Gaming: State of the Art in the Late 1980's*, edited by D. Crookall, C. S. Greenblat, A. Coote, J. H. Klabbers, and D. R. Watson. Oxford: Pergamon.

Crookall, David, Danny Saunders, and Allan Coote. 1987. "The SIMULATION DESIGN GAME: An Activity for Exploring the Simulation Design Process." To be published in the Proceedings of the SAGSET 1986 meetings.

Dillman, Duane. 1970. "The Design and Development of Simulation Exercises." Paper presented at the meetings of the American Educational Research Association, Minneapolis, MN, March.

Duke, Richard D. 1974. *Gaming: The Future's Language*. New York: Halsted.

Duke, Richard D. 1980. "A Paradigm for Game Design." *Simulation and Games* 11(September):364-377.

Duke, Richard D. and Cathy S. Greenblat. 1979. *Game-Generating Games*. Newbury Park, CA: Sage.

Elgood, Chris. 1984. *Handbook of Management Games*. 3rd Ed. Brookfield, VT: Gower.

Elliott, Charles and Brian McKeown. 1985. *It's Not Fair*. Dublin: Christian Aid.

Ellington, Henry, Eric Addinall, and Fred Percival. 1983. *A Handbook of Game Design*. London: Kogan Page.

Feldt, Allan and Frederick L. Goodman. 1975. "Observations on the Design of Simulations and Games." In *Principles and Practices of Gaming-Simulation*, edited by C. S. Greenblat and R. D. Duke. Newbury Park, CA: Sage.

Fuhs, F. Paul. 1986. "The Design of Simulation Models Using Thought Organizers." In *Developments in Business Simulation and Experiential Exercises*, Vol. 13, edited by Alvin C. Burns and Lane Kelly. Little Rock: ABSEL, University of Arkansas.

Gagnon, John H. and Cathy S. Greenblat. 1978. "Pregnancy Before Marriage: Contraception, Abortion, and Out-of-Marriage Births." *Life Designs: Individuals, Marriages, and Families*. Glenview, IL: Scott, Foresman.

Gamson, William. 1975. "SIMSOC: Establishing Social Order in a Simulated Society." In *Principles and Practices of Gaming-Simulation*, edited by C. S. Greenblat and R. D. Duke. Newbury Park, CA: Sage.

Gamson, William. 1978. *SIMSOC: Simulated Society*, 3rd ed. New York: Free Press.

Gamson, William. 1984. *WHAT'S NEWS: A Game Simulation of TV News, Coordinator's Manual*. New York: Free Press.

Glazier, Ray. 1970. *How to Design Educational Games*. 2nd Ed. Cambridge, MA: Abt.

Goodman, Fred L. and Community Systems Foundation. 1970. *The Policy Negotiations Simulation: Leader's Notebook*. Ann Arbor, MI: Learning Activities and Materials, Inc.

Goodman, Fred L. and Larry Coppard, eds. 1979, *Urban Gaming-Simulation*. Ann Arbor, MI: School of Education.

Goosen, Ken R. 1982. *A Comprehensive Guide to ABSEL's Conference Proceedings (1974-1981)*. Little Rock: University of Arkansas.

Gordon, Amy K. 1970. *Games for Growth*. Palo Alto, CA: Science Research Associates.

Gray, Paul and Israel Borovits. 1986. "The Contrasting Roles of Monte Carlo Simulation and Gaming in Decision Support Systems." *Simulations* 47(6):233-239.

Greenblat, Cathy Stein. 1973. "Teaching with Simulation Games: A Review of Claims and Evidence." *Teaching Sociology* 1(October).

Greenblat, Cathy Stein. 1974. "Sociological Theory and the 'Multiple Reality' Game." *Simulation and Games* 5(March).

Greenblat, Cathy Stein. 1975. "Simulating Marital Decision Making." In *The Marriage Game: Understanding Marital Decision Making*, edited by Cathy S. Greenblat, Peter J. Stein, and Norman F. Washburne. New York: Random House.

Greenblat, Cathy Stein. 1980. "Group Dynamics and Game Design: Some Reflections." *Simulation and Games* 11(March):35-58.

Greenblat, Cathy Stein and Richard D. Duke. 1975. *Gaming-Simulation: Rationale, Design, Applications*. Newbury Park, CA: Sage.

Greenblat, Cathy Stein and Richard D. Duke. 1981. *Principles and Practices of Gaming-Simulation*. Newbury Park, CA: Sage.

Greenblat, Cathy Stein and John H. Gagnon. 1976. "Specifications for Design: Blood Money—Report to the National Heart and Lung Institute." New Brunswick, New Jersey. (unpublished)

Greenblat, Cathy Stein, Linda Reich Rosen, and John H. Gagnon. 1978. "Sex Education and Pre-Marital Pregnancy: An Innovative Approach." Paper presented at the 3rd International Congress on Medical Sexology, Rome, Italy, October.

Greenblat, Cathy Stein, Peter J. Stein, and Norman F. Washburne. 1977. *The Marriage Game: Understanding Marital Decision Making*. New York: Random House.

Henderson, Thomas A. and John L. Foster. 1978. *URBAN POLICY GAME: A Simulation of Urban Politics*. New York: John Wiley.

Hoffman, Therese Lemire and Susan Dempsey Reif. 1978. *INTO AGING: A Simulation Game*. Thorofare, NJ: Charles B. Slack.

Hope, Joanne and Peter McAra. 1984. *Games Nurses Play*. New York: Pergamon.

Horn, Robert and Anne Cleaves. 1980. *The Guide to Simulations/ Games for Education and Training*. Newbury Park, CA: Sage.

Inbar, Michael and Clarice Stoll. 1972. *Simulation and Gaming in Social Science*. New York: Free Press.

Jones, Ken. 1980. *Simulations: A Handbook for Teachers*. London: Kogan Page.

Jones, Ken. 1982. *Simulations in Language Teaching*. Cambridge: Cambridge University Press.

Jones, Ken. 1986. *Designing Your Own Simulations*. New York: Methuen.

Kenner, Joseph and Myron Uretsky. 1986. "The Management Decision Laboratory at New York University." In *Developments in Business Simulation and Experiential Exercises*, Vol. 13, edited by Alvin C. Burns and Lane Kelly. Little Rock: ABSEL, University of Arkansas.

Klabbers, Jan H. G. 1984. "Design Characteristics of the Simulation-Game PERFORM." *Simulation and Games* 15(June).

Klabbers, Jan H. G. 1985. "Instruments for Planning and Policy Formation: Some Methodological Considerations." *Simulation and Games* 16(June):135-161.

Lederman, Linda. 1983. "Differential Learning Outcomes in an Instructional Simulation: Exploring the Relationship between Designated Role and Perceived Learning Outcome." *Communication Quarterly* 32:198-204.

Lederman, Linda. 1984. "Debriefing: A Critical Re-examination of the Post-Experience Analytic Process with Implications for Its Effective Use." *Simulation and Games* 15:415-431.

Lederman, Linda and Lea P. Stewart. 1983. *The SIMCORP Simulation Participant's Manual*. Princeton, NJ: Total Research Corp.

Livingston, Samuel A. 1972. "How to Design a Simulation Game." Baltimore, MD: Academic Games Associates.

Livingston, Samuel A. 1973. "Six Ways to Design a Bad Simulation Game." *Simulation/Gaming/News* (March):15.

McClellan, Larry A. 1971. "Simulation Game Development: An Instructional Packet." Chicago: Governors State University.

Meadows, Dennis L. 1985. "User's Manual for STRATEGEM-1, A Microcomputer-Based Management Training Game on Energy-Environment Interactions." Report DSD #509, Thayer School of Engineering, Hanover, New Hampshire 03755.

Meadows, Dennis, William W. Behrens III, Donella H. Meadows, Roger F. Naill, Jorgen Randers, and Erich K.O. Zahn. 1974. *Dynamics of Growth in a Finite World*. Cambridge: MIT Press.

Moore, Omar Khayyam and Alan Ross Anderson. 1975. "Some Principles for the Design of Clarifying Educational Environments." In *Principles and Practices of Gaming-Simulation*, edited by C. S. Greenblat and R. D. Duke. Newbury Park, CA: Sage.

Philliber, Susan and Elane M. Gutterman. 1982. "Playing Games about Teenage Pregnancy." *Evaluation and Program Planning* 3(41).

Raser, John R. 1969. *Simulation and Society*. Boston: Allyn & Bacon.

Rhyne, R. F. 1975. "Communicating Holistic Insights." In *Principles and Practices of Gaming-Simulation*, edited by C. S. Greenblat and R. D. Duke. Newbury Park, CA: Sage.

Richardson, George P. and Alexander L. Pugh III. 1981. "Chapter 2: Problem Identification and System Conceptualization." *Introduction to System Dynamics Modeling with DYNAMO*. Cambridge: MIT Press.

Roberts, Nancy, David Anderson, Ralph Deal, Michael Garet, and William Shaffer. 1983. *Introduction to Computer Simulation: A System Dynamics Modeling Approach*. Reading, MA: Addison-Wesley.

SAGSET (Society for the Advancement of Gaming and Simulation and Training) n.d. Resource lists on the following topics:

(1) Introductory Reading
(2) Game and Simulation Design
(3) Game and Simulation Evaluation
(4) Chemistry
(5) Economics
(6) International Relations
(7) Business and Management Relations
(8) Mathematics
(9) Teaching English as a Foreign Language
(10) Health Education
(11) Education Management
(12) Human Relations
(13) Geography
(14) Music

SAGSET. 1986. *Debriefing Simulation/Games. Simulation/Games for Learning*, guest edited by Morry van Ments, 16, 4 (December).

Sanoff, H. 1979. *Design Games*. Los Altos, CA: William Kaufmann.

Sarason, Seymour. 1971. *The Culture of the School and the Problem of Change*. Boston: Allyn & Bacon.

Schellenberger, Robert E. and Lance A. Masters. 1986. "An Example: The Use of Management Games on Microcomputers by Computer Novices." In *Developments in Business Simulation and Experiential Exercises*, Vol. 13, edited by Alvin C. Burns and Lane Kelly. Little Rock: ABSEL, University of Arkansas.

Sherrell, Daniel L., Kenneth R. Russ, and Alvin C. Burns. 1986. "Enhancing Mainframe Simulations via Microcomputers: Designing Decision Support Systems." In *Developments in Business Simulation and Experiential Exercises*, Vol. 13, edited by Alvin C. Burns and Lane Kelly. Little Rock: ABSEL, University of Arkansas.

Shirts, R. Garry. 1975. "Ten 'Mistakes' Commonly Made by Persons Designing Educational Simulations and Games." Del Mar, CA: SIMILE II.

Shubik, Martin. 1968. "Gaming: Costs and Facilities." *Management Science* 14(July):629-660.

Shubik, Martin. 1975. *Games for Society, Business and War: Towards a Theory of Gaming*. New York: Elsevier.

Stahl, Ingolf, ed. 1983. *Operational Gaming: An International Approach*. Laxenburg, Austria: International Institute For Applied Systems Analysis.

Sterman, John D. and Dennis Meadows. 1985. "STRATEGEM-2: A Microcomputer Simulation Game of the Kondratiev Cycle." *Simulation and Games* 16(2):174-202.

Suits, Bernard. 1978. *The Grasshopper: Games, Life and Utopia*. Toronto: University of Toronto Press.

Suits, Bernard. 1982. "Games and Utopia: Posthumous Reflections." Keynote address at the 1982 NASAGA meetings, Ann Arbor, MI, October.

Taylor, John and Rex Walford. 1978. *Learning and the Simulation Game*. Milton Keynes.

Thatcher, Don and June Robinson. 1980. *A Game Workshop for the Design of Games and Simulations for Teaching*. Portsmouth, England: Mimeographed.

Thiagarajan, Sivasailam and Harold D. Stolovich. 1980. "Frame Games: An Evaluation." Pp. 98-107 in *The Guide to Simulations/Games for Education and Training*, edited by Horn and Cleaves. Newbury Park, CA: Sage.

Van Ments, Morry. 1983. *The Effective Use of Role-Play: A Handbook for Teachers*. London: Kogan Page.

Wolfe, Joseph. 1985. "The Teaching Effectiveness of Games in Collegiate Business Courses: A 1973-1983 Update." *Simulation and Games* 16(2):251-288.

Zelmer, Amy E. and A. C. Lynn Zelmer. 1982. *Simulation/Gaming for Health Teaching*. Canadian Health Education Society Technical Publications.

PERIODICALS

SIMULATION AND GAMES: AN INTERNATIONAL JOURNAL OF THEORY, DESIGN AND RESEARCH

This journal has been adopted as the official journal of ABSEL, ISAGA, and NASAGA. Published quarterly by Sage Publications, 2111 Hillcrest Drive, Newbury Park, California 91320. Editor: Cathy Stein Greenblat, Dept: of Sociology, Rutgers University, New Brunswick, New Jersey 08903.

SIMULATIONS/GAMES FOR LEARNING (formerly SAGSET JOURNAL).

This is the official journal of SAGSET. Published quarterly by The Secretary, SAGSET, Centre for the Extension Studies, University of Technology, Loughborough, Leics LE11 3TU, England. Editor: Alan Coote, Dept. of Management and Legal Studies, The Polytechnic of Wales, Pontypridd, Mid Glamorgan CF37 IDL, Wales.

SIMJEUX/SIMGAMES.

Published in English and in French. Published and edited by Pierre Corbeil, 690, 104c Avenue, Drummondville, Quebec, J2B 49P, Canada.

ORGANIZATIONS

ABSEL—ASSOCIATION FOR BUSINESS SIMULATION AND EXPERIENTIAL LEARNING

President—Joseph Wolfe, Department of Management and Marketing, The University of Tulsa, 6000 South College Avenue, Tulsa, Oklahoma 74104.

ISAGA—INTERNATIONAL SIMULATION AND GAMING ASSOCIATION

Secretariat—Jan Klabbers, Department of Educational Sciences, P.O. Box 80.140 3508 TC Utrecht, The Netherlands.

NASAGA—NORTH AMERICAN SIMULATION AND GAMING ASSOCIATION

Executive Director—Bahram Farzanegan, National Game Center and Laboratory, University of North Carolina at Asheville, One University Heights, Asheville, North Carolina 28804-3299.

SAGSET—SOCIETY FOR THE ADVANCEMENT OF GAMING AND SIMULATION IN EDUCATION AND TRAINING

The Secretary—SAGSET, Centre for Extension Studies, University of Technology, Loughborough, Leicestershire LE11 3TU, England.

GAMING-SIMULATIONS

THE ACADEMIC GAME
Designed by A. N. O'Connell, J. L. Alpert, M. E. Bredemeier, M. S. Richardson, N. G. Rotter, and R. K. Unger (Task Force on Career Development Simulation of the American Psychological Association's Division on the Psychology of Women). Published by Institute of Higher Education Research and Services, Box 6293, University, AL 35846.

ACCESS
Designed by Susan Ebel and Jean L. Easterly. Published by SIMILE II, P.O. Box 910, Del Mar, CA 92014.

ADVANTIG
Designed by Richard D. Duke, John Morris, and Patrick L. Sweet. Published by The Center for Social and Economic Issues, Industrial Technology Institute, P.O. Box 1485, Ann Arbor, MI 48106.

AT ISSUE!
Designed by Richard D. Duke and Cathy Stein Greenblat. Published in *Game-Generating-Games*. Newbury Park, CA: Sage.

BAFA-BAFA
Designed by R. Garry Shirts. Published by SIMILE II, P.O. Box 910, Del Mar, CA 92014.

BALDICER
Designed by Georgeann Wilcoxson. Published by John Knox Press, 341 Ponce de Leon Avenue, N.E., Atlanta, GA 30308.

BLOOD MONEY
Designed by Cathy Stein Greenblat and John H. Gagnon. Published by National Heart, Lung, and Blood Institute, POCE, Bethesda, MD.

THE BUSINESS POLICY GAME (2nd Edition)
Designed by Richard V. Cotter and David J. Fritzsche. Published by Prentice-Hall, Inc., Englewood Cliffs, NJ 07632.

CALAGRANDE
Designed by Drew Mackie. Available from Drew Mackie, 64, The Causeway, Duddingston, Edinburgh, EH15 3P2, Scotland.

CAPJEFOS: A SIMULATION OF VILLAGE DEVELOPMENT
Designed by Cathy Stein Greenblat, with Philip Langley, Jacob Ngwa, Saul Luyumba, Ernest Mangesho, and Foday MacBailey. Information available from Cathy Stein Greenblat, Professor of Sociology, Rutgers University, New Brunswick, NJ 08903.

CARIBBEAN FISHERMAN
Designed by Rex Walford. Published by Longman Resource Units, London, UK. Also available from Cambridge Publishing Services, Oatlands, High Street, Conington, Cambridgeshire, CB3 8LT, Elsworth (09547) 349, England.

CITY 1
Designed by Peter House et al. Published by National Technical Information Service, 5285 Port Royal Road, Springfield, VI 22151.

CLASSROOM EXPERIENCING
Designed by Alice S. Jackson. Published by Academic Games Associates, Baltimore, MD (game now out of print).

COLLECTIVE BARGAINING SIMULATED
Designed by Michael R. Carrell and Jerald R. Smith. Published by Charles E. Merrill Publishing Company, 1300 Alum Creek Drive, P.O. Box 508, Columbus, OH 43216-0508.

THE COMMONS GAME
Designed by Richard Powers, Richard E. Duus, and Richard D. Norton. Suite 4H, 10 West 66th Street, New York, NY 10023.

COMPETE—A DYNAMIC MARKETING SIMULATION
Designed by Anthony J. Faria, Ray Nulsen, and Phillip Roussos. Published by McGraw-Hill Book Company, Avenue of the Americas, New York, NY.

THE CONCEPTUAL MAPPING GAME
Designed by Richard D. Duke and Cathy Stein Greenblat. Published in *Game-Generating-Games*. Newbury Park, CA: Sage.

THE CONDENSED BUSINESS EXPERIENCE PROGRAM.
Designed by Myron Uretsky. Published by Business Simulations, Inc., 283 Hicks St., Brooklyn, NY 11301.

THE CONFERENCE GAME
Designed by Chris Brand and Terry Walker. Published by Maxim Consultants, 6 Marlborough Place, Brighton, Sussex, BNI 3XA, England.

CRISIS
Designed by Western Behavioral Sciences Institute. Published by SIMILE II, P.O. Box 910, Del Mar, CA 92014.

CUSTOD-E
Designed by Dorothy Derzog and Kathleen Lupo. Information available from Dorothy Derzog, Fair Oaks Hospital, 19 Prospect Street, Summit, NJ 07901 or Kathleen Lupo, Middlesex University Hospital, New Brunswick, NJ 08901.

DANGEROUS PARALLEL
Designed by Foreign Policy Association. Published by Scott, Foresman and Company, 1900 E. Lake Avenue, Glenview, IL 60025.

DEMOCRACY
Designed by Academic Games Project, Johns Hopkins University. Published by Western Publishing Company, Inc., School and Library Department, 850 Third Avenue, New York, NY 10022.

EDGE CITY COLLEGE
Designed by Noel Callahan, Dwight Caswell, Larry McClellan, Robert Mullen, and William N. Savage. Published by Urbandyne, Chicago, IL (game now out of print).

END OF THE LINE
Designed by Frederick L. Goodman. Published by Institute of Higher Education Research and Services, Box 6293, University, AL 35846.

THE EXECUTIVE SIMULATION
Designed by Bernard Keys and Howard Leftwich. Published by Kendall/Hunt Publishing Company, Dubuque, IO.

THE FARMING GAME (formerly THE POVERTY GAME)
Adapted from a game by Jim Dunlop. Published by Oxfam Education Department, 274 Banbury Road, Oxford, OX2-7D ZEB, England.

FISH BANKS, LTD.
Designed by Dennis Meadows and Diana Shannon. Available from Resource Systems Group, Box 250, Plainfield, NH 03781.

GENERATION GAP
Designed by Erling O. Schild and Sarane S. Boocock. Published by Western Publishing Company, Inc., School and Library Department, 850 Third Avenue, New York, NY 10022.

GHETTO
Designed by Dove Toll. Published by Bobbs-Merrill Company, Educational Division, 4300 W. 62nd St., Indianapolis, IN 46268.

THE GREEN REVOLUTION GAME
Designed by Graham Chapman. Published by The Green Revolution Partnership, 2A Green End Road, Cambridge CB4 1RX, U.K.

HALLOWEEN GAME
Designed by Cathy Greenblat, John Gagnon, Kevin Greenblat, and Leslie Greenblat. Information available from CSG Enterprises, 34 Bayard Lane, Princeton, NJ 08540.

THE HEMOPHILIA PLANNING GAME
Designed by Cathy Stein Greenblat and John Gagnon. Published by National Heart, Lung, and Blood Institute, OPCE, Bethesda, MD.

THE HEXAGON GAME
Designed by Richard D. Duke, Jeffrey K. Harris, Nancy Steiber, and Jo H. Webb. Published by Multilogue Inc., 321 Park Lake, Ann Arbor, MI 48103.

HORATIO ALGER
Designed by Ann Kraemer, Bob Preuss, and Helen Howe. Published by Citizens for Welfare Reform, 305 Michigan Ave., Detroit, MI 48226.

ICONS (INTERNATIONAL COMMUNICATIONS AND NEGOTIATIONS SIMULATIONS)
Designed by Jonathan Wilkenfeld and Richard Brecht, based on POLIS, by Robert Noel. Information available from Jonathon Wilkenfeld, Department of Government and Politics, University of Maryland, Lefrak Hall, College Park, MD 20742.

IMPASSE
Designed by Richard D. Duke and Cathy Stein Greenblat. Published in *Game-Generating-Games*. Newbury Park, CA: Sage.

INTER-NATION SIMULATION (INS)
Designed by Harold Guetzkow and Cheo Cherryholmes. Published by Science Research Associates, Inc., 155 North Wacker Drive, Chicago, IL 60606.

INTO AGING
Designed by Therese Lemire Hoffman and Susan Dempsey Reif. Published by Charles B. Slack, Inc., Thorofare, NJ 08086.

THE MANAGEMENT DECISION LABORATORY (MDL)
Designed by Myron Uretsky et al. Information available from Myron Uretsky, Graduate School of Business, New York University, 100 Trinity Place, New York, NY 10006.

MANSYM (4th Edition)
Designed by Robert E. Schellenberger and Lance A. Masters. Published by John Wiley and Sons, 605 Third Avenue, New York, NY 10158.

THE MARBLE COMPANY
Designed by Linda Costigan Lederman and Lea P. Stewart. Published by the Department of Communication, School of Communication, Information and Library Studies, Rutgers, The State University of New Jersey, New Brunswick, NJ 08903.

THE MARRIAGE GAME: UNDERSTANDING MARITAL DECISION MAKING
Designed by Cathy Stein Greenblat, Peter J. Stein, and Norman F. Washburne. Published by Random House, Inc., 201 E. 50th St., New York, NY.

MAXIMASIA
Designed by Maxim Training Systems, Ltd. Available from Maxim Training Systems, Ltd., 6 Marlborough Place, Brighton, Susssex BN1 1UB, England.

ME, THE SLOW LEARNER
Designed by Don Thatcher and June Robinson. Published by Solent Simulations, 80, Miller Drive, Fareham, Hants, P016 7LL, England.

METRO-APEX
Designed by Richard D. Duke. Published by Mark James, Director of Computing Services, COMEX, Davidson Conference Center, University of Southern California, Los Angeles, CA 90007.

MODERN BUSINESS DECISIONS
Designed by Richard V. Cotter and David J. Fritzsche. Published by Prentice- Hall, Inc., Englewood Cliffs, NJ 07632.

PERFORM
Designed by Jan H. G. Klabbers. Information available from Professor Jan H. G. Klabbers, c/o Faculty of Sciences, P.O. Box 80140, 3508 TC Utrecht, The Netherlands.

PLANAFAM
Designed by Harold Thomas and Katherine Finseth. Published by ERIC, 855 Broadway, Boulder, CO 80302.

POLICY NEGOTIATIONS
Designed by Frederick L. Goodman. Published by Institute of Higher Education Research and Services, Box 6293, University, AL 35846.

POMP AND CIRCUMSTANCE
Designed by Cathy Stein Greenblat, John H. Gagnon, and Linda Reich Rosen. Published by CSG Enterprises, 34 Bayard Lane, Princeton, NJ 08540.

PRODUCTION LINE, INC.
Designed by Dennis Meadows, Elzbieta Naumienko, Diana Shannon, and Paula Antunes. Available from Resource Systems Group, Box 250, Plainfield, NH 03781.

RADIO COVINGHAM
Designed by Ken Jones. Published by Max Hueber Verlag, Max Hueber Strasse 4, 8045 Ismaning, West Germany.

RED DESERT
Designed by Ken Jones. Published by Max Hueber Verlag, Max Hueber Strasse 4, 8045 Ismaning, West Germany.

RELOCATION
Designed by SIMILE II. Available from SIMILE II, P.O. Box 910, Del Mar, CA 92014.

SHIPWRECKED
Designed by Ken Jones. Published by Max Hueber Verlag, Max Hueber Strasse 4, 8045 Ismaning, West Germany.

SIMCORP
Designed by Linda Costigan Lederman and Lea P. Stewart. Published by the Department of Communication, 4 Huntington Street, New Brunswick, NJ 08903.

SIMSOC (Third Edition)
Designed by William A. Gamson. Published by the Free Press, 866 Third Avenue, New York, NY 10022.

SNUS—SIMULATED NUTRITION SYSTEM
Designed by Richard D. Duke. Published by the Certificate Program in Gaming/Simulation, University of Michigan, Ann Arbor, MI 48109.

STARPOWER
Designed by R. Garry Shirts. Published by SIMILE II, P.O. Box 910, Del Mar, CA 92014.

ST. PHILIP: A SIMULATION ABOUT THE DEVELOPMENT OF A CARIBBEAN ISLAND
Designed by Rex Walford. Published in *Journal of Geography*, Volume 82, Number 4, July-August 1983: pp. 170-175. Also available from Cambridge Publishing Services, Oatlands, High Street, Conington, Cambridgeshire, CB3 8LT, Elsworth (09547) 349, England.

STRATEGEM-1
Designed by Dennis Meadows, Donella Meadows, Diana Shannon, and Ferenc Toth. Available from Resource Systems Group, Box 250, Plainfield, NH 03781.

STRATEGEM-2
Designed by John D. Sterman and Dennis Meadows. Published in *Simulation and Games*, 16,2 (June 1985): 174-202. Also available from John Sterman, System Dynamics Group, E40-294, Massachusetts Institute of Technology, Cambridge, MA 02139 or from Resource Systems Group, Box 250, Plainfield, NH 03781.

STRATPLAN
Designed by Roy W. Hinton and Daniel C. Smith. Published by Prentice-Hall, Inc., Englewood Cliffs, NJ 07632.

THEY SHOOT MARBLES, DON'T THEY?
Designed by Frederick L. Goodman. Information available from Frederick L. Goodman, School of Education, University of Michigan, Ann Arbor, MI.

THE TRADING GAME
Published in *It's Not Fair*, Trocaire, 169 Booterstown Avenue, Blackrock, County Dublin, Ireland.

URBAN POLICY GAME
Designed by Thomas A. Henderson and John L. Fox. Published by MacMillan Publishing Company, 866 Third Avenue, New York, NY 10022.

WHAT HAPPENS WHEN THE GAS RUNS OUT?
Designed by Henry Ellington, Eric Addinall, and Fred Percival. Published by the Chemical Society, Education Division, Burlington House, Piccadilly, London W1V 0BN, England.

WHAT'S NEWS?
Designed by William A. Gamson. Published by The Free Press, 866 Third Avenue, New York, NY 10022.

YOUR NUMBER IS UP
Designed by Joanne Hope and Peter McAra. Published in Joanne Hope and Peter McAra, *Games Nurses Play: Experimental Games for Behavioural Science Programmes*. New York and Oxford: Pergamon Press, 1984.

About the Author

Cathy Stein Greenblat, Ph.D. (Columbia University, 1986) is Professor of Sociology at Rutgers University, and a member of the Rutgers Women's Studies Program. In 1985-1986 she served as Visiting Professor of Sociology at Princeton University and in 1987-88 was a Visiting Fellow at Princeton's Woodrow Wilson School of Public and International Affairs. In her major area of specialization—gaming simulations—she has designed several simulation games, including THE MARRIAGE GAME (Random House, 1973 and 1977); IMPASSE?, AT ISSUE!, and THE CONCEPTUAL MAPPING GAMES (Sage, 1979); THE HEMOPHILIA PLANNING GAMES and BLOOD MONEY (National Heart, Lung, and Blood Institute, 1976); POMP AND CIRCUMSTANCE (development sponsored by the Ford and Rockefeller Foundations); and CAPJEFOS: A SIMULATION OF VILLAGE DEVELOPMENT (development sponsored by UNESCO). She has authored or coauthored several dozen articles and four books in this area of specialization.

Since 1979 Professor Greenblat has been the Editor of *Simulation and Games: An International Journal of Theory, Design, and Research.* She has served on the Executive Boards of the North American Simulation and Gaming Association (NASAGA), the International Simulation and Gaming Association (ISAGA), and the Society for the Advancement of Gaming and Simulation in Education and Training (SAGSET); she is past-president of ISAGA and currently serves as U.S. Secretariat for that organization. Dr. Greenblat has lectured on gaming in the United States, Latin America, Western Europe, Eastern Europe, the USSR, Japan, and China. She has served as an UNESCO expert on missions to the Philippines and to Cameroon, and was part of a 4-person U.S. team under NSF sponsorship that collaborated with a Soviet team of scientists on a project on the use of gaming for training high-level managers in 1976. She is currently working on a cross-national research enterprise involving simulation, with teams in 11 countries; she is designing a game-based training program for use in developing countries; and she is in the planning stage of a series of AIDS-related gaming-simulations for education and policymaking.